Spain in the Middle Ages
From Frontier to Empire, 1000–1500

NEW STUDIES IN MEDIEVAL HISTORY

General Editor: Denis Bethell

Published

J. K. Hyde, *Society and Politics in Medieval Italy:
The Evolution of the Civil Life, 1000–1350*

Angus MacKay, *Spain in the Middle Ages:
From Frontier to Empire, 1000–1500*

Other volumes are in preparation.

Spain in the Middle Ages

From Frontier to Empire, 1000–1500

ANGUS MacKAY

ST. MARTIN'S PRESS NEW YORK

For Linda, Angus John and Anne Marie

Contents

MAPS

Acknowledgements

This book has been written in the intervals of teaching at the University of Edinburgh and its appearance is due not least to colleagues and students whose comments have helped me to clarify ideas which are now less half-baked than they would otherwise have been. I owe a special debt of gratitude to Professor Denys Hay, who first turned my thoughts in the direction of medieval Spain and who has been a source of encouragement and help ever since. The editor of the series, Mr Denis Bethell, has devoted much time to helping me to say what I meant, and the book has benefited greatly from his constructive comments and advice. My father has read successive drafts and has saved me from many a blunder. Dr Richard Hitchcock, Dr Salvador Giner and Mr T. H. Newcombe have commented on sections of the book and have helped me on particular points. Although archival material has been used for the elaboration of ideas and interpretations (particularly in the second half of the book), the use of extended references in a work of this size would be a luxury. Similarly I have drawn on the researches of so many scholars, most of whom are mentioned in the bibliographies, that I can only express my general gratitude here. However, references are given for quotations. My greatest debt is to my wife without whose comfort and help this book would truly never have been written.

The illustration on the dustcover depicts James I of Aragon in battle against the Moors, 1235. Detail from a panel in a fourteenth-century Valencian altarpiece dedicated to St George; reproduced by courtesy of the Victoria and Albert Museum, London.

Chronological Table

711	Muslims win battle of Guadalete and invade Visigothic Spain.
722	Christians under Pelayo win victory at the 'battle' of Covadonga.
732	Charles Martel defeats the Muslims at the battle of Poitiers.
756	'Abd al-Rahmān I establishes emirate of Córdoba which is politically independent of Damascus.
778	Charlemagne besieges Zaragoza and his rearguard is defeated by the Basques at Roncesvalles.
800	The Franks take Barcelona and the Spanish March of the Carolingian Empire is in the process of formation.
816	The Malikite rite is introduced to al-Andalus.
c. 830	The relics of St James are found and begin to focus attention on Santiago de Compostela.
866	Reign of Alfonso III of León (866–910), during which the Christians advance to the Duero.
929	'Abd al-Rahmān III proclaims himself caliph.
931	Count Fernán González of Castile (931–970) and the beginnings of 'independent' Castilian power.
976	Death of al-Hakam II; al-Mansūr the power behind the throne in al-Andalus.
985–97	Al-Mansūr sacks Barcelona (985), León and Sahagún (988), and Santiago de Compostela (997).
1031	Caliphate of Córdoba finally breaks up into Taifa kingdoms.
1037	Castile and León united under Ferdinand I.
c. 1040	Birth of the Cid.
c. 1060	Compilation of the *Usatges* begins.
1064	Crusade against Barbastro and beginnings of the Aragonese reconquest.
c. 1070	Beginnings of the Romanesque cathedral at Santiago de Compostela.
1074	Gregory VII asks Alfonso VI of Castile and León to establish the Roman rite.

1081	Banishment of the Cid by Alfonso VI.
1085	Toledo is taken and the Christians advance to the Tagus frontier; Bernard de Sédirac subsequently becomes archbishop of Toledo and Cluniac influence is strengthened.
1086	The Almoravids arrive in al-Andalus and Alfonso VI is defeated at the battle of Zalaca.
1094	The Cid captures Valencia; he dies in 1099 and the Christians lose Valencia in 1102.
1106	Death of Yūsuf b. Tāshufīn.
1118	Alfonso the Battler takes Zaragoza.
1126–98	Averroes of Córdoba.
1137	Union of Catalonia and Aragon.
1139	Portugal becomes an independent kingdom.
1140	The beginnings of Cistercian foundations in Spain.
c. 1145–7	The end of Almoravid rule in al-Andalus and the beginnings of Almohad power.
1158	Foundation of the Order of Calatrava.
c. 1160	'School of Translators' in Toledo.
1188	Representatives of the towns attend the *cortes* of León.
1195	The Almohads defeat Alfonso VIII at Alarcos.
1212	Christians defeat the Almohads at the battle of Las Navas de Tolosa.
1213	Peter II killed at the battle of Muret and Catalan power in southern France collapses.
1215	Foundation of the university of Salamanca.
1229	James I takes Mallorca.
1230	Final union of Castile and León.
1230–1	End of Almohad power in Spain.
1236	Muslim resistance crumbles and the Christian reconquest accelerates to take Córdoba (1236), Valencia (1238), Murcia (1243), Seville (1248) and Cádiz (1265).
1238	Nasrid rulers establish their power in Granada.
1258	Treaty of Corbeil between James I of Aragon and Louis IX of France.
1264	Mudejar rebellions in Andalusia and Murcia.
1282	Conquest of Sicily by Peter III of Aragon.
1287	*Privilegio de la unión.*

1300	Foundation of the university of Lérida.
1337	Beginning of the Hundred Years War.
1340	Alfonso IX of Castile defeats the Muslims at the battle of Salado.
1343	Peter IV of Aragon annexes the Balearic islands.
1348	The Black Death.
1350	The accession of Peter the Cruel is followed by the beginnings of Trastamaran opposition and propaganda.
1368	Treaty of Toledo between Henry II of Castile and France.
1369	Henry II (of Trastámara) kills his half-brother Peter the Cruel at Montiel.
1371	John of Gaunt, duke of Lancaster, marries Peter the Cruel's daughter, Constance, and assumes the title of king of Castile.
1385	John I of Castile defeated by the Portuguese at the battle of Aljubarrota.
1386	Lancastrian army disembarks at La Coruña, but the invasion of Castile subsequently ends in failure.
1388–9	Treaties with Lancaster and the Portuguese; end of the Spanish phase of the Hundred Years War and of the Lancastrian claims to the Castilian throne.
1391	Anti-Jewish feeling sparks off a wave of pogroms in the towns of the Iberian peninsula.
1406	Death of Ibn Khaldūn.
1410	One of the regents of Castile, Ferdinand, takes Antequera from the Moors; death of Martin I of Aragon raises the problem of succession to the throne of the Crown of Aragon.
1412	The Compromise of Caspe – the regent of Castile, Ferdinand of Antequera, becomes king of Aragon.
1415	Ceuta is taken by the Portuguese.
1442–3	Alfonso V of Aragon gains control of Naples.
1445	John II of Castile and Alvaro de Luna defeat their enemies at the battle of Olmedo.
1449	Anti-*converso* movement in Toledo and rebellion of the town against royal authority.

1453	Execution of Alvaro de Luna.
1454–8	*Cortes* of Barcelona coincides with *Biga–Busca* crisis in Barcelona, continuing tension over the *remensa* problem, and constitutional clashes between the *cortes* and the monarchy.
1462–72	Civil and *remensa* wars in Catalonia.
1465	The effigy of Henry IV of Castile deposed; civil wars in Castile.
1469	The marriage of Ferdinand and Isabella.
1473	Massacre of *conversos* in Andalusian towns; printing begins in Spain.
1478	Setting up of the Inquisition.
1479	Union of Castile and Aragon.
1486	Sentence of Guadalupe deals with the *remensa* problems.
1492	Conquest of Granada; expulsion of the Jews; Columbus discovers America.
1502	*Moriscos* forced to choose between baptism and expulsion.

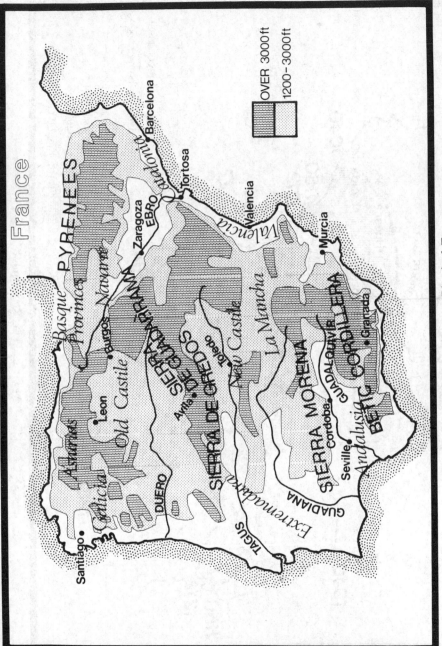

MAP I Medieval Spain: Physical Features

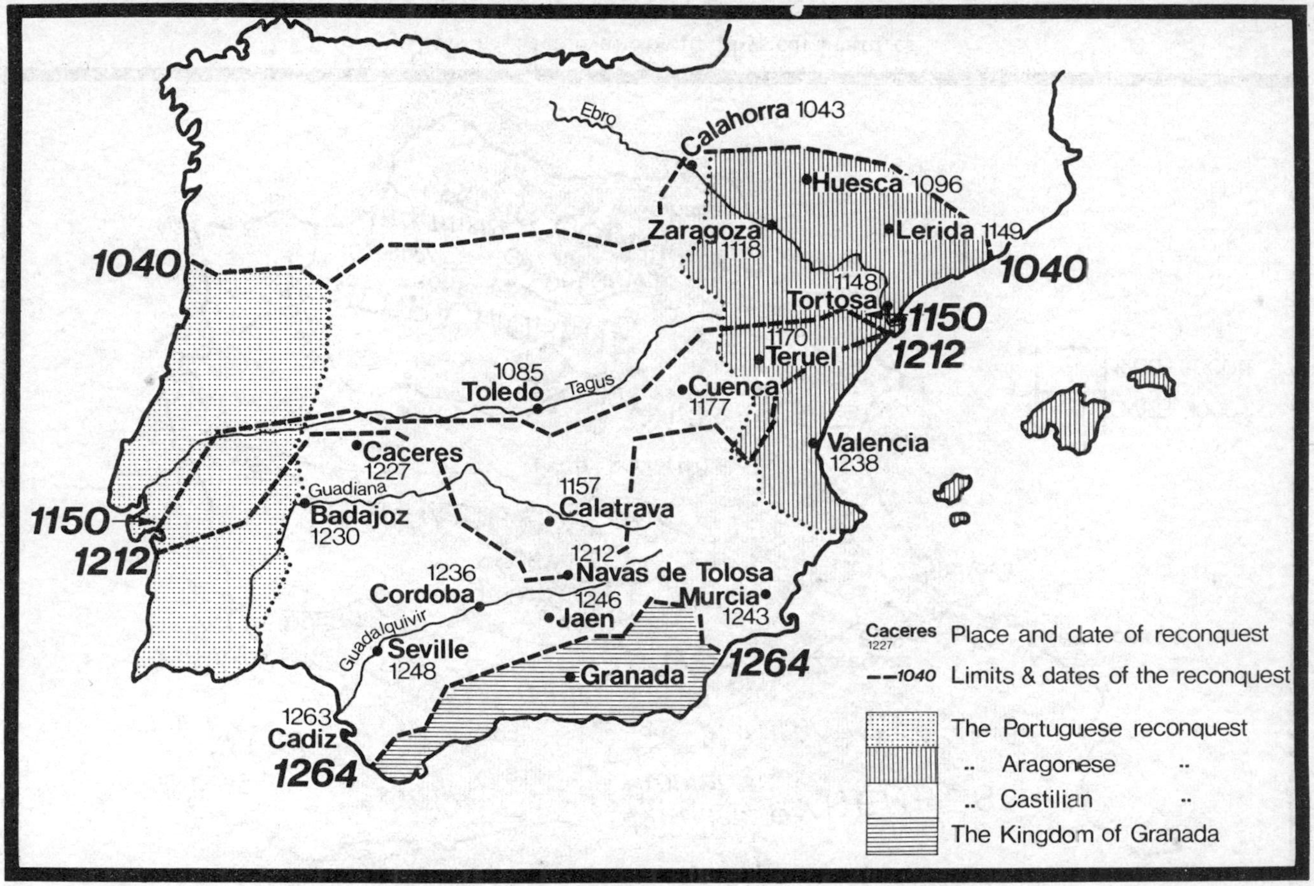

MAP 2 The Reconquest

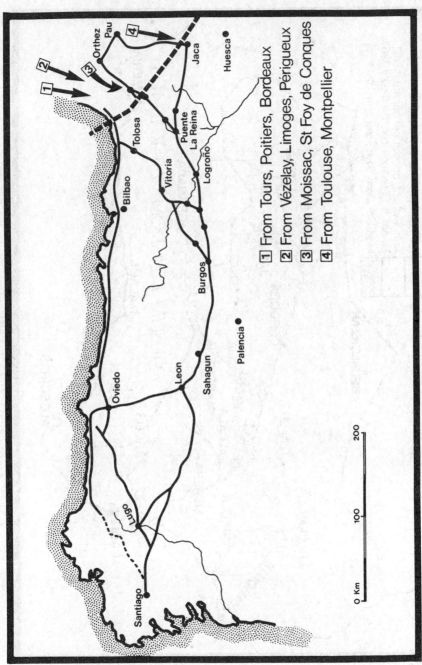

1 From Tours, Poitiers, Bordeaux
2 From Vézelay, Limoges, Périgueux
3 From Moissac, St Foy de Conques
4 From Toulouse, Montpellier

Orthez · Pau · Jaca · Huesca ·
Tolosa · Puente La Reina · Logroño · Vitoria · Bilbao · Burgos · Sahagun · Leon · Oviedo · Palencia · Lugo · Santiago

0 Km · 100 · 200

MAP 3   The Pilgrim Route to Santiago de Compostela

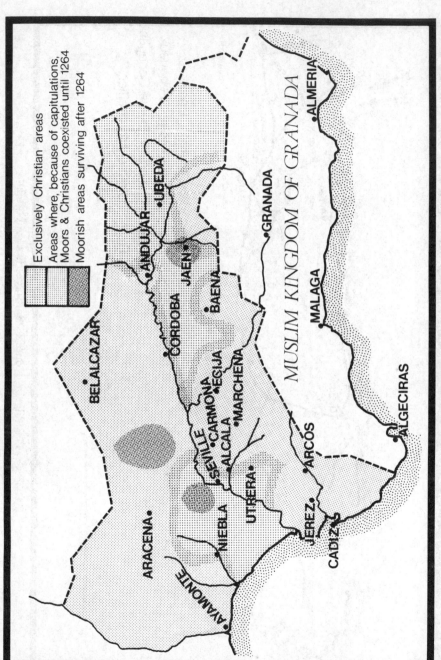

Exclusively Christian areas

Areas where, because of capitulations,
Moors & Christians coexisted until 1264

Moorish areas surviving after 1264

MUSLIM KINGDOM OF GRANADA

ALMERIA

UBEDA

ANDUJAR

JAEN

CORDOBA

BAENA

GRANADA

BELALCAZAR

ECIJA

MARCHENA

CARMONA

ALCALA

MALAGA

SEVILLE

MARCHENA

UTRERA

ARCOS

ALGECIRAS

ARACENA

NIEBLA

JEREZ

CADIZ

AYAMONTE

MAP 4 Andalusia after the Thirteenth-Century Reconquest

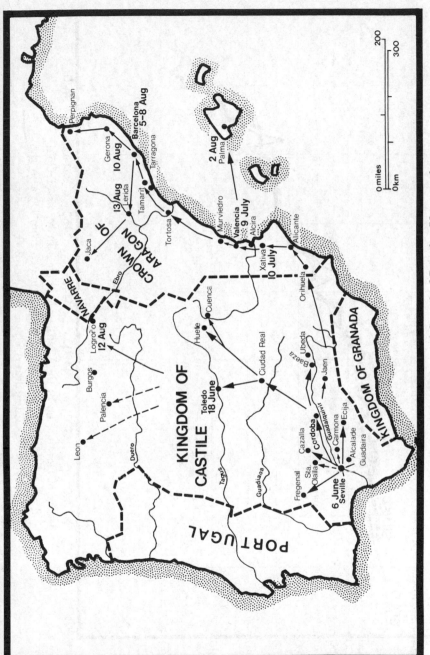

MAP 5 The Geography and Speed of Popular Unrest: the 1391 Pogrom

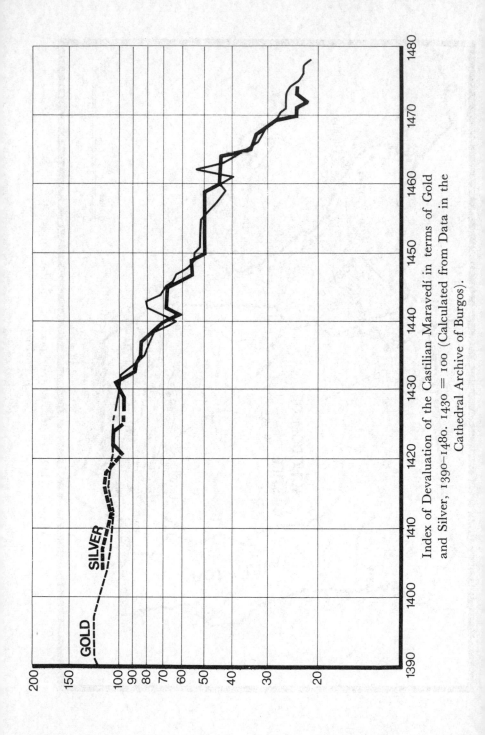

Index of Devaluation of the Castilian Maravedí in terms of Gold and Silver, 1390–1480. 1430 = 100 (Calculated from Data in the Cathedral Archive of Burgos).

Introduction

FROM FRONTIER TO EMPIRE: the sub-title of this book summarises the developments which made medieval Spain unique.
In 711 the Muslims overran most of the Iberian peninsula, and it
was only in 1492, after centuries of frontier warfare, that the
Christians completed their reconquest by taking Muslim Granada.
However, in the same year as the fall of Granada, Columbus discovered America and Spanish troops were also to be found fighting
in Italy. Thus, as Angel Ganivet pointed out at the end of the last
century, no sooner had fragmented Spain achieved some measure of
unity after the struggles against Islam, than she emerged to dominate the European stage and administer a vast Empire. Spain
moved 'from Frontier to Empire' – from, so to speak, 'minus' to
'plus'.

Many historians would agree with the great medievalist, Sánchez-
Albornoz, that the related concepts of the frontier and the reconquest provide the key to Spanish historical development. Indeed,
the idea of 'the Middle Ages' in Spain has differed radically from
that prevailing in the rest of Europe. The Italian humanists of the
Renaissance regarded the barbarian invasions and the sack of
Rome (410) as a turning-point between the civilisation of the Ancient
World and a period of darkness and obscurity, the Middle Ages,
from which Europe was only rescued by the rebirth of learning in
their own day. Moreover, the Spanish presence in sixteenth-century
Italy even led some of these humanists to cast their country in the
image of classical Rome and the Spaniards in the role of new
barbarian invaders. For a man such as the sixteenth-century
Spanish poet and humanist, Fernando de Herrera, the analogy was
totally false: 'civilised' Italy was not threatened by 'barbarian'
Spain. The latter, perhaps, could not quite match Italy in the
number of her scholars because she had been forced to give precedence to arms over letters, but the Spaniards were civilised because
they had no equals as defenders of the faith against the heathen. In
short, the arduous crusade against Islam over the centuries had
elevated Spain to the role of champion of Christian Europe against
the Infidel. Herrera, no doubt, would approve of the way in which

the Spanish medieval period is still today traditionally defined in terms of the duration of the Christian reconquest of the land occupied by the Muslims: the Muslim invasion of 711 and the destruction of the Visigothic state mark the beginning of the medieval period, and the conquest of Granada in 1492 brings it to a close.

Many of the peculiar features of Iberian historical development, therefore, are to be explained in terms of the frontier experience and of the arduousness of an enterprise, the reconquest, which had virtually achieved most of its objectives by the end of the thirteenth century. Consequently the earlier chapters of this book are, on the whole, devoted to the frontier and the reconquest, and to associated problems.

The importance of the reconquest suggests obvious parallels with Turner's thesis on 'The Significance of the Frontier in American History'. Indeed, in the Second International Congress of Historians of the United States and Mexico a great deal of attention was devoted to an analysis of the medieval Spanish frontier as a prototype of those frontiers which later developed in the New World. And, of course, Turnerian terminology can be used to argue that the continuous recession of the frontier and the advance of Christian colonisation southward moulded Spain's historical development, and that when there was no longer a frontier, the formative period of Spanish history ended. Much of the impact of the frontier, indeed, was due to the fact that successive generations were put through the same transforming disciplines – that is, they had to forego luxuries and adapt to those habits and institutions which the reconquest and frontier life demanded. The existence of a permanent military frontier virtually meant that medieval Spain was a society organised for war, and it may be because of this that 'feudalism' never developed properly throughout the peninsula. For, in reality, feudalism offered a set of conventions which made for a relative degree of stability and peace: it was primarily defensive, and from the military point of view it was confined to professional groups of nobles and warriors. But in Spain the problems of frontier warfare affected most sectors of the population and hence endowed society with a curious mixture of 'democratic' and noble characteristics. This was especially the case in Castile where, although the honours, privileges and status of nobility were largely the preserve of warriors, the engagement of a larger number of people in war both entailed a greater number of nobles and brought a greater degree of social mobility into the ranks of the nobility. In this respect a comparison between the *Chanson de Roland* and the *Cantar de Mío Cid* is illuminating. While on the one hand the French epic-fantasy is aristocratic in character and outlook, the Cid and his companions are humbler protagonists engaged in realistic warfare in a society where the military participation ratio and the existence of 'villein knights' make it almost possible to speak of *le peuple en marche vers la noblesse.*

There was not, however, one frontier, but a series of frontiers which varied so greatly from one area to another, and from one century to the next, that successive generations experienced different transforming disciplines. Moreover, the frontier did not entirely master the soldier and the colonist, and since what happened on the frontier was often the product of the cultural habits and institutions that were brought to it, the frontier itself was transformed by the successive and different generations who fought and settled on it. Thus to understand the differences between, for example, the early eleventh-century frontier of tribute-warfare, and the thirteenth-century frontier of systematic reconquest and colonisation, we must turn to those developments in the Spanish backcountry and to those contacts with Europe which produced new institutions, new habits and new religious attitudes. The importance of the frontier, in short, must be balanced by the impact on society of forces affecting developments behind the front lines.

Another fundamental feature of the medieval Spanish frontier which must be constantly kept in mind is that it was always on the move. There were, of course, periods when the impulse of the reconquest slackened, but the general picture is that of the occupation of territories on the margin of an expanding society. Problems of repopulation and colonisation, therefore, inevitably followed on from the process of conquest, and a characteristic feature of much of Christian Spain was a lack of manpower and an abundance of land. As a result the thirteenth-century 'expansion' in Spain was different from that in the rest of Europe. For most of western Europe historians have diagnosed a strain imposed by population growth on food resources, with the result that crises of subsistence became more serious and there was a consequent collapse in the fourteenth century. But for large areas of the Iberian peninsula this Malthusian analysis has, so to speak, to be reversed. The leap forward of the reconquest meant too much land and too few men, and many features of Spain's divergence from European developments are connected with this distinctive land–population ratio. For this reason, problems of repopulation and colonisation are studied in some detail in this book because they formed an inseparable and important aspect of the expanding frontier.

From the eleventh century onwards the frontier was not simply one of relatively empty territories being occupied and colonised. The lands in question were held and defended by the Muslims, and since not all of them withdrew or were forced to withdraw in the face of Christian advances, the course of the reconquest raised problems of assimilation or rejection of cultural and religious minorities. Just as Christian minorities had survived in Muslim Spain after the conquest, so too did Muslim minorities survive within the advancing Christian societies. Hence the abundant references in this book to such cultural and religious minorities as the Mozarabs, the Mudejars, the Jews, and the *conversos*.

Despite the military importance of the reconquest, the processes of assimilation and acculturation must also be studied. The successive generations who manned the frontier were not prompted to action by an overpowering sense of manifest religious destiny. True, the cult of St James at Compostela gave focus to religious and crusading aspirations, but the religious life of the peninsula was unlike that of any other area in Europe. Arians for a long period under the Visigoths, the later Catholics of Spain were in perpetual and intense contact with the Muslim and Jewish religions. Moreover, the Spaniards were aware that they were not waging war against barbarians, and the Iberian frontier was at times an area of fruitful cultural contacts. Indeed, the coexistence of Christians, Muslims and Jews – or, as Américo Castro put it, *convivencia* – and the evidence of a *creative* struggle indicate that, despite the drive of the reconquest or the later medieval persecution of Jews, the degree of acculturation was considerable. Christianity expanded at the expense of Islam, but it was the civilisation of Islam, in many ways richer and more cultivated, which influenced Spain and western Europe in its turn. The interplay of all these influences between Christian, Muslim and Jewish cultures was, of course, an extremely complex process. This book tries to give fairly detailed examples of deliberately directed processes of cultural change, such as the work of the twelfth-century translators, while at the same time taking account of some unconscious episodes of acculturation such as took place on the late medieval frontier.

The later medieval period in Spanish history has traditionally posed something of a conundrum to scholars. This is partly due to the break in the continuity of the reconquest and the impulse of the advancing frontier. Between the thirteenth century and the fall of Granada in 1492, the Iberian peninsula was plagued by a seemingly dismal succession of civil wars, meaningless bouts of anarchy, and nerveless rulers. As a result, historians have tended to turn away with relief from the later medieval 'decline' and acclaim the advent of the Catholic Kings (Ferdinand and Isabella), the creation of the modern state, the restoration of the forces of law and order at the expense of overmighty 'feudal' nobles, and the stern morality of a 'new' monarchy able to prepare the institutions for an Empire that would dominate the sixteenth-century world.

Of course, it has also long been realised that such a sharp contrast between the later medieval and early modern period is misleading. This book presses home the argument for continuity to an even greater extent, in that the later medieval period is presented as constituting, as it were, a laboratory for testing and developing some of the governmental, social and economic institutions and forces which were to be prevalent in early modern Spain and parts of its Empire. It is, for example, a remarkable fact that almost all the institutions of the early modern period were developed during the course of the fourteenth and fifteenth centuries. Indeed, given the long history of some of these institutions it is not at all fanciful to discern an *ancien régime* period in Spanish history which stretches from the fourteenth to the nineteenth centuries.

As in earlier centuries, war constituted a major factor making for governmental and social innovation during the fourteenth and fifteenth centuries. In terms of political and military exploits, the civil and foreign wars of the period could produce little to compare with the heroic deeds of the reconquest; yet the wars arising from English and French intervention in Iberian politics, and the constant dangers posed by civil wars, stimulated a greater degree of institutional reform. Developments in war, government, armies, navies and taxation were inextricably bound up together. And so this book attempts to show the relationship between naval and maritime expansion and Castilian participation in the Hundred Years War, while also setting institutional innovations against the background of monarchs who, faced with civil wars, introduced military reforms, invented new taxes to buy alliances and troops, and tried to win support by governmental and administrative reforms.

In dealing with the civil wars and popular unrest of the later medieval period, this book tends to stress those aspects which link up naturally with features which characterised the social and economic structure of the early modern period. During the fourteenth and fifteenth centuries Catalonia suffered economic and demographic decline, and the Genoese established themselves in strength in a Castile which was to act as a springboard for their activities in the New World. In this period, too, a crisis in incomes provoked the lords of Castile into a feverish search for alternative sources of revenue as a result of which, although the monarchy seemed to be the main victim, the fortunes of the great nobility came to be closely linked to the royal court and the king emerged in a potentially commanding position. At the same time economic and social grievances led, along with religious tensions, to an increasing victimisation of the Jews and *conversos* which ended in the establishment of the Inquisition. By the end of the fifteenth century *convivencia* had come to an end and a closed and rigidly orthodox society was being formally established.

The existence of several Spanish kingdoms and peoples during the medieval period has inevitably presented problems in the writing of this book. It is possible, by a process of arbitrary simplification, to draw a sensible distinction between two groupings of polities in medieval Christian Spain. In the western grouping there were the kingdoms of the Castilian *meseta*. The nucleus of this grouping had been the kingdom of Asturias which, with the transfer of the court to León in the tenth century, became the kingdom of León. The important county of Castile became an independent kingdom in 1035 and ended up by dominating the areas of the western grouping as well as acquiring the lion's share of the lands reconquered from the Muslims. It was on these western or central areas, and especially Castile, that the influence of the frontier had its greatest impact, and it was in the later medieval kingdom of Castile that many of the institutions of the future were to be forged. Inevitably, therefore, Castile figures prominently in this book.

The nuclei of the areas in the eastern bloc were to be found in the Pyrenees. They included the kingdom of Navarre, the county of

Aragon (which became a kingdom in 1035), and various counties intimately connected with the Frankish kingdom. From an early date, some of these counties began to constitute a Catalan entity, with the counts of Barcelona providing the impetus towards unity. Catalonia and the kingdom of Aragon were united in 1137 to form the Crown of Aragon, and the kingdoms of Mallorca and Valencia were later acquired by conquest. Within the space at my disposal I have tried to do justice to the unique features of the Crown of Aragon, and in particular to the development of its socio-economic structure and its remarkable constitution.

Selection has also involved the sacrifice of detailed political narrative. This is not wholly disastrous, for it would require a much larger book than this to give life to all the characters who crowd the Spanish political stage. It has seemed better to use selected individuals who can stand for, or signify, trends of importance: such an individual might be a king, like James the Conqueror, but he might equally be a *caballero*, like Corraquín Sancho of Avila, or a shepherd from Jaén.

The Background of Early Eleventh-century Spain

WHEN the Muslims invaded in 711 and defeated the Visigoths, they called the lands they acquired al-Andalus. Until 756 al-Andalus was ruled by a governor under the political and religious supremacy of the caliphs of Damascus. When in 756 'Abd al-Rahmān I founded an independent emirate in al-Andalus, the fiction of the religious supremacy of the caliphate, now at Baghdad, was maintained; but in 929 'Abd al-Rahmān III assumed the title of 'caliph', and a fully independent al-Andalus now entered an age of splendour which lasted until the early eleventh century. By the late tenth century, however, the caliphs were merely titular rulers, and during the period known as the Amirid dictatorship, which lasted till 1009, power was wielded by the redoubtable al-Mansūr and his successors. Thereafter al-Andalus was plunged into anarchy, and by 1031 the caliphate had officially ceased to exist.

The salient features of the economy of al-Andalus, as it developed during the ninth and tenth centuries, were a relatively sophisticated agricultural system, large and flourishing towns, and the existence of a monetary economy. Most of the country was characterised by poor soil and dry-farming areas which were primarily devoted to the production of cereals, olives and vines, but irrigation agriculture was also practised in the *huertas* of the rich alluvial lands along the Mediterranean coast and in the valleys of the Guadalquivir and Genil. The advanced state of the agrarian economy explains why al-Andalus also enjoyed considerable urban and industrial development. For example, Córdoba, with a population of some 100,000 in the tenth century, was easily the largest town in a western Europe where, in the Christian areas, no town even approached the 50,000 mark. Córdoba was also outstanding for its cosmopolitan and cultural atmosphere: it was an intellectual centre as well as being the capital of the caliphate. Contemporaries were astonished not only by the sophisticated level of life in the capital but also by the fabulous sums of money which the rulers seemed to have at their disposal. Conservative calculations indicate, for example, that 'Abd al-Rahmān III's reserves averaged about 5,500,000 dinars during his reign, and all estimates indicate revenues far in excess of those at the disposal of rulers in feudal Europe. The reasons for this abundance of wealth were the proximity of North African supplies of gold and the fact that al-Andalus enjoyed a flourishing external trade within a buoyant Mediterranean economy where gold currency was reasonably abundant.

Despite its relatively sophisticated economic and governmental structure, however, the caliphate was beset by serious problems which militated strongly against stability and unity. Even at the political zenith of al-Andalus the rulers failed to establish their authority over a country where environmental features encouraged regional autonomy. Nearly half the total area of Spain is taken up by a vast tableland, the *meseta*, around which mountain barriers make communications extremely difficult. Moreover, the rivers of Spain are for the most part unnavigable, and the *meseta* itself is fragmented by even more ranges of mountains. Thus the nature of the terrain encouraged the emergence of regional potentates whose dependence on the caliphs was often signified merely by the payment of tribute and the promise of military support in times of crisis.

An endemic problem of racial and tribal conflict also posed a threat to the unity of al-Andalus. Relations between Arabs and Berbers were usually marked by profound hostility. The Berbers, who formed the bulk of the invaders and came over into Spain in several waves of immigration, numbered several hundreds of thousands – not a large figure when compared to a total Spanish population of some seven million in the tenth century. Although the point is still problematical, it is probable that the Arabs forced a disadvantageous distribution of land on the Berbers. There were, of course, exceptions to this pattern, and Guichard has forcefully argued in support of a Berber settlement in the fertile lands of Valencia. But, on the whole, it seems that the Berber clans settled in the mountainous and peripheral regions – that is, in remote areas which lacked urban centres and which appear only fleetingly in the writings of contemporary observers.

The Berbers adapted to their new environment rapidly, and by the ninth century many had ceased to speak their native language in favour of Arabic or the prevailing romance dialect. Indeed, in the face of further Berber immigration, the original Berbers attempted to obscure their origins by adopting Arabic names which would differentiate them from newcomers.

The number of Arab invaders, most of whom entered Spain during the first half of the eighth century, can reasonably be estimated at between thirty and fifty thousand. They settled in the fertile areas along the valleys of the rivers Ebro, Guadalquivir and Genil, the lands round Toledo and the irrigated *vegas* and *huertas* of the south and east. Although some lived on their estates, many were absentee landlords who used their revenues to support their taste for a life of luxury in the environs of the large towns. The Arabs tended to monopolise official positions, and it was perhaps because of this that they emphasised their ethnic origins and tribal affiliations. Yet, from the very date of the invasion, they had been forced to select their wives and concubines from the indigenous population, and by the tenth century their blood had been inextricably mingled with that of Europeans and Africans – a fact which did not for one minute hinder many of them from perceiving a reality in tribal and racial differences. Indeed, the Arabs themselves were for long divided by feuds of tribal rivalry, especially between the Yemenites and Qaysites.

The majority of the population in al-Andalus was made up of the Muwallads or native Spanish converts to Islam. These people, along with the relatively few remaining Christians or Mozarabs, continued for the most part to speak a romance language which, although it adopted numerous Arabic words, remained the language of greatest usage. Arabic, rather like Anglo-Norman French in post-conquest England, constituted the language of the politically dominant groups but not of the bulk of the population. During the ninth and tenth centuries the native Spanish population of al-Andalus played an increasingly important role in popular movements and rebellions.

The 'slaves' (saqāliba) imported into al-Andalus from eastern and western Europe were relatively few in numbers, but most of them lived in the larger towns, and by the end of the tenth century there were about eight thousand saqāliba in Córdoba alone. The caliphal guard was recruited from their ranks, and since most saqāliba arrived in al-Andulas as children and were brought up as Muslims, they could and did attain important posts in government.

Unrest, therefore, was hard to eradicate in a country where particularism and the creation of local power bases coincided with racial and tribal patterns of land settlement, and the political structure of al-Andalus was characterised by the existence of lordships of Berber brigands in the mountains, federations of Arab tribal groupings in the plains, and Arab-dominated power-blocs based on large towns such as Seville and Toledo. It is hardly surprising, therefore, that when the caliphate collapsed, political units surfaced to become small Taifa or 'party' states which were identified with different ethnic groups. The Berbers dominated the south coast from Cádiz to Granada; the Arabs, by now more or less fused with indigenous Muslims, controlled the states based on the larger towns; the saqāliba gained power in the lands between Almería and Tortosa. In each of the Taifa states the dominant party governed parasitically in its own interests, and this inevitably led to much internal strife, while at the same time the rivalry between rulers led to interminable and complicated wars which encouraged the Christians of the north to advance southwards.

The Muslims had never established more than a precarious military occupation in the northernmost parts of Spain. Indeed, some Basque and Pyrenean areas escaped their control entirely, and as early as 732 a guerrilla band inflicted a defeat on the Muslims at Covadonga. During the ninth century the Christians gradually advanced from the cordillera which protected the mountain kingdom of Asturias, to the defensive barrier of the river Duero; by this time Barcelona had also escaped from Muslim domination, and its counts were busying themselves in acquiring power in the Spanish March which the Franks had established. Thus, slowly and with deter-

mination, the Christian rulers built up the various polities of the
north.

For the Muslims, however, the 'battle' of Covadonga was nothing
but an insignificant skirmish. Moreover, despite the Christian
advance to the Duero, the balance of economic, political and
military power remained heavily weighted in favour of the caliphate.
In contrast to the richer and more productive lands of al-Andalus
those of the Christian north were, on the whole, mountainous,
underpopulated and lacking in towns and cities. When the Christian
frontiersmen moved south to the Duero wilderness they were
settling free land which was uncontested by the Muslims. Indeed, as
early as the mid-eighth century the Berbers who had settled in
Galicia and the Duero valley had migrated southwards and away
from lands which they found inhospitable. Thus there was as yet no
real military reconquest, and the vast no-man's-land which separated the kingdom of Asturias from al-Andalus was an unadmini-
stered desert when the colonists began to move in during the ninth
century. With the collapse of the caliphate in the early eleventh
century, however, political circumstances changed and the military
initiative now lay with the Christians. The new situation was
admirably summed up by an eleventh-century Christian count,
Sisnando Davídiz, whose words were recorded by the Taifa ruler of
Granada, 'Abd Allah:

> All this was repeated to me by Sisnando by word of mouth. . . .
> 'In the beginning al-Andalus belonged to the Christians, until
> they were defeated by the Arabs who drove them back to Galicia,
> the region least blessed by nature. But now that it is possible, they
> want to recover that which was taken from them by force and,
> in order to gain a decisive result, it is necessary to wear you down
> and weaken you. When you have no money and no soldiers left,
> we will take over the country without the least difficulty!'[1]

PART I

THE AGE
OF
THE FRONTIER,
c. 1000–1350

1. Protection Rackets and Crusaders,
c. 1000–1212

RIGHT up to the early eleventh century the Christian kingdoms suffered from the military blows delivered at will by the rulers of al-Andalus. Al-Mansūr (978–1002), dictator of al-Andalus, led some fifty campaigns against the north, many of which cut deep into Christian territory: for example, in 985 the inhabitants of Barcelona were put to the sword and in 997 Santiago de Compostela was sacked. But after the death of al-Mansūr's son, 'Abd al-Malik, in 1008, the caliphate disintegrated, and by 1031 it had been replaced by Taifa states whose rulers were absolutely incapable of presenting a united front against the Christians.

How did the Christians react to the opportunities which the new situation presented? One frontier area, Castile, had become prominent precisely because its geographical position had exposed the inhabitants to constant attacks. Bearing the brunt of Muslim onslaughts, the country became a land of castles and, by the end of the eighth century, this *territorium castelle* was already being referred to by Muslim chroniclers as *al-Qila* (the castles). Even when united with the kingdom of León, it was Castile which dominated the task of reconquest, and her epic hero, the Cid (c. 1040–99), not only typifies specific Castilian qualities but also the frontier virtues of the eleventh century. It was during this period that the Christians advanced from the Duero to the Tagus: Alfonso VI of León and Castile (1065/72–1109) captured Toledo (1085), and the Cid stormed Valencia. All these were magnificent achievements. Yet this was not a crusading frontier. On the contrary, it was a frontier where the Christians, desperately short of manpower, often allied themselves with Muslim rulers while at the same time subjecting them to 'protection racket' systems in order to obtain the precious gold which they coveted so much.

The Eleventh Century:
Warriors and Monks in the Age of *Parias*

'ABD Allah, the Taifa ruler of Granada, was in a good position to observe the realities of eleventh-century frontier politics, and he brilliantly describes the thoughts and strategies of the Christians in his *Memoirs*. He was particularly well informed about Alfonso VI's policy because it was revealed to him by Count Sisnando Davídiz, a Mozarab, who acted as a diplomatic intermediary between the Christian king and the Taifa rulers. Here then is 'Abd Allah's lengthy exposé of Alfonso VI's reaction to the changed circumstances of the eleventh century. It describes the thoughts of the Christian king at a time when he was being enticed into a military alliance with the Taifa state of Seville, which, of course, was to be directed against Granada:

> All these promises [by the ruler of Seville] filled the Christian with greed and he said to himself: 'Here is a pretty business from which I can't fail to profit even if the town [of Granada] is not taken! But how would I gain by taking Granada from one of them and giving it to the other who would thus be provided with further means to oppose me? The more unrest and rivalry that there is between them the better it is for me!' He came away then with the intention of stripping clean his ally, as well as the other against whom he was manoeuvring, and of setting one against the other to their mutual ruin. Besides, he entertained no hope of taking the town for himself and on this matter he reasoned as follows: 'I am a foreigner to them and they all hate me. Why should I decide to take Granada? That it should surrender without a fight is impossible! Thus I would have to wage war, risk the lives of my soldiers, and spend money – and I would then lose more than I could hope to gain if it fell [without a fight] into my hands! Even in the latter case itself, I would not be able to hold it unless I could be sure – and this would be impossible – of the loyalty of the population. I couldn't even massacre the latter and populate the town with men from my own country! No, in reality what must be done is to set the Muslim princes against each other and continually take money from them in order to weaken their resources and exhaust them. Once they have reached that stage they won't be able to do anything except give in and come to surrender to me spontaneously. That is what has happened at Toledo, which I will obtain without trouble, thanks to the impoverishment and dispersal of the population as well as to the flight of its ruler.'[2]

All the evidence supports this remarkably fine analysis by 'Abd

Allah and confirms the Christian strategy of continually extorting money from the Taifa rulers. For a short time after anarchy broke out in al-Andalus in 1009, the Christian rulers had contracted to supply Muslim princes with specific military support in return for cash. But they were soon to step up their demands and, using the threat of war, they forced treaties on the Muslim rulers which stipulated the surrender of fixed amounts of cash, known as *parias*, which were to be paid annually and at regular intervals. These *parias* came to form an essential part of the regular income of Christian rulers who, although short of manpower for reconquest, could use warfare as a lever to induce the Muslim payers of *parias* to increase the sums involved. In their matrimonial projects, pious donations, and political alliances the Christian princes used present and future *parias* to cement the intentions of contracting parties. When, for example, the count of Barcelona wished to repopulate Tarragona, he granted it in fief to Viscount William of Narbonne along with 120 ounces of gold from the *parias* paid to him by the Muslims, and he agreed to continue paying him this gold until such time as further *parias* of the same amount should be paid directly to his vassal. Rulers even included their *parias* in their wills. Ferdinand I of León and Castile (1037–65), for example, distributed his *parias* and kingdoms among his sons in the following manner: Sancho received Castile together with the *parias* paid by the Taifa state of Zaragoza, Alfonso was given the kingdom of León and the *parias* of Toledo, and García gained Galicia and the *parias* of Seville and Badajoz.

Although it is impossible to calculate the total amount paid in *parias*, it is certain that huge amounts were involved. It was the income from *parias*, for example, which enabled Count Ramón Berenguer I to spend 10,000 ounces of precious metals in only ten years during which he bought up those lands, castles and rights which would emphasise the supremacy of Barcelona over the other Catalan counties. And, of course, even then the count could include in his will another 1000 ounces for his daughter and a further 1600 ounces to be spent for the good of his soul. Alfonso VI of León and Castile similarly disposed of vast sums of *parias* income. Quite apart from the *parias* paid by the rulers of Zaragoza, Seville and Badajoz, we have the direct evidence of 'Abd Allah for the *parias* paid by Granada. These consisted of an initial instalment of 30,000 dinars and annual payments of 10,000 dinars, and 'Abd Allah ends his account of the negotiations with a description of the honeyed words and veiled threats so common among those exacting money in exchange for protection:

> An agreement was accordingly drawn up in the presence of Alfonso. . . . For my part, he fixed the annual tribute at 10,000 mitqals. He spoke to me softly, saying: '. . . I will not subject you to anything else except the payment of the tribute, which you will send to me each year without delay. If you hold back payment, you will receive the visit of my ambassador and his stay will occasion you some expenses! It is better for you, therefore, to hurry up and hand over the money!' I accepted his words since I knew that the payment of 10,000 mitqals per year protected me from his misdeeds and was better than Muslim losses and the ravaging of the country. . . .[3]

Parias, of course, did not constitute all the profits to be obtained from the frontier, as the career of the hero of the epic *Cantar de Mío Cid* illustrates. The *Cantar*, probably composed about 1207, is nevertheless strikingly accurate with regard to the historical events surrounding the life of Rodrigo Díaz de Vivar who was also known as *El Cid* and *El Campeador*. The Cid was born in Vivar, near Burgos, round about 1040. In 1079 he was sent by Alfonso VI to collect the *parias* due from the ruler of Seville. Shortly after this embassy, however, Rodrigo fell foul of the king and, exiled by Alfonso VI, set off with his retinue to carve out a prodigious career for himself in eastern Spain. The Cid's title derived from the Arabic *sīd*, meaning 'lord', and in the following years he was as often to be found in the service of Muslim rulers, such as al-Mu'tāmin of Zaragoza, as in alliance with Christian princes. Subsequently the Cid became lord and independent ruler of Muslim Valencia (1094–9).

The *Cantar* or epic is plainly obsessed with the problem of how warriors made a living – a theme which is both historically realistic and yet fits in well with the story. Propertyless and in exile, the Cid tells his men that they must keep moving 'for we must live by our swords and lances. Otherwise, in this lean land we could not survive and, in my opinion, we must move on.' Since *parias* were paid to secure effective protection, however, it was not long before the Cid was receiving tribute in much the same way as the Christian princes. Sometimes, it is true, tribute was paid locally by Muslim frontier areas as a means to avoid the immediate danger of attack. But the Cid also probably ended up receiving as much in regular *parias* as kings and princes. For five years, for example, he acted as the 'protector' of Muslim Zaragoza, and the amounts he was paid for this protection could hardly have been less than the 12,000 dinars per year which previous protectors had exacted for the same services.

Booty and spoils provided another profitable source of income for the Cid and his men. Officials known as *quiñoneros* divided up the booty, and the epic makes it clear not only that a written record was kept but that there were rules about share sizes: the leader, following the Muslim custom, received one-fifth of the spoils, and *caballeros* or knights gained twice as much as footsoldiers. Time and again the *Cantar* dwells on the livestock, gold, silver, horses and clothing which were acquired as booty. Yet in the end success is also measured in terms of land – not the lean land of the arid dry-farming areas, but the rich lands of the Valencian *huertas*.

> They admire Valencia, how it spreads before them, and beyond it the sea, and there the *huerta* lands, vast and thickly planted, and all manner of things to delight them, and they raise their hands and give thanks to God for this gift, so rich and great.[4]

For many of the Christian princes and warriors, therefore, the eleventh century was literally a golden age. Indeed, at one point in the *Cantar* the Cid fills a boot with gold and silver, and sends it off to pay for masses at the church of Santa María in Burgos. The incident is not without its general significance because, although it may be difficult to accept the view that Romanesque architecture in Spain was financed from the *parias*, important donations of gold were certainly made to religious centres both inside and outside the peninsula. One such donation was truly magnificent: Ferdinand I established an annual 'cense' or rent of 120 ounces of gold in favour of the monastery of Cluny, and Alfonso VI doubled this amount to 240 ounces.

The age of *parias*, however, was also one of alliances and close contacts with the Muslims, and this inevitably left its mark on society. The epic of the Cid, for example, convincingly portrays the Cid's Muslim friend, Abengalbón, as being nobler and in all respects worthier than the evil princes of Carrión who inhabit Alfonso VI's court. Alfonso himself, indeed, spent some of his youth in exile at the Muslim court of Toledo, and in his later life took the daughter-in-law of the Muslim ruler of Seville as his mistress. Not surprisingly such a society displayed few signs of a crusading spirit. In 1064, it is true, a 'crusade', which included men from across the Pyrenees, was successfully mounted against Muslim Barbastro; but once the Christians had captured it, they let themselves be seduced by the life-style of the vanquished, surrounded themselves with female slave-singers, and took to dressing in Muslim clothes. After the fall of Toledo in 1085, however, this confusion in attitudes led to a serious conflict within governing circles as to the policies to be adopted towards the vanquished.

In many ways the views of Count Sisnando Davídiz, Mozarab and royal councillor, typified one policy which had for long prevailed at court. In his youth Sisnando had been captured during a Muslim expedition into Christian territory and taken to Seville. There he received a highly advanced education in all aspects of Arabic culture and became an intimate councillor of the Taifa ruler. Then, for reasons that remain obscure, he crossed to the Christian side and became a royal councillor. Thus, as Ibn Bassām put it, Sisnando 'acquired great experience of frontiers and communications and ended up dominating the secrets of politics and government'.[5] Indeed this was the man who had revealed Alfonso VI's thoughts to 'Abd Allah of Granada.

Sisnando was a Mozarab. The term 'Mozarab' derives from the Arabic *musta 'rab*, meaning 'Arabicised' or 'having assimilated Arabic customs', and it came to be used to denote Christians living in al-Andalus – that is, a clergy and laity who had adopted Muslim clothes and spoke Arabic. From the second half of the ninth century groups of Mozarabs had freely chosen to escape Islamic domination, and they had been well received by Christian communities in the north. The case of the eleventh-century Mozarabs of Toledo, however, was different.

There is little doubt that, when Toledo was taken over by Alfonso VI in 1085, Sisnando and a small group of prestigious Mozarabic families in the town contributed to the Christian success. Thus the Christians at first adopted a policy of toleration towards the Mozarabs and Muslims who remained in the town, and Sisnando, the main advocate of this policy, was appointed governor. This attitude of toleration, however, did not last for long, and the change of policy was marked by the forced conversion of the chief mosque of Toledo into a church. It is worth examining Muslim and Christian accounts of this incident because they reveal serious conflicts of opinion in court circles which ultimately contributed to bringing the age of *parias* and tolerance to an end. Here is Ibn Bassām's account of the incident:

> The latter [Sisnando] tried to make the Toledan's misfortunes bearable and to render tolerable the vile condition into which they had been depressed. He demanded little and acted justly in his decisions; thus by this policy he conciliated people of standing and even displayed his care for the lower orders. . . .
>
> Sisnando's idea was to maintain the *status quo* in Toledo. . . . But Alfonso rejected anything that did not fit in with his ignorant conduct, and continued the downhill path which his greed dictated. . . . Sisnando said to him: 'Extend your protecting wings over the inhabitants and win their taxes in exchange for the protection which you provide for them. Be not angered with the [Muslim] rulers of the peninsula because you will not be able to do without them. . . . Remember that if you vent your anger and persecute them without respite, you will force them to escape your control and they will have to seek the intervention of a third party.' But . . . Alfonso followed the opposite course which his passion indicated and he immediately decided to defile the mosque of Toledo – an event which was the culmination of so much ill fortune and desolated all those who saw or knew about it.
>
> Sisnando said to him: 'To act in this way will inflame passions, render useless all policies followed in the past, alienate all those who might help us, and deter all those who are already supporting us.' But Alfonso (God curse him!) was blinded by pride . . . and listened only to the voice of his own madness. . . .[6]

Count Sisnando, then, desperately tried to salvage a Mozarabic policy of mutual understanding and toleration. It was the policy of a man who knew the frontier well and was himself an Arabicised Christian. But a Christian version of the incident does not substantiate the picture of a proud and intolerant king:

> Shortly after Toledo was taken, the Cluniac monk Bernard, abbot of Sahagún, was elected archbishop of the recently conquered town and, at a time when the king had gone to León, Queen Constance induced him [Bernard] to take possession of the chief mosque. Accompanied by Christian knights, he entered into the mosque, set up altars and had bells put into the minaret

to summon the faithful. When Alfonso heard of this, he was saddened and angered, because he had promised the Muslims that he would protect their mosque. Threatening to burn Bernard and the queen, he covered the distance from Sahagún to Toledo in only three days. . . .[7]

This account, therefore, attributes the incident to Queen Constance and Archbishop Bernard, and they represented a different policy opposed to Sisnando's Mozarabic viewpoint. Both the queen and the archbishop were French: Constance, Alfonso VI's second wife, was the daughter of Duke Robert of Burgundy, and Bernard had been born into a noble family of the Agenais. Another common factor linked them together: the queen was the niece of St Hugh of Cluny, and Bernard was a Cluniac monk. The French and Cluniac background of these two, who had only recently entered upon the Spanish scene, inevitably affected their attitudes and they found the 'Mozarabic' policy of tolerance not only strange but abhorrent and suspicious. Indeed, an older generation of historians also identified the activities of Cluniac monks with the policies of Gregory VII and with the origins of the crusading movement against Spanish Islam. Few scholars would now subscribe wholeheartedly to these views, but they still contain much that is useful to an exploration of what lay behind the opposing policies of Bernard and Sisnando.

After the Muslim conquest both the Mozarabic Church in al-Andalus and the independent church in the north-west were cut off from Rome and Europe. One important consequence was that control over ecclesiastical affairs in Christian Spain fell to the monarchy, and important decisions were made in the *curia regis* which, under royal control, was the headquarters of the Church. As the Christians pushed south, therefore, the tasks of restoring and creating dioceses, confirming the foundation of monasteries, and appointing bishops and abbots, fell to the control of monarchs.

In more general terms, the isolation of Spain, with the exception of Catalonia which maintained close links with France, led to the development of differences between Hispanic or 'Mozarabic' religious traditions and the 'Roman' pattern of practices observed in the rest of Europe. After the Muslim invasion, for example, monasticism continued to flourish both in al-Andalus and in Christian Galicia and Asturias, but, being isolated, the monks maintained their identity precisely because they stressed their own

Mozarabic and Visigothic traditions. Thus, they remained largely unaware of monastic developments in the rest of Europe, and when groups of Mozarabs migrated to the Christian north during the ninth century, they reinforced the particularism of religious traditions there. The result was that there was nothing Benedictine about monastic life down to the eleventh century, and it was to the Hispanic *regulae* of men like St Isidore of Seville and St Fructuosus of Braga that the churchmen looked back to for their inspiration. What was true of monasticism was also true of other aspects of religious and cultural life. The liturgy, for example, was different from that of the Roman rite, and even the manner of writing contrasted with the Carolingian script used on the other side of the Pyrenees. It is because of such differences, arising out of Spain's isolated position, that historians such as Maravall have used the term 'Mozarabic' to describe the whole texture of cultural and religious life in the north-west down to the eleventh century. The use of the term in this sense may seem exaggerated, but it underlines those developments which help us to understand the problems arising from the absorption of those who remained behind after the fall of towns such as Coimbra (1063) and Toledo (1085). In short, as well as standing for a policy of political toleration, Sisnando can be viewed as representing a Hispanic or Mozarabic religious and cultural tradition of considerable resilience and independence.

In the eastern kingdoms, where the links with France and Rome were stronger and Benedictine monasticism became established by the tenth century, the imposition of the Roman rite was the work of the papal legate Hugh Candidus. The latter was not a Cluniac, and the changeover had virtually been effected in Aragon and Navarre before Gregory VII became pope. In the western kingdoms of León and Castile, however, the reformed Benedictinism of the Cluniacs began to make headway in the 1070s at a time when Gregory VII was pressing Alfonso VI to replace the Mozarabic or Visigothic liturgy with the Roman rite. Modern research has modified the traditional view of a triumphant papal–Cluniac alliance spearheading an attack on Hispanic religious traditions. It is pointed out, for example, that only some thirty monastic houses in Spain actually placed themselves within the Cluniac dependence and that their regional distribution varied considerably. Thus while some areas of the kingdom of León, such as the Tierra de Campos, were heavily influenced by Cluniac monasticism, Castile was hardly penetrated, and the advance into the Galaico-Portuguese west did not come until the first quarter of the twelfth century. Moreover, the first abbot of Sahagún, Robert, whom Alfonso VI placed there after deposing the previous abbot by his own authority, turned out to be a champion not of the Roman but of the Mozarabic rite. Nevertheless, such qualifications do not substantially alter the general picture. The number of Cluniac monasteries may have been small, but St Hugh, abbot of Cluny, worked through his monastic bishops and legates, all of whom were Frenchmen. Bernard became archbishop of Toledo, and Cluny provided bishops for other dioceses such as Segovia, Palencia, Siguenza, Zamora and Salamanca. Abbot Robert certainly defended the Mozarabic rite, and there may have been other Cluniacs who counselled a policy of gradual change, but Robert was sent back to France after being evicted from both the royal court and Sahagún monastery, and the weight of both the papacy and Cluny was behind the struggle to impose the Roman liturgy.

The opposing viewpoints of Sisnando and Archbishop Bernard, therefore, were not confined to the incident of the mosque of Toledo but reflected a wider controversy between the partisans of the Hispanic or Mozarabic religious traditions and those who wished to establish a monopoly of Roman norms in Spain. In 1080 a council at Burgos decided officially in favour of the Roman rite, but this was by no means the end of the matter, for resistance continued in the extreme west and, above all, in the recently occupied towns of Toledo and Coimbra. In Toledo, the occupation of the mosque and its consecration to the Roman rite led Sisnando to abandon the government of the town which was handed over to Pedro Ansúrez. But the Mozarabic clergy in the Christian churches, accustomed to their own liturgy and Arabicised customs, did not accept the hard line adopted by Archbishop Bernard, and hostility towards the Francophil clergy lasted well into the twelfth century. Sisnando, meanwhile, had retired to Coimbra which was to be the other bastion of resistance to the Roman rite. This town and its region had fallen to the Christians in 1063 and, constituted into a county, had been given to Sisnando who lost no time in welcoming Mozarabic clergy from the south and in proposing that the newly created see be given to Paternus, formerly Mozarabic bishop of Tortosa. With the death of Sisnando in 1091, however, the Coimbran resistance began to crumble, and it was not long before Martin, the Mozarab who held the diocese, stepped down in favour of a new bishop under whom the Roman rite was imposed. Thus, by the end of the eleventh century the Francophil clergy had triumphed, and the Mozarabic liturgy survived only in some of the parishes of Toledo.

Cluniac intervention in peninsular affairs, however, was not prompted solely by religious considerations, as the Burgundian abbey's interest in the politics of the *parias* illustrates. It was Ferdinand I who, at some point during the decade after 1055, established an annual cense of 1000 dinars in favour of Cluny. During the last years of his reign the king was receiving about 40,000 dinars a year from the *parias* of Zaragoza, Toledo, Seville and Badajoz, and the payments to Cluny consequently constituted only about two-and-a-half per cent of this cascade of gold. For the abbey of Cluny, however, the cense represented a fortune which, estimated by contemporaries and modern scholars to be worth 120 ounces of gold a year, was worth more than the total income of the abbey's important landed possessions. By the standards of the age, indeed, the cense was a magnificent gift which put the sums donated by other rulers in the shade.

But Ferdinand I divided his realms and *parias* amongst his sons, and Alfonso VI at the start of his reign only controlled the Toledan *parias*, of which the cense to Cluny would have taken up as much as ten per cent of the total. Moreover the king was by no means a weak and credulous creature who could easily be exploited by foreign monks, and his goodwill had to be gained by active means. Thus, when in 1072 Alfonso VI was defeated and imprisoned by his brother, Sancho II of Castile (1065-72), it was St Hugh of Cluny who secured his release, and it was the latter who was also behind the marriage to Constance of Burgundy in 1079. Furthermore, when Alfonso VI needed military help against the Muslims in the late 1080s, it was from Burgundy that it came, as did the two young cousins, Raymond and Henry, who married the king's daughters, Urraca and Teresa.

As these political and dynastic links were forged, so did Alfonso VI reciprocate. In 1073, shortly after being released from prison through the mediation of St Hugh, the king began to hand over the first monasteries which Cluny acquired in the Leonese-Castilian realms. In 1077 he doubled his father's cense to 240 ounces of gold per year, and when St Hugh himself crossed the Pyrenees in 1090 the double cense was solemnly confirmed in Burgos with the assent of the queen, the ecclesiastical hierarchy and the nobility. By this date, however, the age of *parias* was already ending, and the inability of the Leonese–Castilian rulers to keep up their payments was to plunge Cluny into a financial decline which St Hugh's successors vainly attempted to halt. There remained the political interests of the Burgundians established in Spain, and St Hugh's hand is clearly to be seen in a conspiracy designed to prevent the succession to the throne of Sancho, son of Alfonso VI's Moorish mistress Zaida, to secure the Crown for Raymond of Burgundy and to divide the royal treasure in Toledo between Raymond and Henry of Burgundy. But in the event Prince Sancho, Raymond of Burgundy and the age of *parias* all passed away before Alfonso VI himself died.

The Twelfth Century:
Monks and Warriors in a Crusading Age

IN contrast to the age of *parias*, as will be seen in a subsequent chapter, the twelfth-century frontier world was marked by Christian attempts to ransack al-Andalus for its works of scholarship rather than for its gold. But it was also a century which witnessed a heightening of the antagonisms between Muslims and Christians as a result of the intolerance imported from Europe and Africa respectively.

With the taking of Toledo in 1085, the territory north of the Tagus fell to the Christians, and Alfonso VI, established in the ancient capital of the Visigothic kingdom, appeared to be the arbiter of Iberian politics. Sisnando, as we have seen, advised the king to treat the remaining Taifa rulers benevolently: 'otherwise you will force them to escape your control and they will have to seek the intervention of a third party'. But Alfonso VI ignored Sisnando's advice, pressed for more *parias* and imposed 'governors' on the Taifa rulers to ensure his direct control and the payment of tribute.

The Muslim rulers, of course, disposed of considerable resources of wealth, but the huge sums demanded from them inevitably meant that they imposed greater burdens of taxation on their subjects. Thus, for many Muslims, the Taifa rulers seemed to be encouraging the rapacious Christians. The entry for 'Castile' in al-Himyari's *Rawd al-mi'tār*, for example, ends:

Someone composed the following verses.

'The Christians mount expeditions into the countryside and take away booty: whatever is left to the inhabitants is then taken by the Arabs and the fisc! All the money of the country goes to Castile in tribute payments. May Allah look after his slaves and have pity of them!'[8]

Similarly Ibn Hazm of Córdoba, who loathed the Taifa rulers, bitterly assailed them for their corruption, illegal taxation and alliances with Christians:

By God, I swear that if the tyrants were to learn that they would attain their ends more easily by adopting the religion of the Cross, they would certainly hasten to profess it! Indeed, we see that they ask the Christians for help and allow them to take away Muslim men, women and children as captives to their lands. Frequently they protect them in their attacks against the most inviolable land, and ally with them in order to gain security.[9]

The alternative to the system of *parias*, however, was almost as perilous for the Muslim princes, because an appeal to a 'third party' would entail the intervention of the Berber Almoravids of North Africa, and this might well lead to the disappearance of the Taifa states. It was the ruler of Seville, al-Mu'tamid, who finally took the decisive step of invoking North African help to redress the balance against Alfonso VI. With the intervention of the Almoravids the Christians suffered serious reverses, and the Taifa rulers were swept aside. Alfonso VI, for example, managed to hold Toledo but his army was decisively defeated at Zalaca (1086), and he had to give up Valencia after the death of the Cid. By the end of the eleventh century, after Taifa rulers such as 'Abd Allah and al-Mu'tamid had been sent into exile, the Almoravids had succeeded in imposing a measure of unity on al-Andalus. But their control crumbled in the 1140s, petty rulers reappeared on the scene and unity was only once again imposed, towards the end of the twelfth century, by the Almohads, products of another Berber religious revival in North Africa. Their supremacy, however, was shortlived and, after a crushing defeat at the hands of the Christians in the battle of Las Navas de Tolosa (1212), their power declined rapidly.

What were the forces underlying the unity which was imposed on al-Andalus by the mutually antagonistic movements of the Almoravids and the Almohads? Ibn Khaldūn, the fourteenth-century historian, envisaged the rise and fall of civilisations as invariably taking place between two poles of social organisation – desert life and the urban environment. The initial drive is derived from a feeling of group unity ('*asabiya*) which, based on religious conviction and tribal loyalty, gives the people of the desert the will to conquer and found a state or dynasty. The new state extends its frontiers and uses some of the assimilated labour forces for the production of luxury goods and the fostering of science and the arts, thus increasing its 'civilisation'. But the new conditions corrupt the desert people, and group unity and religious cohesion wither and disappear. Thus urban and sedentary society is more 'civilised', but its structure inevitably leads to political decline and a conquest by a new wave of desert peoples.

In the early stages of both movements the religious austerity and religious cohesiveness of the Almoravids and the Almohads certainly contrasted sharply with the disunited and irreligious climate of al-Andalus. Under the Taifa rulers, for example, the jurists or *alfaquíes*, who regarded themselves as the custodians of the Malikite orthodoxy of al-Andalus, had become sharply critical of the profanity and irreverence of princes and aristocrats. Rulers seemed to delight in the luxurious corruption of their courts, and by the imposition of taxes contrary to the revealed law of Islam they aroused widespread resentment amongst the population. The *alfaquíes*, therefore, encouraged support for the Almoravids, and the latter found their rise to power facilitated by the gulf between the Taifa rulers and their subjects. Indeed, the jurists issued a solemn sentence in which they declared the rulers to be libertines, corrupters of the populace and enemies of religion whose deeds had rendered them unworthy of ruling over Muslims; the emir of the Almoravids, Yūsuf b. Tāshufīn, had not only the right but the duty to depose them and impose religious orthodoxy and unity. Thus the pole of social organisation based on the hardy desert life was invoked to cleanse the corruption characteristic of the princely-urban environment.

The background to both the Almoravid and Almohad movements was one of 'desert austerity', localised in the Atlas region of north-west Africa, which provided the basis for the rapid growth into the empires of which al-Andalus formed a part. There, however, the similarity ends. The nucleus of the Almoravid movement depended on the tribal groups of the Sanhāja, whereas that of the Almohads was constituted by the Atlas highlanders of the Masmūda who were bitter enemies of the Sanhāja. In addition to these tribal differences there were the all-important religious issues. The Almoravid movement represented a strict and total acceptance of the Malikite rite, and it is this factor which stifled the study of sources, excluded the possibility of differing scholarly interpretations, and created an aura of fanaticism. Indeed, the Almoravids excluded allegorical interpretations of the *Qur'ān* and, by insisting on the literal acceptance of such phrases as 'Allah spoke' and 'Allah sees', they ended up with anthropomorphism – that is, God was attributed with a human personality and forms. The Almohads, for their part, insisted that the *Qur'ān* must be interpreted allegorically, placed great emphasis on the concept of *taw'hīd* or 'the assertion of unity', and preached Holy War against the Christian infidel and anthropomorphist Almoravids.

Bitter tribal and religious differences, therefore, opposed the Almohads to the Almoravids. But it was precisely these factors which endowed each movement with unity or *'asabiya* and, since they were both ardently committed to the Holy War against the Christians, their intervention in al-Andalus took on the appearance of two succeeding waves of 'crusading' fervour. It was this factor, indeed, which explained both their presence in Spain and their ultimate failure, for the Andalusians only really accepted the North African presence as long as it guaranteed military success and protection against the Christians.

Meanwhile similar developments had occurred in Christian Europe. Although crusading ideas formed slowly among Christians, the elements for the preaching of a Holy War were all present by the mid-eleventh century. At the Council of Clermont (1095) Urban II's appeal for volunteers to fight in the east drew an enthusiastic response, and the first of many crusades set off for the Holy Land. But the infidel could also be found in the Iberian peninsula, and increasing numbers of 'foreign' knights fought on the Spanish frontiers of Christendom. The life and activities of Alfonso I, 'the battler', king of Aragon and Navarre (1104–34), illustrate the extent to which the crusading impulse affected the Iberian frontier.

At the death of Alfonso VI and the accession of his daughter, Urraca, the Leonese–Castilian realms, which already faced serious military threats from the Almoravids, were plunged into civil wars. Thus, the brunt of the reconquest struggle passed to Alfonso I of Aragon who, although he had married Urraca and had to play a leading role in the social convulsions of León–Castile, brought to the frontier task a crusading fervour and military qualities of a high order. It was during his reign that most of the Ebro valley was taken, and important towns such as Zaragoza (1118), Tudela and Tarazona (1119), and Calatayud (1120) fell to the Christians. An examination of one of these episodes – the conquest of Zaragoza – will reveal the change of circumstances on the 'crusading' frontier.

In the conquest of Zaragoza the Aragonese received invaluable help from French forces. Even a Muslim writer like al-Maqqarī stressed the extent of this participation by soldiers from across the Pyrenees:

> At last in 512 [1117] when he thought the time had come to deal the decisive blow, Alfonso sent messengers to the lands of France, summoning all the Christian nations there to come and help him in his project; and the men of those lands, answering his call, rallied to his standard like swarms of locusts or ants. Soon Alfonso found himself at the head of countless forces with which he encamped before Zaragoza.[10]

Alfonso I, of course, was not the first monarch to appeal for such help for, as we have seen, Alfonso VI had received military and political support from the Burgundians. But by this time there was a decisive difference in that French help was envisaged within a crusading context. In 1118 a Council meeting in Toulouse, and attended by the archbishops of Arles and Auch and the bishops of Pamplona, Bayonne and Barbastro, elevated the expedition against Zaragoza into a crusade. Such an action was natural in the south of France: the memory of the First Crusade was still fresh, and there were many who, like Gaston of Béarn, Centulo of Bigorre, and Bernard Aton, viscount of Carcassonne, had already been to the Holy Land as crusaders and who now prepared for the Zaragoza expedition along with others such as Bishop Guy de Lons, and Auger, viscount of Miramont. The French, indeed, probably arrived at Zaragoza before Alfonso I himself, and it was Gaston of Béarn who, because of his experience with siege machines at Jerusalem, organised the wooden towers and catapults for the attack on the town. In the event it was starvation which forced the Muslims to surrender in December 1118, but, given the extent of the help from the Midi, it was only natural that Alfonso I should have granted the lordship of Zaragoza to Gaston of Béarn.

The example of the Zaragoza campaign, therefore, shows how the reconquest of the Ebro valley was to a certain extent the result of a deflection of the crusading impulse to the Iberian side of the Pyrenees. On no one was the influence of the crusading spirit greater, however, than Alfonso I himself. In his later years the king dreamed of taking Lérida, Tortosa and even Valencia, which he hoped to use as the port of embarkation for an expedition to Jerusalem. But above all it was in his astonishing will, drawn up in 1131, that Alfonso I revealed the extent to which the crusading 'fever' had taken hold of him. In it he declared that 'I grant and give all my kingdoms completely to the Sepulchre of Christ, the Hospital of the Poor and the Temple of the Lord so that they have it and possess it in three equal shares. . . .'

Veneration of the Holy Places and the lack of an obvious heir help partly to explain the king's action, but there can be little doubt that he was also prompted by the idea of heavily involving the military orders in the struggle against the infidel. His attempts to establish his own orders of Monreal and Belchite had not been successful and, by the terms of his will, he placed his hopes on the Templars. In the event, the terms of the will were not carried out, and after his death the Aragonese succession went to his brother, Ramiro.

In terms of the needs of the frontier, however, Alfonso I had certainly been thinking along the right lines. The Templars had already established themselves in Aragon during his lifetime, and before long the indigenous and powerful orders of Alcántara, Calatrava and Santiago appeared in the rest of the peninsula. These military orders owed their existence to a combination of military and religious enthusiasm, the objective of which was the struggle against the infidel. It has been argued that their emergence was influenced by the Muslim *ribāt* – that is, the house of retreat or frontier convent whose inmates combined a religious way of life with military service against the enemies of Islam. Indeed, the term 'Almoravids' is derived from the Arabic *al-Murābitūn* meaning the 'inhabitants of the *ribāt*'. There is no direct evidence to support this argument, but the very formulation of the theory serves as a reminder of the rise of crusading fervour on both sides of the Iberian frontier.

Nevertheless, even if the *ribāt* did influence the origins of the military orders, historians such as Lomax and Forey are surely right in stressing the Christian rather than the Muslim context. It was above all Cistercian monasticism which left its imprint on the organisation of the orders. Indeed, the origins of the earliest Spanish order, Calatrava, were in this respect spectacular. When in 1158 the Templars professed themselves incapable of holding the town of Calatrava against the Almohads, a group of knights and Cistercian monks, led by Raymond of Fitero, stepped into the breach and defended the town heroically, and these were the men who formed the Order of Calatrava which subsequently gained papal approval in 1164.

The origins of the Order of Santiago, on the other hand, show that the Christian background was a complex mixture of both indigenous and European influences. Shortly after taking Cáceres in 1170, Ferdinand II of León founded a brotherhood or *hermandad* of 'the knights of Cáceres' into whose custody he entrusted the town. The appearance of this group of *freiles de Cáceres*, dedicated to helping in future campaigns against al-Andalus and to defending newly reconquered lands in Extremadura, was by no means a unique phenomenon in twelfth-century Spain. Many towns had an *hermandad* of knights in which religious and military motivations and duties were mingled together: the *freiles de Avila*, for example, appeared on the scene about the same time as the *hermandad* of Cáceres. From the start, however, the latter stressed the fusion of religious and military discipline, and within a year it was being referred to as the 'Order of Santiago', a change which is to be explained by the archbishop of Santiago's donation of a standard of the saint, and his entry into the order as an honorary knight. Yet despite these indigenous factors, the constitution or rule of Santiago was a conscious imitation of that of the Templars and, of course, it had to receive the confirmation of the papacy (1175).

The military orders were invaluable in resisting the onslaught of the Almohads and in wresting and holding lands on the frontier. Consequently they were granted fortresses and areas of military importance as well as territory behind the front lines. At a local level the lands acquired by the orders were organised on a basis of strategic castles and convents where communities of knights followed a partly military, partly monastic, way of life. There were, of course, important variations in the distribution of the landed power of the orders. The Templars, for example, possessed great power and wealth in the eastern kingdoms, but in Castile, León and Portugal the international orders could not match the political and economic predominance of Santiago, Calatrava and Alcántara. From its humble origins in Cáceres, for example, the Order of Santiago grew until its possessions covered large areas of the north-eastern, central and southern regions of the peninsula.

Contemporaries undoubtedly envisaged the frontier role of the military orders in crusading terms. Thus, an account of the foundation of the Order of Santiago, written about 1175, relates how a group of nobles, moved by the Holy Spirit, turned away from their sinful lives and, embracing the Cross and the badge of Santiago, vowed to defend the Church, avoid fighting other Christians, and devote their energies to defeating the infidels.

All the evidence which has been presented, therefore, provides eloquent proof of the rise of a crusading spirit. But frontier warfare frequently remained a matter of individual enterprise, relations with Crusaders from across the Pyrenees sometimes reached breaking point, and Christian rulers clashed over their respective spheres of frontier possession and control. Thus, although the crusading endeavour was a dominant characteristic of the age, it by no means excluded policies and episodes which were contrary to its spirit. Indeed, in one such episode the founder of the Order of Santiago, Ferdinand II of León (1157–88), allied with the Almohads in order to prevent the town of Badajoz falling to the Portuguese.

No better example of that peculiar blend of idealism and practical politics which characterised the crusading age can be found than those events relating to the *terminus ad quem* of this chapter, the battle of Las Navas de Tolosa (1212). This encounter, which finally shattered the power of the Almohads and tipped the balance of power decisively in favour of the Christians, illustrated both the strengths and the weaknesses of the crusading impetus.

Three men were of outstanding importance in organising the Crusade of 1212 – Alfonso VIII of Castile (1158–1214), Rodrigo Ximénez de Rada, archbishop of Toledo (d. 1247), and Pope Innocent III (1198–1216). It was the Castilian king who, by stressing the peril posed by the Almohads, persuaded Innocent III to elevate a projected royal expedition into a Crusade. For his part Ximénez de Rada, who had travelled to Rome on Alfonso VIII's behalf, preached the Crusade in Italy, northern France, Germany and Provence, and also prepared for the convergence of the crusaders at Toledo towards the end of May 1212. Innocent III played an indispensable role in two ways. Papal backing for the preaching of a Crusade attracted large numbers of men from across the Pyrenees, and, by using the threat of excommunication, the pope also imposed a semblance of peace and unity among the Spanish rulers themselves.

At first all these preparations proved remarkably successful. Peter II of Aragon's arrival in Toledo, accompanied by a goodly array of bishops and crusaders, was followed by that of Alfonso VIII with 60,000 men, and Sancho VII of Navarre joined up with his forces once the expedition was under way. Moreover, although Alfonso IX of León, mindful of bitter feuds with the Castilian ruler, refused to answer the call, many Leonese nobles and knights made their way to Toledo. Here, too, there arrived almost 70,000 French, Provençal and Italian knights and soldiers under ecclesiastical and lay leaders such as the archbishops of Narbonne and Bordeaux, the bishop of Nantes, Count Centulo of Astarac, Viscount Raymond of Tourraine and Theobald of Blazon. However, once the combined armies had left Toledo, unity did not last long, and, as the *Primera Crónica General* relates, crusaders from across the Pyrenees turned back *en masse*:

> While all this was happening, the enemy of humanity – that is, the Devil, who hates all men and never ceases to be angered by their good deeds – entered among the ranks of Christ's faithful and agitated the hearts of the greedy who had prepared to come to this battle. And he made them turn round and leave and depart from the good conduct which they had hitherto observed. Almost all the tramontanes agreed to remove the signs of the cross which they had embraced, and to withdraw from the labours of the campaign and return to their lands. The noble King Alfonso, maintaining his courage and refusing to take all this into account, shared out all his supplies, gave all that was necessary to those who remained and, despite these events, refused to be moved from the project which he had undertaken. But these tramontanes . . . began to turn round and all of them left – apart from the honourable Archbishop Arnaud [Amalric] of Narbonne . . . and Theobald of Blazon. . . .[11]

Several reasons have been given by chroniclers and historians for this desertion by the foreign crusaders. They were unused to the climatic conditions south of Toledo and they certainly found the great heat, the lack of water and the resulting outbreaks of disease almost unbearable. But, above all, the differences between Iberian and French attitudes to the frontier once again came to the fore. We have already discussed the clash which took place over a century earlier between Count Sisnando and Archbishop Bernard. Now a similar disagreement manifested itself. The Spaniards, like the French, wished to defend Christendom, defeat the infidel and acquire booty and land. But they knew and respected their enemies, and they observed the terms of capitulations when the Muslims agreed to surrender towns and strongpoints. The French found such toleration scandalous and insisted that all infidels should be put to the sword and their lands and possessions looted. Long ago Menéndez Pidal pointed out how this difference of attitude towards the frontier can be seen not only in the various episodes involving the French crusaders in Spain but also by contrasting the *Chanson de Roland* and the *Cantar de Mío Cid:* in the former, Muslims who refuse baptism are killed forthwith, but in the latter they are treated with such respect that they even pour blessings on the Christians.

The campaign of 1212, therefore, started as a carefully prepared international crusade, but when the Christians and Almohads finally fought at Las Navas, the victory was due to the combined might of the Hispanic armies. The Christians of León, Castile, Aragon and Catalonia had been forced to rely on their own crusading spirit, and as the *Te Deum Laudamus* arose over the corpses of the defeated Muslims it was led by the Spanish bishops – Rodrigo of Toledo, Tello of Palencia, Rodrigo of Siguenza, Melendo of Osma, Domingo of Plasencia and Pedro of Avila.

2. Society and the Frontier, c. 1000–1212

THIS chapter discusses the effects which the frontier had on shaping Iberian society during the eleventh and twelfth centuries. Since the frontier did not remain stationary, these effects varied in terms of both area and time. The first stage of the reconquest, taking place between the mid-ninth and early eleventh centuries, witnessed a Christian expansion, based on Asturias and Galicia, which covered almost all the regions of León and Old Castile, and entailed occupation and resettlement of lands as far south as the Duero river. During the second stage of the reconquest, the fall of Toledo (1085) and Zaragoza (1118) enabled the Castilians to advance to the Tagus and the Aragonese and Catalans to the Ebro. But we must also bear in mind subsequent advances to areas such as Cáceres, Cuenca and Tortosa, as well as the fact that Muslim military might revived under the Almoravids and Almohads, and was not crushed until the battle of Las Navas (1212). Thus from the late eleventh to the early thirteenth centuries the frontier areas, straddling the Tagus and the Ebro, were affected by constant warfare and raids of destruction.

During the first stage of the reconquest, then, the effects of the frontier would be felt in the Duero valley regions rather than in Galicia; but during the second stage the Duero was left behind and the frontier regions of New Castile and New Catalonia developed differently from Old Castile and Old Catalonia respectively. Variations in the effects of the frontier also resulted from changes in the historical circumstances at different times. Thus, to take an obvious example, the first phase of the reconquest had already ended when town life began to flourish and the military orders came into existence. Such kaleidoscopic variations at different times and in different areas left important marks on Christian society.

The Moving Frontier, Colonists and Problems of Manpower

THE pattern of slow population growth in Spain between the tenth and the thirteenth centuries was not unlike that in the rest of Europe, but it must be set against the background of a receding frontier; and, while the advance southwards may at times have stemmed from a search for better land, the new territories which were made available by conquest more than matched population growth. Indeed, the shortage of manpower at times acted as a brake on frontier expansion and repopulation, and the lack of colonists which led eleventh-century rulers to opt for a policy of *parias* rather than conquest was followed by a desperate shortage of men to hold and settle the lands of the Tagus and the Ebro.

Of course, to the slowly growing population of Hispano-Christians in the north, there must be added the soldiers and colonists who came from other areas. In the ninth and tenth centuries Mozarabs migrated to the north from al-Andalus, and many colonists and townsmen, as well as crusaders, crossed the Pyrenees into Spain during the course of the eleventh and twelfth centuries. Men from Toulouse, for example, played an important role in repopulating Lérida and its region in the twelfth century.

Considerable numbers of Muslims, Mozarabs and Jews also remained on their lands during and after the second phase of the reconquest. Toledo and Zaragoza lost almost all their Muslim population after they fell to the Christians, but the Mozarabs who remained in the Toledan region outnumbered new colonists from the north, and many Muslims remained in the territories of the Ebro. Indeed, Muslims constituted between 30 and 35 per cent of the population of Aragon, and the same seems to have been true of some areas of Catalonia, such as the region of Tortosa.

Yet, even after taking into account these other groups, the evidence for a continuous shortage is overwhelming. The Duero desert swallowed up vast numbers of colonists, and the same was true of the lands further south. For centuries the documents would continue to refer to the *lugares yermos* or unpopulated areas of Castile, and the many *ad populandum* charters which were granted do not in themselves indicate either an abundance of colonists or the continuing existence of population in any given area. A charter grant of 978 relating to Bañuelos de Calzada, for example, seems to infer a process of repopulation, but the same place was described as being deserted when, in 1202, Alfonso VIII granted it to the monks of Santo Domingo de Silos. Not surprisingly many such grants stipulated that areas given *ad populandum* should not draw their colonists from the lands of the donor. Such attempts to 'reserve' manpower, however, were often ineffectual in the face of the inducements which enticed men to frontier areas. It was in these latter territories that colonists were desperately needed since, despite the numbers of Muslims or Mozarabs who might stay on their lands, the process of reconquest usually involved a sharp drop in the population. The rhythm of repopulation, therefore, lagged well behind that of the reconquest, and continuous migration drastically retarded the process of colonisation. The lands of the Duero were still under-populated when the frontier moved to the Tagus, and the resettlement of New Castile and New Catalonia had hardly started when, in the thirteenth century, the frontier again advanced into Andalusia and Valencia.

Only the existence of special opportunities and privileges could attract colonists to the frontier lands. Sánchez-Albornoz has force-fully argued that 'a whirlwind of liberty shook the frontier of the valley of the Duero', and it is certainly the case that these lands were for long worked by free men, some of whom had shaken off serfdom by moving south. The next stage of the frontier was similarly marked by 'a whirlwind of liberty', but this time it was organised from above by the granting of *cartas pueblas* and *fueros* – that is, charters which laid down the guide lines and conditions for the resettlement of the countryside and the towns. Often these were given by the kings and princes themselves, but others, who had received large grants of frontier lands, also issued charters for the same purpose. In the early thirteenth century, for example, the bishops of Tortosa and the Hospitallers granted charters to stimulate the repopulation of their lands in the lower Ebro valley. The outstanding feature of such charters, down to about 1170, was that they attempted to attract population by granting exemptions to all colonists. Here, for example, are some of the provisions of the charter granted by Alfonso VII to Colmenar de Oreja in 1139 'in order to prevent the Moors from retaking it':

> If someone should have a house or piece of land in Oreja and stays there for one year, he is not to pay any taxes; after one year he may sell or give the land to whoever he wishes.
> If the settler of Oreja should have some land anywhere else, he is to hold it freely and is to make use of it as he wishes and is not to pay any taxes for it.
> The settlers of Oreja are not to pay any *portazgo* in any town of my kingdom save in Toledo.

And if any of them should sell anything of their own in Toledo, they are not to pay *portazgo*, but if they should buy or sell anything there which is not their own, or for their own use, they are to pay *portazgo*.

If anyone who incurs the *ira regis*, or is evicted and thrown out of his land, should wish to settle in Oreja, he is to be allowed to go there safely, and the lord of Oreja, whoever he may be at the time, is to receive him without fear unless he is a great nobleman with princely powers. The land of a man who incurs the *ira regis* and comes to settle in Oreja is to be securely his and is to be exempt in the same way as the lands of the other settlers. . . .

If someone should flee to Oreja with a woman, who is not his relation, is not married, and has not been taken by force or ravished, and he wishes to be one of the settlers, then he is to go there safely, and the lord of Oreja need not fear to accept him, and neither he nor the man who seduced her has to answer to any of the woman's relatives.

The settler in Oreja – be he knight or soldier – who goes out on a foray or expedition . . . does not have to pay any share of his booty to anyone, save to the lord of Oreja, and no one should dare to ask for it. . . .[12]

The colonist of Oreja, therefore, was offered substantial benefits: he was exempted from taxation and was allowed to retain his own profits of war, no restrictions impeded his ability to dispose of his lands freely, and the rigours of royal justice, as well as the restrictions of kinship and sexual morality, were relaxed in his favour.

Bearing in mind the opportunities and privileges afforded by the frontier, is it not possible that the reconquest was due to under-population? 'Hear me, my knights,' the Cid told his men, 'and I will tell you the truth: he who stays in one spot will see his fortunes diminish.'[13] In the *Primera Crónica General* the legendary Bernardo de Carpio echoes the Cid's advice in a blunter form: 'I gain more in war than I do in peace, for the poor knight lives better in times of war than in times of peace.'[14] In terms of earning a living, therefore, fighting for booty on the frontier might represent an easier and more profitable alternative than trying to work an underpopulated and lean landscape. But the warriors were not the only ones whose fortunes depended on movement rather than staying in one spot, for those engaged in pastoral farming found that the deserted landscape provided them with better opportunities than those regions which were relatively well populated. In some areas of the Ebro and Tagus valleys, such as the region round Toledo, the pattern of settlements and population distribution was already partly determined by the agrarian and urban structure inherited from the Muslims. Thus, the Muslim *alquerías* dotting the landscape round Toledo were not dissimilar to that complex of lands and houses which made up a hamlet, and they were often simply referred to in Christian sources as *aldeas* or villages. The *alquería* pattern of agriculture was surprisingly diverse and might include grain-lands, vineyards, poultry-yards and even small orchards, as well as abandoned or uncultivated areas and grass-lands. It was not in these *alquería* regions, but in the lands of Extremadura and the area stretching from Guadalajara and Soria down to Cuenca, that underpopulation reinforced those factors of land and climate which encouraged pastoral farming. After 1085 there was an expansion of sheep-herding round frontier settlements such as Avila and Salamanca, and shortly afterwards Muslim geographers noted the existence of large flocks between the Duero and Tagus. Moreover, the provision made by some twelfth-century *fueros* for livestock routes fomented transhumance to the pasture lands to the south-west and south-east of Toledo, and the bishop and chapter of Cuenca even levied taxes on flocks which were taken across the frontier for sale in al-Andalus. It is possible, therefore, that the advance of the frontier may have been stimulated not only by nomadic warriors in search of a living but by ranchers in search of pasture lands which would allow for transhumance on a large scale.

The equality of privileges and freedoms which attracted colonists to frontier areas was inevitably destroyed with the passage of time. During the process of repopulation inequalities of land distribution emerged, and the functional importance of the mounted warriors meant that they gained socially and politically at the expense of the other colonists. Differences also emerged between the towns and the villages, and between the original settlers and those who arrived subsequently. The frontier, in short, removed legal and fiscal impediments, but it also created the opportunities for social mobility and new conditions for social stratification. Above all, this modification of the initial 'whirlwind of liberty' was accelerated when any given area had been left behind by the frontier, but it was not necessarily modified to the extent that conditions became similar to those prevailing in regions even further removed from the frontier.

In the examples that follow it should be remembered that, although the erosion of frontier 'liberties' is illustrated by reference to sectors of the rural population in the Duero and Tagus lands, conditions in these regions remained markedly better than in Galicia or Old Catalonia.

Down to the eleventh century an important factor in shaping the features of the rural economy was the way in which land was colonised by pioneers. Kings, counts and monasteries played an important role in establishing Christian control in the lands of the kingdom of León and the county of Castile; but the crucial element was *presura* – that is, repopulation, colonisation, and exploitation of the deserted rural landscape by Galicians, Asturians, Basques and Mozarabs. Most of these colonists lacked the means to work large areas of land, and the result was the emergence of numerous and small holdings along the frontier. These were lands worked by free men, and their estates were not enmeshed, either economically or juridically, in larger agrarian units. Thus, whereas in France the ninth and tenth centuries witnessed the disappearance of many free rural communities at the expense of great seigneurial estates, in most of Christian Spain small and medium-sized estates predominated until the eleventh century. Nevertheless, both in feudal Catalonia, which followed a Frankish pattern, and in Galicia, dominated by powerful monastic and episcopal lords, large estates or *villae* certainly increased in size and numbers. These estates consisted of two elements. In the first place there was the manorial demesne – that is, land which the lord reserved for direct exploitation and for his house, farm buildings and servants' living-quarters. Secondly, there were the *mansi* or holdings, which were granted to dependent cultivators and their families in return for specified duties and services.

What happened in these lands when, from the late eleventh century onwards, the frontier moved south to the Tagus? In general terms the emphasis of the agrarian social structure changed from one of small and independent landholders to one of lordships. This change was accompanied by a levelling out of some of the sharper distinctions among sectors of the rural population. By the end of the twelfth century, for example, serfdom had disappeared from almost all areas of Christian Spain. But although military service offered magnificent opportunities for social mobility, the majority of the free peasantry found their liberties restricted in the course of time by varying degrees of dependence on lords. There were differences in the ways in which smallholders and peasants commended themselves and, consequently, the various forms of commendation gave rise to differences in the status of free men. In Galicia, for example, the prevalent form of commendation, the *incommuniatio*, was one in which a man surrendered the ownership of land to a lord, in exchange for protection, in an arrangement which was envisaged as lasting indefinitely. Hence seigneurial power was established over succeeding generations of 'free' men, and the services and payments which they rendered could be sold by one lord to another. The *incommuniatio*, therefore, facilitated the consolidation of large lordships and estates and severely curtailed the freedom of those who commended themselves. At the other end of the scale, the prevalent form of commendation in Castile and León prior to the twelfth century, known as *benefactoría* or *behetría*, hardly impinged upon the independence of free men, since powerful magnates were in relatively short supply and the numerous small landowners were in a strong bargaining position. Not only did the latter freely choose their lord but they could, if they so wished, freely seek a new lord 'from sea to sea' (*de mar a mar*) – that is, any lord throughout the length and breadth of the kingdom. In practice, however, the choice of a new lord tended to be restricted to members of a particular family; hence the *behetrías* were usually seigneurial areas in which men retained their freedom of movement and their right to choose a lord from among the members of a lineage grouping.

The repopulation of the lands of the second stage of the reconquest was stimulated by the imposition of liberties from above, within the context of institutions such as the lordships granted to towns, nobles and military orders. By looking at the example of the Tortosa region we can see how this situation led to important differences between the newly colonised areas and the lands behind the front lines. The acquisition of the regions of Tortosa (1148) and Lérida (1149) by Count Ramón Berenguer IV of Barcelona (1131–62) was the crowning achievement of the Catalan reconquest. From the very beginning the rulers made grants of lordships which served the dual purpose of rewarding those who had participated in the conquests and arranging for the defence of the new frontiers. Thus, within a century, the creation of lordships had swallowed up most of the available land, and the major beneficiaries were those whose help was essential for the military or religious organisation of new territories – the Templars, the Hospitallers, great noble families like the Moncada and, to a lesser extent, ecclesiastical lords such as the bishop of Tortosa. The town and lands of Tortosa itself, for example, constituted a lordship which was shared by the Order of the Temple and the house of Moncada.

The lands of these regions, however, formed part of those territories to the west of the Llobregat known as New Catalonia and, having been reconquered at a relatively late date, they developed along socio-political lines which in many ways were significantly different from Old Catalonia. In the regions of the latter territory, lordships and fiefs had emerged as a result of the fragmentations or usurpations of sovereign power carried out from below by land-owners and officials in the localities. The nature of seigneurial power and the prevalence of a manorial economy restricted the freedom of some of the peasantry considerably and in the long run raised the spectre of a 'new serfdom'. In the Tortosa region, on the other hand, lordships were specifically set up and granted out by the ruler by means of charters which regulated the framework within which seigneurial or lordly powers could be exercised. The creation of lordships constituted only one aspect of the task of repopulation and colonisation, and the existence of seigneurial power was mitigated by the *cartas de población* which granted liberal conditions of tenure to colonists. The restrictions and impositions prevalent in Old Catalonia were out of the question in these territories, and the lands of the peasantry were held under conditions which allowed the holder to retain his personal freedom. Thus the peasantry usually had to pay an annual cense in recognition of lordship, and if a peasant wished to alienate his land, the lord had either the right of resumption, provided he paid the same price as that offered by third parties, or the right to levy a percentage of the sale price in token of his approbation and consent. Such conditions, of course, were hardly onerous, and in general terms they entailed the existence of a quasi-ownership of the land by the rural population. The opportunities and freedoms of the initial period of colonisation were subsequently restricted, but the peasantry of these areas would never be subjected to the kind of seigneurial burdens and impositions which affected some of the *payeses* of Old Catalonia. However, in considering the erosion of the initial 'whirlwind of liberty' in the lands of the second stage of the reconquest, the region of Toledo provides us with a better example because socio-economic changes in this area paralleled some of the religious and political developments examined in the previous chapter.

After the conquest of Toledo a serious dislocation of population affected the balance between town and countryside. The Christians showed a marked preference for establishing themselves in the towns and, as large numbers of Muslims retreated to the south, the Mozarabs came to constitute the most important grouping in an underpopulated landscape. Furthermore, the Mozarabic peasantry, many of whom enlarged their landholdings by right of *presura* or purchase, found that the monarchy not only defended them against the arbitrary actions of the conquerors but even allowed them access to that modified form of nobility known as *caballería villana* (below, pp. 47–50). Such measures were socially and economically favourable to the Mozarabs, and when Alfonso VII gathered all the various privileges of the Toledan region into one *fuero* in 1118, these were envisaged as applying equally and without distinction to all Castilians, Mozarabs and Franks. Nevertheless, although these privileges were routinely confirmed by Alfonso VII's successors, important changes weakened the position of the Mozarabs, and their declining social and economic fortunes accompanied their gradual loss of religious identity.

The decline in Mozarabic fortunes was linked to rapid turnovers in land ownership which occurred during the late twelfth and early thirteenth centuries. Several factors were responsible for creating an active land market in which the sellers were predominantly the small landed Mozarabic proprietors of the rural population. The years in question were marked by a series of natural catastrophes, widespread devastation of the countryside resulting from the campaigns of the Almohads, and a severe price inflation which was largely caused by debasements of the coinage. In many cases, therefore, small landowners had to sell part or all of their properties in order to survive and pay off their debts. The market was flooded with property which mainly consisted of lands already being exploited, but also included houses, shops and taverns in Toledo itself. Times were bad, but for those with capital attractive investments in land were available at bargain prices.

Who profited from this buyers' market? Certainly not all Mozarabs were in the same desperate straits, and a few rich and influential families from among their ranks did well for themselves. This was particularly the case with some of the urban Mozarabs who actively supported each other into important positions in the urban and ecclesiastical hierarchy. Such a family was that of the Polichení, some of whose members, starting with Domingo Ben Abdala el Polichení, archpriest of the cathedral, held high ecclesiastical offices over three generations. The Polichení invested a good deal of money in buying up rural and urban property. Between 1177 and 1196, for example, the Archpriest Domingo Ben Abdala bought arable land and vineyards in several of the *alquerías* round Toledo, and purchased two taverns to add to the two shops and seven houses which he already owned in the town. But the case of the Polichení was exceptional, and even their investments were small when compared to that of the really important purchasers. These included the cathedral church and rich Castilians, such as Archbishop Rodrigo Ximénes de Rada who alone invested almost ten times more money in property than Domingo Ben Abdala. The cathedral, of course, received a constant flow of donations of lands and revenues from the monarchy and individuals, but from about 1170 the chapter began investing large sums of money in buying the best lands of the irrigated areas in the surrounding countryside as well as houses and shops in the town. Thus, by the end of this period of crisis, the cathedral disposed of a vast income which, in 1234, brought in 4330 *mrs* from land and 1138 *mrs* from urban property. Such examples help to explain why, once again, the initial equality of frontier opportunities was subsequently undermined, and how, from the 1170s onwards, the great rural properties of the Toledan region were formed at the expense of the smaller landowners.

The Militarisation of Social Groupings

THE effects of the frontier on the Church and the military orders have already been partly discussed. During the first stage of the reconquest the monasteries had played an important role in colonising the free lands of the frontier. From the late eleventh to the early thirteenth centuries, on the other hand, the lands of the Tagus and Ebro valleys were affected by a series of destructive wars, and the relatively few monasteries which established themselves in these frontier zones were politically and socially less prominent, and relatively less well endowed with lands, than monastic foundations in the areas north of the Duero. Certain Cistercian monasteries provided an exception to this decline of the monastic impulse on the frontier. In 1140 Alfonso VII of Castile, by granting some land to the white monks, contributed to the creation of the first Cistercian foundation in Spain – Fitero. Seeking solitude and autarky, the Cistercians shunned the towns and used their agrarian expertise to bring into use large tracts of unexploited land. That the Cistercians were invaluable in the task of colonisation and repopulation can be seen in the foundation of three of their monasteries in recently reconquered areas – Poblet and Santas Creus in Catalonia (1150), and Alcobaça in Portugal (1153). At the time when these monasteries were founded, the rulers of Catalonia and Portugal were hostile to the growth in their realms of religious organisations which depended on foreign superiors. Afonso Henriques of Portgual even resented the foreign linkages of the military orders. Yet the Cistercians were realistically encouraged by these rulers to establish these three monasteries, which were to become among the greatest and wealthiest of the peninsula, precisely because the white monks provided the necessary organisation and manpower for colonisation. Indeed, in the foundation charter of Alcobaça, Afonso Henriques warned the Cistercian monks that they would have to return the lands granted to them if they failed to bring them into cultivation.

In general terms the Cistercians failed to make a serious impact on the lands across the Tagus frontier, but it must be remembered that they also initiated those heroic actions which led to the foundation of the Order of Calatrava. The convent-fortresses of the various military orders, in fact, counterbalanced the monasticism of the north and represented the Church militant at strategic sites on the frontier itself – for example, the Templars and Hospitallers in the regions of Lérida and Tortosa, the Order of Santiago in advanced positions in the areas of Cuenca and Cáceres, and the knights of Calatrava in the region of Ciudad Real.

In what ways were the nobility affected by the frontier? It is possible, of course, to describe the nobility without any specific reference to the frontier. The most powerful nobles were the great magnates who were closely associated with the task of government, held extensive immunities and were linked by special ties of fealty to the ruler. By the twelfth century these men were known as *ricos hombres.* Among the magnates the counts were of special importance but, with the exception of feudal Catalonia, the comital title was not necessarily hereditary and never became firmly attached to public office. Thus, an area of regional government in León or Castile was only called a county if the king happened to appoint a count to administer it, and in theory the count remained a royal servant who could be removed from office at the king's pleasure. Nevertheless, by the eleventh century comital authority was feudalised to the extent that the title of count and an area of territorial authority (*mandatio*) were usually entrusted by the Crown to an individual as a non-hereditary benefice. And the tendency for the title and office to be linked together was so strong that we find a twelfth-century count confirming a document and emphasising his anomalous position by using the expression *comes sine terra*.

Below the *ricos hombres* there existed a larger group of nobles who were known as *infanzones, hidalgos* or *caballeros*. The generic name of *hidalgos*, however, also tended to be used to describe all nobles in general, and nobility itself was *hidalguía*. The *hidalgos* were exempt from taxation, received benefices from the king or great magnates and performed mounted military service for their lords. Their privileges, along with their knightly style of life and their personal relationships to their lords, differentiated them from the rest of society. By the mid-twelfth century there emerged also the concept of the noble order of knighthood (*orden de caballería*) which attempted to restrict true knightly status to those who were born noble and who, in their youth, underwent a symbolic ceremony marking their entry into the order – thus emphasising lineage rather than function as the determining criterion for *hidalgo* or *caballero* status. Terminology apart, therefore, the concept of *hidalguía* was not dissimilar to that characterising the French nobility, and in the case of the Catalan nobility the similarities were even greater.

But in a society organised for frontier warfare, the Iberian nobility inevitably acquired characteristics for which it is not easy to find parallels elsewhere in Europe. The demands of constant war meant that the nobility were identified with the all-important mounted military service so indispensable to the frontier, and this factor ensured that many free men, who were not themselves the sons of nobles, could attain noble status by performing a legitimising military role. Thus the nobility constituted a rather fluid social grouping, and their privileges and honour did not always derive exclusively from birth and lineage. In the tenth and eleventh centuries, as has been seen, the rural society of León and Castile was one in which the lesser nobility and *villani* for long escaped subjection to seigneurial control. Hence, once the Christians had descended from their mountain fastnesses and there was an imperative need for cavalry, some noble privileges were granted to those *villani* or non-noble freemen who could serve as *caballeros*. Many of these frontiersmen consequently rose in status to become *caballeros villanos* – that is, 'commoner knights'. To become *caballeros* these *villanos* had to possess enough wealth to maintain a horse and armour, and they enjoyed their privileges not by virtue of their lineage but because of their military value. But, since one of these privileges was the important noble characteristic of exemption from taxation, the ability of a family to provide *caballero* service over two or three generations ensured that the 'villein knights' were easily assimilated into the ranks of the *hidalgos*.

Within the ranks of the nobility, social mobility also depended on the honour and wealth arising from military success. In this respect the term *hidalgo* is itself extremely interesting for, deriving from *fijodalgo*, its literal meaning may be translated as 'son' (*fijo*) of 'fortune' or 'wealth' (*algo*). Thus, although the term *hidalgos* came to be used to denote the nobility in general and the lower ranks of the nobility in particular, its origins refer to those men whose wealth and military function enabled them to acquire the same status as the *infanzones* who were born into the lower nobility.

While some nobles derived their status from birth and lineage, therefore, there were many others who owed their social advancement to the economic and military opportunities provided by frontier life and warfare. The contrast between these criteria for social status is a theme which is magnificently handled by the *Cantar de Mío Cid*. The drama of the epic arises not from the struggle against Islam but from the antagonisms and hatreds between the princes (*infantes*) of Carrión, worthless men of great lineage, and the Cid, who fights his way to honour and glory.

The upward social mobility of the Cid and his followers was due to military success and the spoils of war. Here, for example, is the Cid's appeal for men to help conquer Valencia:

> He sent criers through Aragon, Navarre and Castile to spread this message: 'Those who wish to shake off their problems, let them accompany Mío Cid to war. He wants to lay siege to Valencia and win her for Christendom. . . .' His message, know you, was heard everywhere and, thirsting after wealth, many men from Christendom hurried to join him.[15]

But the results of the campaign were social as well as economic:

> Great were the rejoicings there when the Cid won Valencia and
> entered the city. Those who had been on foot now became
> *caballeros*. And the gold and the silver, who can count it?[16]

Success and wealth, then, enabled men to become *caballeros* and,
shortly after, the poem also refers to their acquisition of *algo* in such
a way as to make it evident that both wealth and social status were
involved.

Being an *infanzón* from Vivar, the Cid himself was noble by birth,
but he was by no means a magnate or an aristocrat. Yet this
humble *infanzón* is presented in the epic as being superior to men of
great lineage. For example, a great magnate, Asur González, is
described as a 'troublemaker and loose of tongue, and otherwise of
little worth', and the princes of Carrión are depicted as cowards.
These magnates hate the warrior who gains fame, honour and status
by his military prowess on the frontier. At court, Count García
bitterly comments on the Cid's success:

> 'It is a strange thing how the Cid's honour increases so much. The
> honour which he acquires is an affront to us here, because on the
> battlefield he defeats Moorish kings as easily as if they were
> already dead and gains their horses! Everything that he does will
> be to our detriment.'[17]

But the real clash over social differences comes as a result of the
marriages arranged between the Cid's daughters and the worthless
princes of Carrión. After the princes have abused and tried to kill
their brides, they justify their actions by pointing to their lineage:

> 'We are by birth of the lineage of the counts of Carrión. We are
> worthy of the daughters of a king or an emperor – the daughters of
> an *infanzón* were not our equals. When we abandoned them we did
> the right thing and, know you, we now hold ourselves in greater
> honour, not less.'[18]

Of course, as might be expected, the great men of lineage are
humbled in the end, and the Cid's daughters become the wives of the
rulers of Aragon and Navarre.

In general social terms, therefore, one of the most important
effects of the frontier was the overwhelming importance of the
warrior nobility over other social groupings. Of course, it may be
that the *Cantar de Mío Cid* gives an exaggerated view of the virtues

of the fighting noble, but it should also be remembered that this frontier-orientated society not only exalted the role of the warrior but also demanded the same martial qualities from the rest of society. Knightly and monkly characteristics, for example, were fused together in the military orders, and commoners performing knightly service constituted a social group, unique in Europe, of *caballeros villanos*. Moreover, the greatest military contribution of these villein knights came in the late eleventh and twelfth centuries in the lands between the Duero and the Tagus, and since the frontier defence in these regions devolved on the towns, these *caballeros* came to dominate urban life as well. It was these men who formed the urban audiences for songs and tales which dwelt on the merits and courage, not of the magnates, but of *caballeros* and *hidalgos* like themselves – that is, warriors like the Cid, or that Corraquín Sancho whose exploits we will soon have cause to consider. Town life in Spain, however, did not develop according to a uniform 'frontier' pattern.

As elsewhere in Europe the commercial renaissance of the eleventh and twelfth centuries stimulated the development of town life. The most obvious sign of expansion was the decline of barter, the beginning of minting in the Christian states of the north, and the increase in the number of coins in circulation. But whereas Aragon and Catalonia formed part of the 'Carolingian sterling area', which used the pound of 240 silver pennies as a money of account, the monetary system of the Castilian–Leonese kingdoms was strongly influenced by that of al-Andalus. The first Castilian coins were minted by Ferdinand I (1035–65), but after the fall of Toledo Alfonso VI was faced, as in his religious policy, with the problem of choosing between two alternatives. He opted for a Christian or 'western' minting pattern for his realms. Yet Muslim influences remained very strong, and by 1130 the Castilian–Leonese realms appeared to be divided into two monetary zones: that of the silver penny, which characterised the regions to the north of the Duero, and that of the Almoravid gold *morabitín*, which prevailed in the frontier areas to the south of the central *cordillera*. Subsequently, however, the influence of the *morabitín* expanded to the north of the Duero as well, and when Alfonso VIII began to mint Castilian *maravedís* in 1172, they were not only patterned on the *morabitín* but they actually displayed Arabic lettering. By 1221 the *maravedí* was no longer minted but it continued to be the Castilian money of account. Thus the frontier monetary zone in the end prevailed over that of the north. Some contrasts in urban development formed a curious parallel to these monetary developments.

The axis of the northern zone of towns was the important pilgrim route leading to Santiago de Compostela, where legend asserted that the body of St James had been brought from Jerusalem and buried in a place indicated by a star (*campus stellae*). Covering the north of the peninsula, the route – aptly described as the French road or *camino francés* – allowed European influences to penetrate Spain and, cutting across political boundaries, it imposed a unity on the regions from the French border to Galicia. (See Map 3.) Along the *camino francés* there came all sorts of foreigners – pilgrims, merchants, nobles, clergy and artists. Many towns of this region grew up naturally as a conglomeration of houses, shops, churches and hostels which lined both sides of a street which formed an integral part of the pilgrim route. Monarchs encouraged the growth of these urban centres, and as towns such as Pamplona, Burgos, León, Logroño, Sahagún and Santiago grew in wealth, so too did their colonies of foreign and native artisans and merchants.

Developing well behind the front lines, the towns of the northern zone contrasted with the predominantly military towns of the frontier and shared many of the characteristics of urban centres elsewhere in Europe. Risings of burghers against their ecclesiastical and lay lords in some of these northern towns, for example, not only evidenced the growing importance of such groups in society but also took on that archetypal form of communal movement which was also to be found in northern France, northern Italy, Flanders and some of the Rhine towns. Indeed, the richly detailed accounts of such movements, which are contained in the *Historia Compostelana* and the *Crónicas Anónimas de Sahagún*, are remarkably similar to the classic description which Abbot Guibert of Nogent gave of the communal struggle in the northern French town of Laon. In the *camino francés* region, the towns principally affected by the disturbances were Santiago, Sahagún, Lugo, Carrión, Burgos, Palencia and Tuy. The troubles began in some cases as early as 1087, reached an acute stage between 1109 and 1117, and thereafter only recurred spasmodically in one or two towns during the remainder of the twelfth century.

What were these struggles about? Fundamentally the tension was created by the presence of relatively large numbers of merchants and artisans in towns where they were constrained by the structure of ecclesiastical or noble lordship. The anonymous chronicler of Sahagún describes the background to this problem well:

> Accordingly, inasmuch as the said king [Alfonso VI] had ordered ... that there should be a town there, townsmen (*burgueses*) of many and various kinds and trades came from all parts of the world – smiths, carpenters, tailors, furriers and shoemakers. These men also included many from foreign provinces and kingdoms – Gascons, Bretons, Germans, English, Burgundians, Normans, Toulousains, Provençals, Lombards and many other merchants of divers nations and strange languages. And thus he populated and created a considerably sized town. Then the king decreed and ordered that none of those living in the town should have a field, vineyard, orchard, plot or mill within the lands of the monastery unless the abbot should grant it on terms and conditions; but they could have houses in the town, provided that they each paid a yearly sum of money to the abbot as a rent and in recognition of his lordship. . . . Furthermore, he ordered that all should bake their bread in the monastery's oven, and this was such a vexing and troublesome matter for the townsmen and inhabitants that they entreated the abbot with many prayers to make it legal and permissable for them to bake their bread wherever they wished, provided that they each paid him a yearly sum of money. This was granted to them and written up in a signed document whereby every year all the townsmen and inhabitants would each pay two sums of money to the monastery: one sum at Christmas for the oven, and another at All Saints as rent and recognition of lordship. . . . And because the merchants and *burgueses* of Sahagún disposed of their merchandise peacefully and traded without fear, they came and brought goods from all parts, such as gold and silver and even all kinds of fashions of clothes. Thus the townsmen and inhabitants were very rich and well supplied with many delightful things.[19]

The various groups of French and native merchants and artisans who established themselves in these towns, therefore, often found that economic wealth and status was not paralleled by any participation in the local power structure. In Sahagún, for example, the *burgueses* were favoured by fiscal, military and market privileges, but the powers of lordship were firmly vested in the abbot and monastery.

The rebellions, however, were not simply clashes between the townsmen and their lords and, as elsewhere in Europe, the issues were complicated by other problems. Quite apart from the important distinctions between rich and poor townsmen, and between *burgueses* and mere inhabitants (*moradores*), urban unrest came to form part of the civil wars arising out of the stormy marriage between Alfonso I of Aragon and Alfonso VI's daughter, Urraca. Thus the 'conjurations' or 'brotherhoods' (*hermandades*), whose members were bound together by oath, were not simply confined to restive groups within the sector of the *burgueses*. But groups of *burgueses* were certainly the most active in fomenting unrest, and their aims were not limited to resisting the lords of towns but included the replacement of one form of authority by another, and the establishment of their 'laws' within urban society. In a typical episode in Sahagún, for example, the townsmen:

> ... entered into the chapter of Sahagún, showed the monks a document on which were written down new laws and customs, which they themselves had decreed and drawn up and which abolished the customs established by King Alfonso of blessed memory, and began to compel the monks to sign these laws with their own hands.[20]

There is little doubt, in fact, that the objective of the rebellions was to establish communal power, although this was envisaged in practical terms and never as a 'democratic' or political ideal worth striving for as such. Indeed, the confused situation was in itself advantageous since it allowed active groups among the townsmen to recruit help from other discontented sectors of society, and in Compostela it enabled them to exercise *de facto* communal power for a whole year, during which the political and administrative authority of the episcopal lord virtually ceased to exist.

The development of urban society in the northern zone differed sharply from that of many of the frontier towns established between the Duero and the Tagus and along the Ebro. Towns such as Salamanca, Avila, Segovia, Cuenca, Guadalajara, Calatayud and Daroca not only played a vital military role in the twelfth century but also undertook repopulation in the lands under their control by establishing new communities and settlements. Many of these powerful towns controlled or dominated invasion routes and important passes in the mountain ranges.

Avila was the archetypal example of such a frontier town.

Defending an area of the frontier behind the Tagus, Avila 'of the knights' commanded the approaches through the central sierras and stood at the highest altitude of the *meseta* (3400 feet). Its granite walls, built during the years 1090–9, were reinforced by eighty-eight towers, and the apse of the cathedral was built into these defences and itself formed part of the fortifications. Not surprisingly the *Crónica de la población de Avila* describes a society which was different to that of the towns of the northern zone.

The chronicle begins with the settlement of the town, carried out by Count Raymond of Burgundy, and relates how from the beginning functional divisions were of fundamental importance to the urban social structure. There were merchants and artisans but, being indispensable to the defence of the town and the frontier, it was the group known as the *serranos*, made up of knights or *caballeros*, which dominated society and monopolised municipal offices. Moreover, the bellicose frontier ethic accorded kudos, not to the bishop or merchant, but to the bold *caballero* who performed his exploits in a professional yet modest manner. Each frontier area had its heroes who, although their exploits were on a smaller scale than those of the Cid, symbolised those qualities of courage, integrity and professional skill which earned them an honourable grave and lasting fame in the local memory. Such a man, for example, was Corraquín Sancho of Avila:

On another occasion when this Corraquín Sancho went on an expedition with other *caballeros*, he forgot something in Avila and returned for it. Then, while going to catch up on the rest, he saw sixty Moorish *caballeros* who had captured twenty Christian shepherds on a hillside and were tying them up. So he picked on a spot where he might reach them without being seen . . . and he moved to the attack shouting, 'Avila, *caballeros*!' The Moors allowed themselves to beaten: he killed one or two of them, and those shepherds who had still not been properly tied up undid the others, and they helped him well with the result that the Moors were defeated. Then he went after his companions, but he did not tell them what had happened.

Later, when he had returned to Avila, these shepherds came soon after and brought him sixty pigs as a present. At the time, Corraquín Sancho was in the company of other *caballeros* at the gate of San Pedro. The shepherds passed by there and, when asked to whom the pigs belonged, they replied that they were taking them to Corraquín Sancho. The *caballeros* asked why they were doing this, and the shepherds told them what had happened. In this way the facts became known, even though Corraquín had never wanted to reveal them. After this when people had a get-together they would sing:

'People sing of Roland and Oliver,
But not of Corraquín who was a fine *caballero*.
They sing of Oliver and Roland,
But not of Corraquín who was a fine young man.'

This Corraquín Sancho lies in the most honoured of the burial places in San Silvestre. Sancho Ximeno and Gómez Ximeno, the captains (*adalides*), lie buried in the church of Santiago. The deeds which they performed along with the *caballeros* of Avila are carved on the stones covering them. . . .[21]

Warfare not only produced individual heroes but also stimulated the development of municipal armies in the frontier towns of the *meseta*. The urban militias were invaluable when summoned for defensive action (the *apellido*) and also supplied the monarchy with sizeable military contingents for offensive expeditions and campaigns (the *fonsado*). In general, military service was an obligation of citizenship in León and Castile, but the practice quickly grew up of levying a tax, the *fonsadera*, in lieu of service. Thus the brunt of fighting fell on the towns nearest the frontier, and in some of these areas the armed and mounted *caballero* was not allowed to buy exemption by paying *fonsadera*. Both Christian and Muslim sources reveal that these municipal armies frequently operated deep in the south, and urban contingents from towns such as Segovia and Avila were present at the decisive battle of Las Navas in 1212.

Up to this point little attention has been paid to urban institutional developments precisely because social aspects were of such great importance. In fact, from the eleventh century onwards, towns began to play a part in local government as quasi-independent administrative units with legal personality. The *fuero* was the written expression of a town's juridical status and degree of autonomy. It usually recorded the town's privileges, some or all of the precepts of the customary law of the area, and some of the regulations relating to the practical administration of urban life. Many municipal *fueros* were simply copies of the *fuero* of another town, or perhaps derived their inspiration from a common source of customary unwritten law. There were, therefore, 'families' of *fueros*. The elaborate *fuero* granted by Alfonso VIII to the frontier town of Cuenca in 1190, for example, was the key 'relation' in a 'family' which included Teruel (in Aragon), Béjar, Plasencia and Sepúlveda.

The emergence of royal or autonomous municipalities, characterised by judicial and administrative independence and the power to elect magistrates and officials, was accomplished during the course of the eleventh and twelfth centuries in León and Castile, and somewhat later in the eastern realms. But the development of urban institutions must be viewed within its social context. As has been seen, economic expansion and the increasing importance of trade had a marked effect on the towns of the northern zone. Similarly, by the thirteenth century, Barcelona had developed in a way which was not dissimilar to that of the great mercantile towns of northern Italy (below, pp. 77–8). But elsewhere in the peninsula the militarised towns provided the prevailing pattern for urban society. In fact, the most powerful lords between the Duero and the Tagus during this period were the towns themselves, and within these towns many municipal offices were reserved for the knights. Thus these urban patriciates, where offices were reserved to *hidalgos* and *caballeros*, were militaristic in nature and contrasted sharply with most of those elsewhere in Europe. The knightly class set the tone of society, controlled urban government, and lorded it over the peasantry and the groups of merchants and Jews who engaged in moneylending and small-scale trade. Moreover, given the importance of the frontier and reconquest, it is hardly surprising that these same military and noble values influenced the towns north of the central belt in the same way as the *maravedí* had prevailed over the silver penny. How could it be otherwise in the land of the Cid? As far as the *caballeros* of Avila were concerned the point was axiomatic:

> For the *serranos* maintain that they are pure Castilians, that their sort has never included any artisans but only *caballeros* and *escuderos*, that they have always lived by *caballería* and not in any other way, that they never married with artisans, *ruanos*, or any other men save *caballeros fijosdalgo*, and that they would not do otherwise for anything in the world.[22]

The eleventh and twelfth centuries were the golden age of epic heroes, individual adventurers and religious enthusiasm, and frontier life was characterised by the enterprise of colonists, *caballeros*, lords, military orders and townships. In the thirteenth century the scale and nature of warfare and government, as elsewhere in Europe, changed. The reconquest, like everything else, became more centrally directed. In the thirteenth century we must begin with the kings.

3. The Problems and Opportunities of Reconquest, *c.* 1200—1350

Reconquest and Repopulation

DURING the thirteenth-century phase of the reconquest the Christians made dramatic advances which appeared to eliminate Islamic political power from the peninsula. Two rulers dominated these events and stood out head and shoulders above their contemporaries – Ferdinand III of Castile and León (1217/30–52) and James I of Aragon (1213–76). Like his cousin, Louis IX of France, Ferdinand III was to be canonised. His saintliness was not of the same exalted calibre as that of St Louis and was not officially recognised until 1671, but his firmness of purpose and his practical achievements made him a greater and more successful ruler than the French king. The *Primera Crónica General* tells us how St Ferdinand dedicated himself to his kingly and religious duties, among which the reconquest was of the greatest importance:

> Never did he surrender himself to great vices but always wished to serve God and destroy the infidels. As soon as he had made one conquest he prepared for the next; for he did not wish to eat his bread at rest or to sit around doing nothing, but wanted to give a good account to the highest judge as to how he had used his time.[23]

Unlike St Louis, Ferdinand III was not easily drawn into grandiose but hopeless crusading schemes. It is true that, once he had completed his Spanish conquests, the king's thoughts did turn to fighting the infidel in Africa, but during his reign he had always set himself specific objectives and concentrated on attaining them. Even on his deathbed he revealed that streak of realism which had characterised Castilian heroes from the time of the Cid onwards. Turning to his heir and successor, Alfonso, Ferdinand III gave him a simple and realistic way of determining kingly success or failure:

> 'Son, you are rich in lands and in many good vassals – more so than any other king in Christendom. Strive to do good and be

good, for you assuredly have the means to do so.' And he also said to him: 'Sir, I leave you all the lands on this side of the sea which the Moors won from King Roderick of Spain. All this now lies within your power, one part of it conquered and the other laid under tribute. If you should manage to hold it all in the way in which I leave it to you, then you are as good a king as I; and if you should enlarge it, you are better than I; and if you should lose any of it, you are not as good as I.'[24]

James the Conqueror was a different and more flamboyant crusader for God. Certainly, as his own *Book of Deeds* (*Llibre dels feyts*) illustrates, the king had a high opinion of himself and found it easy to reformulate the will of the Almighty in order to suit his own public designs and private conduct. James was a confirmed adulterer and fornicator, but he thought that such matters were mere trifles in comparison to his crusading deeds and intentions. He himself, for example, describes how, just before a battle with the infidel, he had to convince his confessor to consider the larger issues involved, grant absolution, and overlook his unrepentant liaison with one of his mistresses, Berenguela. However, not all the royal misdeeds were so easily forgiven. The pope found it difficult to overlook attacks on the archbishop of Zaragoza or the fact that James cut out the tongue of the bishop of Gerona. Yet, judged by the standards of the age, the king's assessment of priorities was completely successful. His resounding successes over the infidel in Spain led Innocent IV to view him as the Christian champion who might yet recover Palestine, and the Byzantine emperor and even the khan of the Mongols offered James their alliance for a crusade in the Holy Land.

What were the decisive turning-points in the reconquest successes achieved by these two monarchs? In 1229, urged on by a papal legate, James I conquered Muslim Mallorca and subsequently acquired the other Balearic islands of Menorca and Ibiza. In 1236 Córdoba, the former capital of the caliphate, fell to Ferdinand III. Two years later James the Conqueror took Valencia. Murcia was invested by the Castilians in 1243, and in 1247 Ferdinand III gained Seville. Apart from the Muslim kingdom of Granada, the Christians were now virtually masters of all Spain. To understand the full import of these events, however, we must look more closely at specific aspects related to them.

Undoubtedly crusading zeal, individual courage, sieges and

battles all contributed to splendid victories of profound military and psychological importance. The taking of Córdoba after a siege lasting several months, for example, not only led to what might be described as a ritual religious cleansing of the town but also enabled Ferdinand III to redress the affront which al-Mansūr had inflicted on the Christians when, in 997, he had triumphantly carried off the bells of Santiago de Compostela to the mosque at Córdoba.

On the feast day of the apostles Peter and Paul the city of Córdoba . . . was cleansed of all the filthiness of Muhammad and given up and surrendered to King Ferdinand. King Ferdinand then ordered the cross to be put on top of the chief tower where the name of the false Muhammad was wont to be called upon and praised, and then the Christians all began to shout with happiness and joy: '¡ Dios, ayuda !' . . . And he [the king] found there the bells of the church of St James the Apostle in Galicia, which were brought there by Almanzor . . . and placed in the mosque of Córdoba to the shame of the Christians; and there the bells remained until this conquest by King Ferdinand of the city of Córdoba. . . . King Ferdinand then had these same bells taken and returned to the church of Santiago of Galicia. Thus, the church of Santiago was once more happily adorned and some other smaller bells were also added which gave a very pleasing sound, and the pilgrims who went there heard them and knew the reason for them . . . and they praised King Ferdinand, blessed him, and prayed to God that he might be preserved and given a long life.[25]

The fall of Córdoba, therefore, was viewed within the general context of a victory for Santiago, Spain and Christendom. The frequency with which such passages occur in the chronicles with respect to other similar triumphs is hardly surprising, given the amount of time and military effort which was expended. In general terms, for example, it took James I some fifteen years to win the kingdom of Valencia, and in a more specific sense the siege of Seville lasted sixteen months.

These dramatic military episodes, however, help to create an illusion of complete victory for the Christians at the expense of Islam. This illusion is further strengthened by the natural tendency of chroniclers to concentrate on battles and sieges, and by the fact that surviving documentation reflects the victors' preoccupation with the setting up of Christian civil and ecclesiastical institutions over the reconquered territories. But in fact much of the Christian success must be explained by the willingness of the monarchs to come to terms with the Muslims and allow them to retain some of their own religious and civil institutions. This was especially the case in Valencia where, as Burns points out, 'the majority of the conquered remained in the kingdom, their society and institutions wounded and withdrawn but still omnipresent'.[26] Lack of manpower and the formidable strength of the Valencian realm's defences dictated such an outcome, and James I, forced to concentrate on key military positions, bypassed the majority of Muslim defences and, by isolating these areas, used the threat of potential violence to induce their inhabitants to come to terms. The king himself describes many such negotiations and, on one occasion when he was dealing with Murcian Muslims, he summarised what his policy had been:

> I told them my reasons for sending for them. They knew very well that I had many Saracen vassals in my dominions, and that in old times the royal family from which I was descended had them also in Aragon and in Catalonia, and I myself in the kingdoms both of Valencia and Mallorca, lately conquered. All had their laws, and had been respected as if they lived in the land of the Saracens, that is the people who had put themselves at my mercy and had submitted to me, for those who would not surrender I took their land by force and peopled it with Christians.[27]

James I was not exaggerating as, for example, the 'winning' of the castle of Peñíscola illustrates. An extraordinary degree of diplomatic delicacy surrounded the negotiations on this and other occasions. The sheiks of the town presented the king, encamped at night outside the castle, with 'a hundred loaves, two pitchers of wine, raisins, figs, and ten fowls as a present'. James himself took elaborate precautions to avoid giving offence to the Muslims. As night fell he ordered protective screens against dampness to be made out of carpets and blankets, and prohibited the felling of trees because 'it would have offended the Saracens if at our first entry we had begun to waste their land'. When discussions began next day the Muslims offered to 'make a treaty with me and surrender the castle at once, provided I allowed them their religion, and the liberties they were wont to have under their Saracen kings'. To these terms the king readily agreed and within two days scribes had drawn up a capitulation in due form.

The document of the capitulation of Peñíscola no longer exists, but the fall of this castle led to the 'conquest' of the region of Chivert, and in this case the original document has survived. Before its surrender the Chivert area had been allocated to the Templars, and it was they who undertook the negotiations which resulted in the agreement of 28 April 1234. The capitulation recognised the local Muslim authorities and the customary laws and usages of the area. The existing pattern of property-holding and social and religious organisation was upheld. Of course, the Chivert Muslims had to pay tribute in the form of one-sixth of their crops as well as a tax on their cattle, and the Christians did requisition part of the town. Yet Muslims deprived of houses were compensated with the properties of fugitives who, in their turn, were encouraged to return and were to be given compensation if they came back within one year.

These arrangements at Chivert were typical of the pattern of 'conquest' of many areas of the kingdom of Valencia. And subsequently, when the Christians had to deal with problems relating to the new order, they had recourse again and again to such formulas as 'according to immemorial custom', 'as was the custom in the time of the pagans', and 'as was done in the time of the Saracens'. Although not referring specifically to Valencia, a passage from James I's description of his negotiations with the Muslim authorities of Murcia may be taken as a final example to illustrate the spirit of many such arrangements.

They asked me to divide the town as had been agreed between me and them. I said that from that mosque near the Alcázar down to the gate facing my camp should belong to the Christians, and that the principal mosque itself should fall to our lot. To this they objected, saying that the agreement, as stipulated in the capitulation, was that they were to have their mosques and hold them as in the time of the Saracens. I replied that such was the agreement, but they had not understood the words of the capitulation, for if I were to grant them all their mosques, what would the Christians do without a church to go to? 'The Christian church', said I to them, 'will be at the very gate of the Alcázar. That a muezzin should proclaim the sabbath or the name of Allah close to my head, where I am sleeping, may seem to you a fit thing, but is not one of my liking. You have ten more mosques in the town; you may have your prayers in all of them, and leave that one to us.' They said that they would consult on it.[28]

The agreements made with capitulating Muslims were usually interpreted by the Christians in quasi-feudal terms, and regional Muslim leaders of importance were often required to do homage. At Játiva, for example, it was the military governor ($q\bar{a}'id$) and the hundred most important men of the town who formally did homage to James I as their lord, and subsequently the king made it clear that he regarded the $q\bar{a}'id$ as a vassal who should 'protect and defend me and my interests' and 'take justice at my hands'. In Islamic terms, the kissing of the feet or hands expressed obedience and allegiance, while in Spanish-Christian usage the kissing of hands was the essential symbolic act of vassalage. The act of vassalage usually reinforced a dependent relationship between 'conqueror' and 'conquered' which had arisen as a result of surrender agreements. But there were also cases of tributary or *paria* vassalage between independent Muslim leaders and the Christian kings. Ferdinand III, it will be remembered, had told his son, Alfonso, that all the land 'now lies within your lordship – one part of it conquered and the other laid under tribute'. In using the word 'tribute' the king was referring to the Nasrid kingdom of Granada, whose founder, Muhammad I or Ibn al-Ahmar (1232–73), had entered into a vassalage relationship years before at the time when Ferdinand III was laying siege to Jaén. According to the *Primera Crónica General*, Muhammad I secured his independence by surrendering Jaén, kissing Ferdinand III's hand and becoming his vassal. The Castilian king, for his part, merely stipulated that while the Moorish king should retain his lands and sovereignty as before, he should also 'give 150,000 *mrs* each year as tribute, make war and peace for him, and come each year to the *cortes*'. In fact, Muhammad I turned up to serve in Ferdinand III's campaigns in the Seville region and proved to be of considerable assistance:

> While King Ferdinand was at Carmona, the king of Granada, his vassal, came there with five hundred *caballeros* in order to serve him. After King Ferdinand had laid waste Carmona, he moved on with his army and went to Alcalá de Guadaira. When the Moors

of Alcalá learned that the king of Granada was present, they came out and surrendered to him, and he then gave up the castle to his lord, King Ferdinand.[29]

The crusading St Ferdinand, therefore, secured valuable service from his Muslim ally and vassal, and in 1254 the latter even sent a ceremonial guard of Moorish knights to attend his lord's funeral.

The continuing existence of the independent Muslim state of Granada and the nature of the surrender capitulations serve as a reminder that the crusading successes of James I and Ferdinand III were not as overwhelming as might at first sight appear. Indeed, the fact was that, quite apart from the manpower problems which faced the Christians, the Islamic cause was by no means completely lost. In some of the areas reconquered by the Christians there survived a Muslim aristocracy, many of whose members continued to hold extensive lands and castles, and had at their disposal considerable resources of military power. The Muslim lord of Játiva, for example, was described by a Catalan as being accompanied by 400 horsemen and as looking 'in truth to be a noble, for he came riding upon a splendid horse and his saddle and breast leather were inlaid with foil of gold'.[30] The most famous of these men was al-Azraq, a resistance fighter who rallied many of the Mudejars of Valencia into successful guerrilla action and open warfare against James I's forces during the years from 1247 to 1258. In addition to such rebels there was the kingdom of Granada which, despite its status as tributary to Castile, played a masterly game of alternating war and peace in order to avoid being swallowed up by its more powerful neighbours in Christian Spain and Muslim North Africa. It is true that the victories of Ferdinand III and James I had marked the end of Almohad power not only in Spain but also in Morocco where the Berber empire disintegrated into its tribal parts. Yet, although the unity of the Maghrib was over, by 1269 the dynasty of the Marinids had established itself at Marrakesh as the successor of the Almohads in Morocco, and it was to the Marinids that the Nasrids of Granada turned to redress the balance against Castile. The Marinid sultans, for their part, were only too willing to combine the idea of a Holy War with the opportunity of sending over to the peninsula those military leaders and their followers whose presence in Morocco posed a threat to their authority. On occasion the sultans themselves crossed over and, at the head of large armies, they consolidated

Muslim control over the vital straits of Gibraltar, intervened in the internal affairs of Granada, and invaded Christian Spain.

Mudejar rebellions and invasions by allied Nasrid and Marinid forces, therefore, could endanger Christian control of the reconquered lands. In 1264, for example, the Mudejars of Andalusia and Murcia rebelled while at the same time the armies of Granada, including Marinid troops, moved into an offensive which almost succeeded in wresting back the kingdom of Murcia for Islam. But, above all, the Christians were faced with the task of preventing the easy passage of North African armies across the Islamic bridgehead at the straits of Gibraltar. This problem began to assume serious proportions during the reign of Alfonso X of Castile (1252–84). In 1275 the Marinid sultan, Abū Yūsuf Ya 'qūb, crossed over to Spain with a large army, inflicted humiliating defeats on the Castilians, and secured his control of the straits by occupying Algeciras. Subsequently, although Alfonso X failed in 1277 to recover this vitally strategic area, the Christians managed to weaken the Muslim bridgehead by capturing and holding Tarifa. The struggle did not come to a head, however, until the third and fourth decades of the fourteenth century. In 1333 combined forces from Granada and Morocco reconquered Gibraltar, and the greatest of the Marinid sultans, Abu'l Hassan, began preparations for the invasion of Castile. In the face of this danger Alfonso XI of Castile (1312–50) feverishly sought Aragonese military and Catalan naval support. In 1340 a Christian attempt to prevent Muslim forces crossing the straits ended in a naval defeat at Algeciras, but a few months later the African army suffered a disastrous reverse at the battle of the river Salado. Determined to break the Islamic bridgehead, Alfonso XI now went on to explain to a European as well as a Spanish audience how the capture of Algeciras would solve the problem of the straits. His envoys, for example, explained to the pope:

... that he [the pope] well knew that from this city [Algeciras] much evil and destruction had formerly been inflicted on Christendom. Because of this, and also because it was the last city on the European side and was very close to Ceuta, which is the first city on the African side and was also the place where Abu'l Hassan, king across the sea and lord of the greater part of Africa, was collecting great armies and many ships to cross over in order to conquer the land of the Christians, the king had come to lay siege to Algeciras in order to avoid the evils which could befall Christendom.[31]

The siege of Algeciras, which lasted from 1342 to 1344, became one of the most publicised military operations of the fourteenth century. Chaucer's knight was one one of many men who turned up to the siege from all over Christendom, and financial aid was provided by the monarchs of France and Portugal as well as by the papacy. And this time the Christian success did mean that Marinid expansionism was halted, the Spanish side of the straits was put firmly under Castilian control, and the possibility of an Islamic reconquest was seen to have come to an end.

How did the Christians repopulate the vast territory which passed into their control during the thirteenth-century phase of the reconquest? Like the military conquest, the colonisation of Valencia, Murcia and Andalusia was a lengthy process. The impression given by the chronicle evidence is that colonisation and repopulation was carried out according to a well-established and familiar pattern. Here, for example, is a brief description of post-conquest reorganisation in Jaén:

> When King Ferdinand had taken Jaén . . . he entered it along with a large procession organised by all the clergy. Then he went directly to the chief mosque, to which he gave the name of Santa María, and then had an altar raised up there to the honour of Santa María, and had Don Gutierre, bishop of Córdoba, sing mass. He established a seat and bishopric there, and provided very well for the church, and gave it towns, castles and lands. He also sent out everywhere for populators, promising great liberties to all those who should come to colonise. Many men from all over the land came there, and he ordered the town and the lands to be shared out among them all. . . .[32]

Liberties and exemptions, therefore, once again had to be granted in order to attract colonists. By now a well-established and tested set of institutions was also available for transfer to the frontier. In this case the chronicle dwelt on the most obvious manifestation of such a policy – namely, the conversion of the chief mosque into a church, and the erection of a bishopric which, although not so magnificently endowed as the passage would have us believe, was accompanied by the setting up of episcopal, capitular and parochial organisation.

The same picture holds true of civil institutions. For example, the *fuero* of Toledo, drawn up in the eleventh century and subsequently modified, was used by the Castilian monarchy to structure the urban life of the south, and from the redistribution centres of Córdoba and Seville the *fuero* not only spread out to cover the Andalusian towns but was even transferred subsequently to towns in the New World.

The novel feature about colonisation was the system of land allocation. On the one hand, since manpower was still in short supply and a frontier defence system was still needed, the process of resettlement in Andalusia and Murcia favoured the rise of great estates or latifundia which the Castilian kings granted to powerful nobles and military orders. In some regions, on the other hand, a system of land allocation, imposed from above, shared out urban and rural properties in a detailed manner among the colonists. Commissions of *partitores* or *divisores* carried out repartitions, and recorded the results in registers of *repartimientos* relating to each particular area. This type of repopulation was particularly apt for complex urban areas and their surrounding lands, and *repartimientos* were carried out in Mallorca and parts of Valencia, Murcia and Andalusia. But in examining the repopulation of the newly conquered lands, other important problems must also be considered. Where did the colonists come from and what was the general situation with respect to manpower? What effect did Christian reaction to rebellions have on the relative strength and distribution of Mudejar patterns of settlement?

On specific occasions and in determinate areas there was no lack of colonists. In the early stages after the fall of Córdoba, for example, the legendary prosperity of the town and the fertility of its lands attracted so many settlers from all over the peninsula that a crisis in food and housing developed. But in general terms there can be no doubt that the Christians suffered from a serious shortage of manpower. It would not be too far off the mark to posit a figure of five million for the population of the Christian states of Spain towards the end of the thirteenth century. But Spain was unique in thirteenth-century Europe in that the advance of the reconquest made available large tracts of land which more than matched population growth. Of course, in some areas large numbers of Muslims were incorporated into Christian society. But at a time when elsewhere in Europe population growth caused pressure on food resources, the kingdom of Castile doubled the size of its territory and was faced with an abundance of land and a lack of colonists. In the Guadalquivir valley, for example, lands which had previously been exploited were abandoned during the course of the thirteenth century. The distribution of population throughout the reconquered areas, however, varied considerably.

In the early stages of the conquest of Valencia the Muslims were expelled from Burriana and the city of Valencia, and Mudejar rebellions subsequently led to further expulsions in places like Morella, Murviedro, Alcira and Játiva. In general terms the resulting pattern was that the northern part of the kingdom was almost entirely cleared of Muslims, whereas the central and southern regions, apart from the town of Valencia and its countryside, remained predominantly Mudejar. Into the reconquered lands there also came Christian settlers from Aragon, Catalonia and southern France, who, while preferring to live in the towns, also acquired farms in the surrounding rural areas. But these settlers were relatively few in number, and in the 1270s James I was to complain that, although the minimum number of colonists required for security reasons was 100,000, only 30,000 had come to help in the task of repopulation. Thus the kingdom of Valencia came to contain several predominantly Christian cities (of which the largest was Valencia itself with some 10,000 inhabitants), many towns in which Muslims and Christians lived together, and a countryside which, although under the ultimate control of Christian lords, was mainly tenanted by Mudejars living in Moorish villages.

Despite rebellions, therefore, Mudejars continued to constitute the majority of the Valencian population. It was quite otherwise in Andalusia. (See Map 4.) Here, too, the conquest initially resulted in the expulsion or acceptance of the Muslim population according to the degree of resistance offered to the Christians and the strategic value of key areas. Whereas resistance in Córdoba and Seville led to the expulsion of Muslims from these regions, there were many areas where immediate capitulation earned the inhabitants the right to retain their lands and customs. But the seriousness of the rebellion of 1264 changed Castilian policy in this respect completely, and in place after place the Muslims were expelled until only a few *morerías* of any importance remained. Consequently, the need for settlers to colonise the deserted landscape became even more acute. The *repartimiento* of Ecija, for example, shows the *partitores* trying to reconstitute life in the deserted town, and then moving out to the rural areas to create villages or *alquerías* which usually contained between four and ten settler-families, although cases of one-household *alquerías* were by no means uncommon. Similarly, in the Guadalete region, the *repartimiento* of Jerez in 1266 revealed that there were more houses than settlers, Cádiz had a population of only 800 inhabitants, and even after its colonisation Chiclana was once again abandoned and depopulated for a time. The town of Seville, on the other hand, proved so attractive to settlers, and was to become so politically and commercially important, that its case merits special attention.

In calculating a repopulation total in the order of 24,000, Julio González has shown that Seville attracted enough colonists to make it the largest town in the peninsula after Barcelona with its 25,000 inhabitants. The origins of the settlers who poured into Seville were extremely varied. The vast majority, of course, came from other areas of Christian Spain and, in particular, from places in the northern *meseta*, such as Burgos, Valladolid and Palencia. Catalans came in fairly large numbers, but Aragon, Galicia, Portugal and areas recently reconquered provided few colonists. Although there is no evidence of the presence of Jews in Almohadic Seville, many came to the town after its reconquest, and their community became one of the largest and most prosperous of its kind in the peninsula. On the other hand, no Mozarabs had remained after the Almohadic persecutions, and after the region fell into Christian hands almost all the Muslims were expelled: a small *morería* continued to exist in Seville itself and some Mudejars remained in the smaller outlying towns, but their numbers were few. Although in a minority, the number of foreigners who helped in the repopulation of Seville was surprisingly large. Many of their names figure in the *repartimiento*, and it is clear that the Italians, and in particular the Genoese who settled in the area of Genoa street (*calle de Génova*), were prominent. Most of the *francos* in the *repartimiento* were, of course, French, but Germans and English were also included in their numbers. Peter Arnot or Arnold of London, for example, settled in Bayonne street, and both a 'John of London' and his son figure in the *repartimiento*.

Why did men choose to settle in Seville? As we have seen, the settlers generally preferred the towns to the countryside, and the ordered manner of the *repartimiento* of Seville served as an additional attraction. However, as we shall see, economic incentives and opportunities also induced men from all nations to come and settle in the town.

The Reconquest and the Economic Structure

THE reconquest of the thirteenth century, as we have seen, aggravated the shortage of manpower. What was the economic significance of the varying land–population ratios of the Iberian peninsula? The question is best answered by a comparison with thirteenth-century England or France. In these countries the conditions of an expanding economy prevailed – for example, population growth, rising production, ˙capital investment, high-farming landlords, and a degree of efficient estate management. But there was also land-hunger, fragmentation of peasant holdings, and a sharp decline in *per capita* production and consumption. In terms of the land–population ratio, the economy of western Europe in the thirteenth century has been described as suffering from a progressive 'saturation' of population which in many areas was straining the 'carrying capacity' of land to its limits.

Along the Levantine coast of Spain pressure on the attractive landed resources of some areas was not dissimilar to that in the rest of western Europe. Thus in the *huerta* regions of Valencia, where land distribution had been organised in relation to important towns and their surrounding *alquerías*, the structure of the rural economy was largely determined by a sufficiency of manpower and by an extremely sophisticated irrigation system in which thousands of small canals, divisors and ditches drew water from the larger canals and distributed it over large areas of territory. The patchwork effect of this irrigation system imposed itself on a rural society where small farms rather than large estates predominated, and where a high degree of co-operation characterised all those who depended on water distribution for their living. James I described a typical *huerta* landscape round Játiva:

> When we arrived at the top of it [a hill], we had the finest prospect that could be imagined; we saw the most beautiful *huerta* round the town and castle; there were more than two hundred flat-roofed cottages in it, the finest that man could devise, and several pretty villages (*alquerías*) besides, thickly set all round. . . . I afterwards learned from prisoners we made, that great harm had been done by cutting the water-courses (*cequías*), and destroying the mills. I, who knew what a great evil it was for

the town, so populated as Játiva was, to take away their water, tried to cut off the streams and *cequias* wherewith they watered their lands and worked the mills; but I could not entirely succeed for I had few men with me. . . .[33]

How different was the situation in other areas of Spain! The colonisation of the lands reconquered in the thirteenth century was far from complete even on the eve of the Black Death, and the northern areas of the peninsula felt the effects of the population drain southwards. In the heart of Old Catalonia, the plain of Vich in the thirteenth century still presented a semi-deserted landscape undergoing active colonisation, and in some places in Old Castile, such as Calatañazor, the monarchy had to continue offering privileges and exemptions to settlers in order to prevent depopulation. Indeed, it was precisely because of the continuing migration of men that the great nobility complained to Alfonso X in the *cortes* of 1271 about colonisation policies in the south which depleted their manpower and revenues in the centre and north. The acceleration of the reconquest and the resulting drop in land prices, it is true, reinforced the existing trend towards the formation of large land-holdings and lordships. But the shortage of manpower had favoured the peasantry, and it is this situation which explains the absence of some of the fundamental features so typical of the economies of other areas of western Europe. Even as early as the eleventh century the receding frontier had placed an enormous strain on the arable demesne economy. For example, the monastery of San Millán de la Cogolla, south-west of Logroño, had undoubtedly possessed demesne lands which were worked by a peasantry owing labour services. But the striking feature is the rapidity with which the monks had changed from a regime of demesne exploitation and labour services to one of rents and seigneurial dues, and significantly enough the beginnings of this change dated from the latter years of the eleventh century – that is, in the years after the fall of Toledo (1085), when manpower was at a high premium, and colonists migrated south. When taken in conjunction with the much greater expansion of the frontier in the thirteenth century, this pattern in the agrarian economy of the great lords helps to explain why the rural economy was not characterised by effective estate management, high-farming landlords or excessive fragmentation of peasant holdings. In thirteenth-century Castile and León, unlike England, there was little incentive for landlords to expand demesne cultivation, and there was no Walter of Henley to produce treatises on estate management and accounting.

Ecclesiastical lords were probably more efficient than their lay counterparts, and their records afford the best available evidence as to the nature of 'management' in the century prior to the Black Death. Salustiano Moreta has ably analysed some of the economic problems affecting nine Benedictine monasteries of the ecclesiastical province of Toledo in the early fourteenth century. All these monasteries were possessed of large estates and lordships. Accounts for 1338, for example, show that the revenues of the monastery of Oña were derived from lands and rights in at least two hundred places scattered over the large region between the north coast and Burgos. Similarly, although most of the possessions of the monastery of Silos were concentrated between the rivers Arlanza and Duero, the totality of this monastery's revenues, rights and lands was scattered over a vast area which reached as far south as the regions of Seville and Cartagena.

How did these monasteries exploit their landed and seigneurial possessions? Although seigneurial dues constituted an important element in the income of these nine monasteries, they tended to be fixed in nature and amount, and were less important than the rents. Most of the monastic lands were leased out to tenants, and direct exploitation was generally confined to vineyards and orchards, and, in a few cases, to those cereal lands nearest the monastery. Labour services hardly existed, and when direct exploitation was undertaken by a monastery it was carried out by wage labourers and servants attached to the monastic *familia*. Thus, although the monks took care to ensure that capital equipment, such as mills and houses, was maintained in good order, direct demesne exploitation hardly existed. In general terms the monastic finances were clearly in a parlous state, and the monasteries had been forced to pledge lands and income in order to raise loans to cover their expenditure. In such cases the creditors were frequently townsmen, from places such as Burgos or Valladolid, or tenant farmers of substance from places like Covarrubias or Belorado. Clearly circumstances were not always favourable to the lords, and with leases and debt playing a significant role in the evolution and stratification of rural society, it is difficult to envisage the agrarian world simply in terms of a society whose exploiters and exploited were conveniently divided from each other by the structures of a solidly established seigneurial regime.

This was even true of Old Catalonia where the issue of seigneurial exactions was to play such an important role in the *remensa* wars of the later middle ages.

Pedro Albert in his *Costumbres*, written about the middle of the thirteenth century, emphasised the way in which the legal status of the Catalan peasant or *payés* varied regionally. In Old Catalonia the *masover* (peasant farmer) and his children could not abandon their farmstead or *masia* unless they bought the right to do so from their lord. In New Catalonia, on the other hand, the seigneurial peasants were not tied down in this way and could abandon their lands whenever they wished. It was this situation which subsequently formed part of the background to the *remensa* wars of Old Catalonia. But even in the thirteenth century in Old Catalonia it was common for villages to be enmeshed, as in Old Castile, in several seigneurial jurisdictions or co-lordships, and this fact alone enabled sectors of the rural population to escape from the worst effects of personal ties of dependence. Indeed, unlike some of the nobility, the ecclesiastical lords displayed little interest in tying peasants to the land, and the *remensa* problem was as yet far from becoming a burning issue. On the contrary, as Cuvillier has shown with respect to the region round Taradell, a common concern over land exploitation and profit seems to have led to a fruitful association between some of those with the usufruct of the land, and ecclesiastical lords who encouraged the peasantry to colonise lands and market their products. Consequently within the village hierarchies, based on the distribution of peasant wealth and prosperity, there emerged a *bourgeoisie rurale* of substantial tenant farmers who were relatively unhindered by seigneurial restrictions and concentrated on profits.

Given the surfeit of land and the lack of manpower in many regions of the peninsula, it is hardly surprising that great lay and ecclesiastical lords should have turned their backs on direct arable exploitation and concentrated on obtaining other sources of income. Lordships, for example, came increasingly to be viewed as a means of obtaining income which had previously gone to the Crown, and bishops and monasteries clashed bitterly over the control of tithes. Already the great lords of Castile were beginning to display those attitudes which later hardened into the view that profits were to be derived from lordships over men rather than land, and that land itself gave social prestige rather than economic benefits. However, there was one striking exception to this general picture in that the vast increase in pastoralism which took place during this period attracted the attention of the great lords.

It was only when the Christians won the grass-lands of the plains and steppes of La Mancha and Extremadura that an integrated ranching economy emerged. The grass of these regions was abundant not only in the spring but in autumn as well, and this made possible the great seasonal migrations of transhumant sheep along the routes, known as *cañadas*, and the creation of an authentic ranching frontier. Moreover, the problems of frontier warfare in the steppe-lands not only swung the balance in favour of pastoralism, but also led to the creation in the plains of the great lordships of the military orders.

The military orders owned large flocks. In 1243, for example, the Templars and Alcantarans quarrelled over the control of 42,000 sheep in the Tagus valley, and during the century the Order of Calatrava actively protected its brand against other ranchers and clashed with northern towns over the transhumance routes. The townsmen of the few urban centres in the plains also derived their wealth from pastoralism rather than from their small arable holdings. Royal provisions and *fueros* of towns like Cáceres show that alongside the wealthy ranchers with large flocks there existed a class of small stockmen with flocks of between forty and one thousand sheep. Both the northerners and those who colonised the Manchegan and Extremaduran grass-lands engaged in pastoralism.

Not all graziers, of course, were involved in large-scale trans-humance, and this led to quarrels with rival pastoral interests engaged in short-distance flock movements. Thus the seasonal and prolonged absence of flocks from home territories necessitated escorts of armed riders, as well as some machinery to adjudicate between rival interests, deal with strays and enforce pastoral law on brawling herdsmen. From an early date, therefore, towns like Cuenca and Cáceres made provisions – such as the appointment of special judges to accompany the herdsmen – for pastoral disputes. The famous *Real Concejo de la Mesta*, probably set up by the Crown in the 1260s, in a way sanctioned these local arrangements, and also protected northern flocks in their use of southern pastures. The monarchy, of course, reaped fiscal benefits from this creation of a royal *Mesta* which, in effect, was a privileged association of stockmen whose interests were upheld in the *cortes* by the representatives of those towns, such as León, Burgos, Segovia, Soria and Cuenca, which were most involved in the business of sheep and wool.

The phenomenal expansion of Castilian transhumance, however, cannot simply be explained in terms of an accelerating frontier, a crisis in manpower, and the opportunities for movement between alternative pastures. Without markets the growth in sheep-farming would have been pointless and, indeed, impossible. Such markets did exist in textile centres like Cuenca, Soria, Segovia, Córdoba and Seville, and the volume of cloth production was large enough by the late thirteenth and early fourteenth centuries to stimulate royal intervention in the form of privileges and rudimentary controls. Several factors may have stimulated the growth of these textile centres during the thirteenth century: the Christians seem to have inherited capital equipment and perhaps skilled Mudejar artisans from the Muslims, exports to Portugal may have acted as an early stimulus to production, and the needs of the home markets were matched by cheap wool of a good quality. But the decisive factor was that, by the early years of the fourteenth century, the demand for Castilian wool was increasing in the textile centres of the Low Countries and Italy, and it is to the wider context of commercial expansion that the concluding pages of this chapter are devoted.

The acquisition of a southern coastline in the thirteenth century was to provide the Castilians with great opportunities for commercial and maritime expansion in subsequent centuries. The *Primera Crónica General*, after describing the conquest of Seville, goes on to sing its praises, and a passage from this eulogy helps to explain why the town became the economic capital of the south:

There are many other noble and great features [about Seville] apart from all those which we have already described. There is no town so pleasant or so well situated in the world. It is a town to which the ships come daily up the river from the sea. Ships and galleys and other sea vessels dock there inside the walls with all kinds of merchandise from all parts of the world. They arrive there frequently and come from all kinds of places: from Tangier, Ceuta, Tunis, Bougie, Alexandria, Genoa, Portugal, England, Pisa, Lombardy, Bordeaux, Bayonne, Sicily, Gascony, Catalonia, Aragon, and even France and many other places from across the sea, and from the lands of both Christians and Moors. So how can such a city, which is so perfect and plentiful and where there is such an abundance of goods, not be so excellent and so prized? Her olive oil alone is sent throughout the world by sea and land –

and this is to omit all the other plentiful riches which are to be found there and which it would be tedious to recount here. . . . [34]

This extract helps to explain the attraction for settlers of a city and port which was at the crossroads not only of the European and African economies but of those of the Mediterranean and the Atlantic as well. In fact, direct sea communications between the Mediterranean and Southampton and Bruges were opened up by the Genoese in the 1270s, and as the fairs of Champagne declined the maritime route through the straits came to carry the densest commercial traffic of the later middle ages. For these reasons, and also because Andalusia had a great variety of marketable commodities to offer, the future prosperity of Seville was guaranteed.

However, as we have seen, the commercial renaissance of the eleventh and twelfth centuries began in the north where, at a time when the Almoravid and Almohad invasions tended to hinder commercial links with al-Andalus, the *camino francés* encouraged the circulation of merchants and goods along the route from the Pyrenees to Santiago. During the course of the twelfth century the shippers and fishermen of the north-coast towns, such as San Vicente de la Barquera, Laredo, Castro and Santander, also laid the foundations of their formidable commercial operations. By the second decade of the thirteenth century the Basques were exporting iron and specialising in transporting Gascon wine to England. Ships from the north coast participated in the campaigns leading to the conquest of Seville, and in 1296 the north-coast towns formed what was in effect a league similar to that of the Hansa – the *hermandad de la marina de Castilla con Vitoria.* The growth of the pastoral economy of central and southern Castile was of momentous importance for the *hermandad.* Expanding wool production supplied the north-coast shippers with export material and, shortly after the mid-thirteenth century, a Castilian commercial colony established itself in Bruges. Meantime, the foundation of Bilbao in 1300 marked the beginnings of that rivalry with Burgos which was to symbolise the conflict between northern shippers and inland wool merchants. In a sense such conflicts of interest were inevitable for, as the great age of the frontier drew to a close, the Castilians turned increasingly to the new opportunities provided by ports and commercial centres on the northern and southern coasts.

These beginnings of Castilian commercial expansion, however, were overshadowed at this time by the range and sophistication of Catalan mercantile activity. The merchants of Barcelona were men of initiative who were prepared to participate in all kinds of foreign and domestic trade. Like their Italian counterparts they formed various kinds of partnerships which lasted for a specific length of time. *Commenda* contracts, for example, were much in vogue by the thirteenth century and stimulated enterprise by providing capital for travelling merchants who, sharing in the profits in return for their labour, subsequently accounted for the goods or money entrusted to them *in commenda*. Then, as well as common and limited partnerships for one trading venture, Catalan merchants also formed commercial companies for periods up to five years, with the profits being shared out yearly in proportion to the partners' investments.

Catalan trade reached its apogee in the late thirteenth and early fourteenth centuries. By this time the Catalans were to be found all over the Mediterranean, in North Africa and in the Atlantic. In Provence and Languedoc they cornered the spice trade, sold textiles and grain, and more or less established Catalan as the official language of trade. From the reign of James II (1291–1327) the islands of Corsica, Sardinia and Sicily provided one side of triangular trading routes which included north-west Italy and southern France to the north or, alternatively, North Africa to the south. In fact Catalans were trading in Alexandria as early as 1219, and from 1272 the spice trade gave rise to a Catalan colony under the authority of a consul. Further west, Catalan merchants for a time exercised a virtual monopoly of Christian trade with Tunis, Bougie and Tlemcen – to such an extent, indeed, that in the treaty of 1301 with Tunis, James II reserved to himself half the profits of customs charges paid by his subjects in Tunis. In the mid-thirteenth century the Catalans also ventured into the Atlantic trade and established a colony in Bruges.

Active everywhere from Alexandria to Bruges, the merchants of Catalonia established colonies abroad which, adapting themselves to local circumstances, provided stability for the trading routes. In Muslim towns, for example, they were granted their own settlements or *alfóndigos* which, apart from the warehouses and attached living quarters (the *funduqs*), usually included a church, bakery, baths, space for a market and, in the seaports, a landing-stage.

Although not as closely related as has sometimes been thought, the political and economic factors behind Aragonese–Catalan expansion tended to complement each other. When, for example, the papacy invited James I to intervene in Italy in the mid-1230s, Catalan and Genoese trading interests had already clashed in the Mediterranean, and the importance of Barcelona as the economic centre of the Crown of Aragon was manifest. From mid-century the town's government was restructured in favour of the mercantile oligarchy, and Peter III (1276–85) began his reign by crushing a revolt of those Catalan nobles who opposed his design for a Mediterranean expansion which would benefit the merchants of Barcelona as well as the monarchy. It is not surprising, therefore, that when the Sicilians appealed to Peter III for help against the Angevins in 1282, the subsequent acquisition of Sicily by the Crown of Aragon was a venture in which the Catalans predominated. The Catalans had introduced their language into Mallorca and Valencia, and the acquisition of new territories, together with the commercial primacy of Barcelona, resulted in a situation in which the Aragonese played the minor role in a political federation which bore their name.

4. The Frontier and Cultural Change

ALTHOUGH the reconquest of the twelfth and thirteenth centuries was at times elevated to the level of a crusading 'manifest destiny', the frontier did not act as an insurmountable barrier to the flow of cultural influences. We have seen how, at a practical level, even kings like Ferdinand III and James I had to come to terms with infidels and accord them a place in Christian society. Cultural developments were similarly affected by both elements of 'hostility' or 'rejection' and by those processes of accommodation or accultura-tion which were continually taking place between the Christians, Muslims and Jews. Some of these processes were, so to speak, accidental, but there were also cases of deliberate and conscious cultural borrowing in which individuals of authority played a positive role. This chapter is largely devoted to examining cases of both these types of acculturation, but it is only fair to warn the reader that some aspects of these problems have aroused heated controversy. Perhaps the first and most important pitfall to avoid is that of exaggerating the impact of Islam on cultural developments in Christian Spain.

It is obvious that the reconquest endeavours of the Christians were accompanied by cultural developments which owed little to Islamic Spain and were fundamentally Christian and European. As the Christians pushed south they restored bishoprics, built Romanesque and Gothic cathedrals, celebrated their victories in chronicles and epics, and turned to the European heart-land for material and spiritual support. It was along the *camino francés* or pilgrimage route, for example, that Romanesque architecture penetrated into Castile–León. (See Map 3.) Almost all the early Romanesque churches and monasteries lay close to the *camino francés*, and many were built by Frenchmen and in the 'pilgrimage style' which also characterised the architecture of the French routes leading into Spain. It is a style which links together churches as far apart as St Martin at Tours, St Foy at Conques, St Sernin at Toulouse, the cathedral at Jaca, San Martín of Frómista, San Isidoro at León, and the cathedral of Compostela itself. The very sculptures of these churches, of which the most famous are those of the *Puerta de las*

Platerías and the *Pórtico de la Gloria* at Compostela, bear witness to the efforts made to instil the tenets of the Christian religion into the minds of contemporaries. Nor were such influences solely French or confined to the regions of the pilgrimage route. The Romanesque, for example, spilled over from the *camino francés* and influenced evolving regional architecture in places such as Segovia, Salamanca and Avila. In Catalonia, as the twelfth-century cathedral at Seo de Urgel illustrates, Romanesque architecture owed much to Italian influences and to the work of Lombard masons. And what are we to make of the wall paintings of Old and New Testament scenes which were executed in the chapter house at Sigena about the year 1200? The artists responsible were almost certainly trained at Winchester, and yet they were also familar with the Byzantine artistic traditions of Sicily and even Constantinople.

Although similar points could be made about 'European' influences in the thirteenth-century transition from Romanesque architecture to the new style which produced a perfect example of French Gothic in the cathedral of León, language and literature must also claim our attention briefly. As will be seen below, many scientific and philosophical works were translated from Arabic during the course of the twelfth and thirteenth centuries. However, the very fact that translations had to be carried out is some indication of the barriers to Muslim influences in a society where the Romance vernaculars were even challenging the supremacy of Latin. Alfonso X of Castile (1252–84), at whose court the work of translation flourished, deliberately promoted the rise of the vernacular. Works in the vernacular, of course, predated Alfonso's reign, but the 'official' support for Castilian at court was truly impressive. It, and not Latin, was to be the language of law and history as well as of official records and chancery documents. The king, indeed, seems to have set out consciously to provide a measure of cultural, legal and linguistic unity for a kingdom which contained such diverse areas as Galicia and Andalusia. Thus the synthesising and unifying influences, which were at their most obvious in the law code of the *Siete Partidas*, are also discernible in Alfonso's two major historical enterprises in the vernacular – the *History of Spain* (*Estoria de España*) and the unfinished *General History* (*General Estoria*). Taken together, such works clearly bear witness to a flourishing vernacular tradition with an independent and conscious identity. But the content of much of the literature of the period likewise points to the dominating influences of the European and Christian inheritance. The so-called *cuaderna vía* poems of the thirteenth century, for example, were written in a learned metre adapted from either French or Latin, and the content of many of them was designed to inspire a religious reverence which would attract pilgrims and badly needed cash to specific monasteries such as San Pedro de Arlanza and San Millán de la Cogolla. Moreover, even when Arabic influences can be detected in literary works, they are usually less important than the European elements. Alfonso X's *Estoria de España*, for example, not only drew upon Arabic historians but also upon Latin and Spanish chronicles, classical authors, the bible and epic material. The same is true of the *Cantar de Mío Cid* which at first sight presents us with an ambiguous frontier world of bewildering fluidity. While the extant version of the poem was probably composed in the early thirteenth century by an anonymous author with a legal turn of mind, the story must be set within the context of the epic tradition of the Germanic peoples, and the Cid himself, although he is refreshingly practical and realistic, is fully aware of the larger issues at stake in the struggle between Christians and Muslims.

The Translators

BEARING in mind the predominantly European background which has just been briefly sketched in, the recognition by Christians of the advanced cultural and technological achievements of Islamic Spain can now be considered. Let us begin with the famous case of Gerard of Cremona (*c.* 1114–87), an Italian scholar, who was probably the most prolific translator into Latin of works in Arabic. According to a biobibliographical note which Gerard's students inserted into one of his translations:

> He was trained from childhood at centres of philosophical study and had come to a knowledge of all of this that was known to the Latins; but for love of the *Almagest*, which he could not find at all among the Latins, he went to Toledo; there, seeing the abundance of books in Arabic on every subject, and regretting the poverty of the Latins in these things, he learned the Arabic language, in order to be able to translate. In this way, combining both language and science . . . he passed on the Arabic literature in the manner of the wise man who, wandering through a green field, links up a

crown of flowers, made from not just any, but from the prettiest; to the end of his life, he continued to transmit to the Latin world (as if to his own beloved heir) whatever books he thought finest, in many subjects, as accurately and as plainly as he could.[35]

Here, then, was a scholar who deliberately moved to the frontier and devoted his life to translation. Indeed his students listed the titles of seventy-one works which he translated: three on dialectic, seventeen on geometry, twelve on astronomy, eleven on philosophy, twenty-one on medicine, three on alchemy, and four on geomancy. Gerard was only one of many such scholars who participated in the widespread movement of translations during the twelfth and thirteenth centuries. What was their purpose and how is their interest in such a task to be explained?

Islam was a bridging civilisation. Her conquest of Persia and some Byzantine provinces, as well as her contacts with China and India, enabled her to act as a transmitter of culture to Europe. Islam also provided a cultural bridge linking Latin Europe with certain aspects of its Greco-Roman past because, when the fall of the Roman Empire and the barbarian invasions imposed a break on the European classical tradition, it was Islam which succeeded to most of the heritages of the Greco-Persian and Greco-Roman Empires. We have seen, for example, how Gerard of Cremona went to Toledo in search of the fundamental work on Greek astronomy, known by its Arabic title as the *Almagest*, which Ptolemy had put together in Alexandria during the first half of the second century. Much of the lost luggage of the classical past was to be collected in this way by the Latin scholars of the twelfth and thirteenth centuries.

Since the scientific knowledge of the school of Alexandria had been of marginal interest to the intellectuals of Rome and Byzantium, the true heirs of this cultural tradition were Baghdad and Córdoba, and the heritage of the Greeks was translated into Arabic, Syrian or Hebrew. But the scholars of Islam were not merely translators, and the store of Alexandrian science was enriched by their intellectual contributions. Thus, as well as producing philosophers, historians and poets, the Islamic world improved a scientific tradition of which Latin Europe was largely ignorant.

The cultural greatness of al-Andalus dated from the ninth century and continued, with varying fortunes, down to the twelfth century. The anxiety of successive rulers to patronise intellectuals undoubtedly acted as a powerful stimulus to learning. Even after the collapse of the caliphate the tradition of enlightened patronage was maintained in the small Taifa courts, such as that of the 'Abbādids of Seville whose rulers were themselves poets. To a certain extent this cultural tradition was blunted by the regimes of the Almoravids and the Almohads, but their intolerance towards learning has frequently been exaggerated. Under the Almoravids, for example, fine poets like Ibn Khafāja and Ibn Quzmān flourished, and Malikite theologians broadened the scope and range of their studies. Similarly, under the Almohads a strong philosophical tradition culminated in the work of Averroes of Córdoba (1126–98).

Much of the scholarship of al-Andalus during these centuries consisted of studies in Greek science and philosophy within an Islamic and Arabic-language setting. But since the *Qur' ān* imposed a complex of specific beliefs and actions on Muslims, the study of the Greek sciences inevitably raised tensions in those areas of scholarship which clashed with orthodoxy. This was not generally the case in the empirical sciences, which orthodox theology hardly touched upon, and consequently the study of subjects like mathematics and astronomy flourished from an early date. For example, the work of the great scholar Maslama (d. 1007), who was renowned for his study of Ptolemy's *Almagest*, exemplified the salient characteristics of Muslim mathematical and astronomical scholarship – that is, the use of meticulous observation to verify and correct the works of predecessors. Maslama had a school of disciples who, in their turn, established new schools in which outstanding scholars continued to study astronomy and mathematics in the courts of the Taifas. Like Maslama, these scholars had at their disposal accurate instruments which were essential to the practical application of learning. For example, specific problems related to the calculation of tithes or the division of estates according to the precepts of orthodoxy called for the application of practical mathematical skill. But the use of precision instruments and careful observation was particularly developed in astronomy, which fulfilled the command of the *Qur'ān* to contemplate the glory of God and was also indispensable to religious observance. Thus the scholars of al-Andalus made extensive use of astrolabes and quadrants, and constructed globes of the heavens. Surviving examples of these instruments indicate that the craftsmen of Muslim Spain displayed a high degree of skill in producing precision equipment.

In contrast to subjects such as mathematics, astronomy and medicine, the study of Greek philosophy appeared dangerous to *Qur'ān*-centred theology because it claimed to demonstrate truths in much the same way as the Greek empirical sciences did. Thus, when philosophers who admired Plato or Aristotle spoke of the world and the destiny of man, they ran the very real danger of clashing both with the teachings of the *Qur'ān* and the Malikite jurists who were the guardians of an orthodoxy which was summed up by the saying: 'Knowledge is threefold: the clear book of God, past Tradition (*Sunna*) and "I know not".' In such an unfavourable climate philosophers took care to harmonise their opinions, and the continuation of such studies depended to a large extent on the attitude of rulers. The career of Ibn Rushd, or Averroes as he was known in Christian Europe, not only illustrates the real dangers which confronted the philosophers but it also serves as a reminder that the twelfth century, despite being dominated by the Berber regimes, produced some of the most outstanding scholars in the history of Islamic Spain – men, for example, like Avenpace, Ibn Tufail and Maimonides. Between them these scholars developed a neo-Aristotelian school which was to have a considerable influence on Christian Europe.

Towards the end of his life Averroes suffered from the persecution of philosophers which was carried out by the Almohad ruler Abū Yūsuf in 1196. In the general supression of philosophical activities Averroes was banished to the small town of Lucena, and all but his scientific works were ordered to be burnt. The incident, of course, provides another example of Almohad intolerance, but against it we should balance both the fact that similar difficulties had affected philosophical studies in previous centuries and that Averroes's studies had been promoted by Abū Yūsuf's predecessor, Abū Ya 'qūb. The enlightened patronage of this Almohad ruler, indeed, does much to demolish the charge of barbaric intolerance which has sometimes been levelled against the Berber regimes in general. For it was Abū Ya 'qūb who, with his friend and councillor Ibn Tufail, author of the *Autodidact Philosopher*, encouraged Averroes to write commentaries on the work of Aristotle. Indeed, Averroes's reported account of how Ibn Tufail introduced him to Abū Ya 'qūb conveys perfectly the curious blend of constraint and official encouragement which characterised the atmosphere of the philosophers' world:

When I entered into the presence of the Prince of the Believers, Abū Ya 'qūb, I found him with Abū Bakr Ibn Tufayl alone. Abū Bakr began praising me, mentioning my family and ancestors and generously including in the recital things beyond my real merits. The first thing that the Prince of the Believers said to me, after asking me my name, my father's name and my genealogy was: 'What is their opinion about the heavens?' – referring to the philosophers – 'Are they eternal or created?' Confusion and fear took hold of me, and I began making excuses and denying that I had ever concerned myself with philosophic learning; for I did not know what Ibn Tufayl had told him on the subject. But the· Prince of the Believers understood my fear and confusion, and turning to Ibn Tufayl began talking about the question of which he had asked me, mentioning what Aristotle, Plato and all the philosophers had said, and bringing in besides the objections of the Muslim thinkers against them. . . . Thus he continued to set me at ease until I spoke, and he learned what was my competence in that subject. . . .

Abū Bakr Ibn Tufayl summoned me one day and told me, 'Today I heard the Prince of the Believers complain of the difficulty of expression of Aristotle and his translators, and mention the obscurity of his aims, saying, "If someone would tackle these books, summarize them and expound their aims, after understanding them thoroughly, it would be easier for people to grasp them." So if you have in you abundant strength for the task, perform it. . . .' This was what led me to summarize the books of the philosopher Aristotle.[36]

In this brief discussion of scholarship in al-Andalus the importance of the Greek empirical sciences and the twelfth-century flowering in the study of the Greek philosophers have been deliberately emphasised at the expense of other branches of Muslim learning. For, what kind of works did the Christian translators in Spain seek out from the cultural world of al-Andalus? Although the Christian scholars displayed an almost uncritical veneration with respect to the 'secrets' possessed by the Muslims, the process of transmission was in fact fairly selective, and many of the translations were from works relating to Greek philosophy and science. Of course, there were famous exceptions. For example, Peter the Venerable, abbot of Cluny, recorded how he had the *Qur'ān* translated during his visit to Spain in 1142, although significantly enough he had to lay out considerable sums of money in order to secure the help of translators who were engaged on other work. Even within the field of the empirical sciences the process of transmission included a fair amount that was not related to the Greek heritage: the Hindu numerical system, which we call Arabic numerals, for example, owed nothing to Greek science. But as far as the translators themselves were concerned, their efforts were on the whole directed at extending their knowledge of Arabic-Greek learning. The English scholar Daniel of Morley summed up the situation succinctly when, after returning from studying in Spain, he declared his intention of teaching everything he had learnt in Toledo 'in order not to remain the only Greek among the Romans'.

The process of transmission itself has frequently been viewed within the context of a 'School of Translators of Toledo' which was allegedly founded by Archbishop Raymond (1124–51). In fact there were various centres and phases of translating. As early as the tenth century, for example, mathematical and astronomical works from Córdoba, dealing with such scientific novelties as astrolabes and quadrants, were being collected and translated in the Catalan abbey of Ripoll. But these early contacts were not maintained by subsequent generations, and it was only in the twelfth century, after the frontier had advanced to the Tagus and the Ebro, that a continuous tradition of translating was established. Even then, however, the earliest translations were not produced in Toledo which, as we have seen, was dominated by Archbishop Bernard's policy of intolerance towards the infidel and all his works. Instead, scholars set to work in places along the Ebro valley almost immediately after the conquest of Zaragoza (1118). Subsequently the activity of translators, preoccupied chiefly with astronomy, astrology and even the occult, spread outwards to encompass other centres from Pamplona to Toledo and from Logroño to Barcelona. Prior to the middle of the twelfth century, therefore, Toledo enjoyed no special primacy as a centre for translation, and although scholars kept in touch with each other, they did not constitute a 'school'. It was only after 1165 that such a school emerged in Toledo round the figure of Gerard of Cremona, and it was not until this late date that interest in the scientific and philosophical works of Aristotle began to manifest itself. In the final phase of cultural transmission Alfonso X (1252–84) provided royal patronage for a revival in the work of translating.

Everything from history to chess seems to have interested the king, but the results were particularly directed towards astronomy, and works such as the *Alfonsine Tables* and the *Books of Astronomical Knowledge* bear witness to the continuing interest in the scientific heritage of al-Andalus.

The Iberian frontier of cultural transmission by selected translations was not exclusively Spanish in its effects. The various translations made in Spain of the works of men like the Persian Avicenna are evidence of the extraordinary degree to which ideas and scholars travelled within the Islamic world. The same was true of Christian Spain and Europe, and the list of scholars who, excited by the possibilities of Arabic–Greek learning, came to the Spanish frontier from other European countries during the course of the twelfth century is impressive: for example, Gerard of Cremona, Adelard of Bath, Herman of Carinthia, Robert of Chester, Plato of Tivoli, Daniel of Morley and Rudolph of Bruges. Moreover, since some of these men, as well as Spanish scholars, worked at the behest of others, the translations can also be regarded as a deliberately directed process of selective acculturation. For example, Hugh of Santalla, a Spaniard, translated works on astronomy and astrology for Bishop Michael of Tarazona, who was almost certainly a Frenchman. Thus, Spain was not the major beneficiary of this process of selective transmission, and its greatest impact was felt in such centres as Chartres and Paris – where the Aristotelianism imported from the peninsula was condemned in 1210 – or in the English scientific tradition which, espoused by men like Daniel of Morley, subsequently found its greatest exponents in Robert Grosseteste and Roger Bacon. Indeed, it was only in the thirteenth century that the intellectual developments usually associated with the twelfth-century renaissance affected Spain. However, quite apart from the fact that the transmission of Greek and Arabic writings constituted an essential element of the twelfth-century renaissance, Spain was affected in other and more profound ways by the interpenetration of cultures, and an important aspect of the work of the translators, which has still to be considered, provides a useful starting point for a more general discussion of acculturation.

Informal Acculturation

TRANSLATION from Arabic presented formidable obstacles to scholars because of the complicated terminology of scientific treatises, the nature of the concepts to be translated and, above all, the problem of mastering the language itself. That these obstacles were overcome was largely due to the unique opportunities of a frontier world where Christians, Mozarabs, Mudejars and Jews were thrown into contact with each other. Peter the Venerable, for example, tells us that the group of scholars which he recruited for the translation of the *Qur'ān* consisted of four men – two 'foreign' Latinists, Herman of Carinthia and Robert of Chester; Peter of Toledo, a Mozarab; and Muhammad of Toledo, a Muslim. The preface to the Latin version of one of Avicenna's works sheds further light on the process of transmission: a Jewish scholar translated the Arabic into Castilian, and then his Christian counterpart, in this case the Spaniard Domingo González (Dominicus Gundissalinus), translated the Castilian into Latin. Jews and Mozarabs, therefore, were 'hinge' men who could both translate and mediate between the different cultures. And, like Count Sisnando Davídiz, some of them were men who 'acquired great experience of frontiers and communications'. Such men were not only to be found in Toledo or other translating centres of Christian Spain. In Ibn 'Abdun's treatise on Muslim Seville in the early twelfth century there is a remarkable passage which suggests that the work of cultural transmission began in al-Andalus rather than in Christian Spain:

> Men should not sell scientific works to the Jews or Christians [Mozarabs], unless such works deal with their own faiths; in effect, they translate scientific books and then attribute the authorship to men of their own faith and to their bishops, even though they are the work of Muslims![37]

These Mozarabic and Jewish scholars were not simply the artisans of the world of learning but were men of learning who, in their own way, were as important as the Mozarabic Count Sisnando was in the world of high politics. Indeed, R. Lemay has convincingly suggested that one of the most outstanding scholar–translators, Juan of Seville or Juan David of Toledo, was Count Sisnando's relation and may even have been his son. Clearly such men knew both sides of the frontier world well, and since they did not always work for specific patrons, the process of cultural diffusion was more general and less 'official' in character. Pedro Alfonso's *Disciplina Clericalis* bears witness to this point.

In 1106, at the age of forty-four, Moses Sephardí had himself baptised in Huesca and took the name of Pedro Alfonso. The fame of this converted Jew rests on his *Disciplina Clericalis*, a book containing a collection of fables and anecdotes of Indian and Arabic origin which he translated for the instruction of clerks. It was the first book of its kind to introduce oriental tales to the West, and being eventually translated into French, English, Spanish, German and even Icelandic, it became a source-book for fiction which was used, among others, by Chaucer, Boccaccio and the Archpriest of Hita. There were two striking features about scholars like Pedro Alfonso. In the first place they were intimately acquainted with the cultural heritage of al-Andalus. Several works on astronomy, mathematics and philosophy, for example, can be attributed to Pedro Alfonso, Juan of Seville (the putative relation of Count Sisnando), Rabbi Abraham bar Hiyya (who was probably educated in al-Andalus) and Rabbi Abraham bar Ezra of Tudela. Secondly, some of these scholars were extraordinarily mobile. Pedro Alfonso lived for a time in England and was a physician at Henry I's court; Abraham bar Hiyya settled in Barcelona after leaving al-Andalus; and Abraham bar Ezra and Benjamin of Tudela between them seem to have covered almost the whole of Europe in their peregrinations. With their mixed cultural background, Jews and Mozarabs not only helped in the technical task of translating but also played a major role in the diffusion of learning.

The mingling together of Christians, Mozarabs, Mudejars and Jews also makes it obvious that informal acculturation must have been particularly marked during the twelfth and thirteenth centuries. By its very nature this process is hard to analyse, but it was perhaps most striking in its effects on the language and customs of Spain. Only Latin has provided the Castilian language with more words than Arabic, and the 'borrowing' of vocabulary, most of which occurred during these centuries, related mainly to warfare and to those customs and skills in which al-Andalus displayed greater sophistication than the Christian north: for example, agriculture, irrigation, house-building, and the organisation of aspects of urban life such as markets, luxuries, furniture and ornaments. What was true of the words was also true of the objects and customs which these words designated. For example, the very fact that many of the techniques, concepts and definitions of the irrigation system of Valencia were new to the Christians is indicated by the extensive acquisition of arabisms by the vernacular during the thirteenth century.

The atmosphere of this mixed cultural world is brilliantly depicted in the miniatures which illustrate Alfonso X's *Book of Chess (Libro de Ajedrez* and his *Songs in Praise of St Mary (Cántigas de Santa María).* As might be expected, the miraculous powers of the Virgin Mary constitute the dominant theme of over 1000 miniatures which illustrate the *Cántigas.* But the various artists from towns like Toledo and Seville, who collaborated on the work, faithfully depicted the acculturative details of dress, weapons, architecture and customs in the daily life of a mixed world of Christians, Jews, Mudejars, Muslims and even Negroes. Of special interest is the miniature which pictures two jongleurs, one of them a Moor and the other a Christian dressed in the Provençal fashion, singing a duet and playing lutes together. This juxtaposition, as we shall see, is not without significance for the vexed problem of the rise of Provençal troubadour music, but it also helps to explain why, as late as 1321, the council of Valladolid had to prohibit the entry of Muslim jongleurs into churches.

Of course, acculturation affected social groups in different ways, as is shown by the varieties of ecclesiastical architecture. The great Romanesque and Gothic cathedrals and abbeys, although not untouched by Muslim influence, were built in expensive stone in styles imported from the European hinterland. But the Church as a whole was far from wealthy, especially in the thirteenth century, and the small parish churches had to rely on cheap materials and labour – that is, on brick instead of stone and on the skill of Mudejar bricklayers, plasterers and carpenters. This was particularly true of the brick ecclesiastical architecture of Aragon which derived its inspiration from the Almohad style of al-Andalus. So striking is the process of acculturation in this case that the belfries of many thirteenth-century Aragonese parish churches are patently imitations of Muslim minarets. Mudejar influence is also apparent in the interiors, and inscriptions such as 'There is no God but Allah; Muhammad is the messenger of Allah' have been found next to gospel texts on the plasterwork of some churches.

The emergence during the twelfth and thirteenth centuries of the Mudejar architectural style was paralleled by the beginnings of other manifestations of acculturation which we will have occasion to examine later (below, pp. 197–205). In the present discussion, the whole background of acculturative detail is relevant to a consideration of the controversial problem of the origins of troubadour poetry. The view presented here is that, although Provençal lyrical poetry – the poetry of the troubadours – developed out of an existing European popular tradition, its evolution prior to maturity was dominated by the influence of Spanish-Arabic poetry. If the reader is not fully convinced by the argument, the evidence put forward should at least persuade him of the importance to be attached to the processes of informal acculturation.

The earliest surviving lyrics in Provençal are those by William IX of Aquitaine (1071–1126), and it was for long believed that all Romance lyrical poetry derived from Provençal origins. In the late 1940s, however, poetic fragments were discovered which, dating back to the tenth century, were composed in Mozarabic – that is, the dialect of Spanish which was spoken in al-Andalus. To understand the significance of these Romance fragments of lyrical poetry we must begin by considering their relationship to the Arabic poetry of al-Andalus.

Broadly speaking there were two types of poetry in al-Andalus. In the first place there was the classical poetry of the *qasīda*, which was cast within the confine of subjects relating to the traditional desert life of the Arabs – the nomadic life, desert revenge, love and the details of nature. This poetry was written in Arabic, the language of revelation and conservative orthodoxy, and tended to become fossilised by a critical theory which stressed mastery of technique and rules of composition rather than innate poetical talent. However, there were also two forms of poetry which grew up in al-Andalus itself, and, having no ancestry in Arabic poetry outside Spain, they differed sharply from the *qasīda* while at the same time sharing many characteristics with the later lyrics of Christian Europe. These two forms, the *muwashshaha* and *zajal*, were metrically similar and they consituted the popular lyric poetry and song of al-Andalus. There were important language differences between the two forms. The *zajal*, although it might contain isolated words in Romance, was composed in vulgar Arabic. The *muwashshaha*, on the other hand, was composed in classical Arabic (or Hebrew), but its concluding lines, known as the *kharja*, were in the Romance language of al-Andalus, colloquial Arabic, or a mixture of both. It is these *kharjas* which constitute the fragments of Romance lyrical poetry to which reference has already been made.

The existence of *kharjas* as early as the tenth and eleventh centuries demolishes any theory that Romance lyric poetry originated with the twelfth-century troubadours. But since the *muwashshaha* and *zajal* developed in al-Andalus and did not derive from Arabic poetry outside Spain, arguments in favour of an Arabic origin for Romance lyrics are equally implausible. Indeed, the weight of the evidence seems to point the other way, for the particular poet who, according to twelfth-century evidence, 'invented' the *muwashshaha*, constructed his poems on the basis of popular verses – that is. he *started* with the *kharja*. Thus an existing oral and popular tradition of Romance lyrical poetry served as the basis for the 'invention' of the *muwashshaha* and *zajal*. This development is understandable when it is remembered that the Muslim invaders brought few women with them and the children of mixed families were bilingual. Consequently, the Romance dialect – the domestic and maternal tongue – was both the language of emotions and of women's love-songs which were assimilated by the invaders. It may well be the case, therefore, that the similarities between the European lyric tradition and that of al-Andalus were not due to a process of cultural diffusion from Muslim Spain but reflect a common derivation from an earlier popular tradition. On the other hand, bearing in mind the overwhelming evidence of other examples of acculturation, the theory that the earliest Provençal troubadours owed much to the Andalusian lyrical tradition, as evidenced particularly by the popular and easily translated *zajal*, cannot be lightly dismissed. What evidence is there for such Spanish-Arabic influences on the Provençal troubadours?

The miniature of Alfonso X's *Cántigas* which depicts the Muslim and Christian jongleurs playing lutes serves as a reminder that with few exceptions, such as the zither and the harp, the musical instruments of Europe were of Moorish origin. Moreover, the importance of acculturation in the music, singers and entertainers of Christian Spain not only emerges from the miniatures of the *Cántigas* but is also amply demonstrated by other evidence: for example, at the court of Sancho IV (1284–95) a group of twenty-seven jongleurs was made up of thirteen Muslims, twelve Christians and two Jews. Of particular interest for the early development of Provençal lyrical poetry is the evidence which links William IX and his father to the Spanish frontier. In 1064 William VIII of Aquitaine, accompanied by his vassals from Limousin and Poitou, was among those who participated in the 'crusade' which captured Muslim Barbastro. The count, however, was apparently himself captivated by his Muslim prisoners and, in particular, by the female lute-playing singers. He was even reputed to have shared out these female singers among the nobles of his lands in southern France. Subsequently, according to his expressed wish, William VIII was buried at Santiago de Compostela. The succeeding generation maintained the family's close connections with Spain. William IX, the troubadour, married the young widow of the king of Aragon, and her retinue would almost certainly have included some jongleurs or female singers similar to those who had been captured at Barbastro. By this time, too, William IX's sisters had respectively married Peter I of Aragon and Alfonso VI of Castile and León. William IX was too young to participate in Alfonso VI's conquest of Toledo, but in 1125 he accompanied Alfonso I of Aragon ('the battler') in a campaign during which the Christians thrust down as far south as Granada and brought back with them several thousand Mozarabic families who were resettled along the Ebro valley.

Given the circumstances, therefore, there was certainly no lack of contact opportunities with the lyrical and musical traditions of al-Andalus, and this lends credence to the theory that the troubadours imitated a Spanish-Arabic model. The earliest troubadours, such as William IX, Cercamon and Marcabrun, not only used the type of stanza which was typical of the *zajal* but they also composed poems with close parallels to pornographic *zajales*. It has even been plausibly argued by some scholars that, just as William VIII is reputed to have conversed with his female captives in broken Arabic, so William IX's fifth poem illustrates that he was acquainted with the spoken Arabic of the peninsula.

Even if the arguments in favour of Spanish-Arabic influences are accepted, however, it is important to note that, in passing from Spain to Provence, the poetical art-form underwent important changes. In the feudal society of Provence the lyric-songs, from being popular, became the preserve of noble and princely circles, and subsequently the new poetic form, elevated to the art of courtly love, was reimported into Spain with resounding success during the late twelfth and thirteenth centuries.

This argument in favour of a 'through-passage' of poetic influences and their subsequent 'reimportation' in a new guise may at first sight appear highly improbable. It must also be admitted that it is impossible to prove. After all, the problem with acculturation (or cultural diffusion) is that, since it was so often informal and since the fusion that resulted was inevitably different from its constituent elements, it is sometimes impossible to document or record its progress. But did not Aristotelianism, in an Arabic guise, have to travel through Spain to the northern schools of France in a similar fashion, before being reimported into the Iberian peninsula during the course of the thirteenth century? In the last chapter of this book other examples of criss-cross frontier patterns of cultural influences will be examined when we come to consider the late medieval art-forms of the potters and ballad-singers.

5. Constitutional Developments: Kings and *Cortes*

BY the mid-fourteenth century there was as yet no royal theocracy in the Castilian realms which embodied in itself the principle of legislative sovereignty. Yet Castilian–Leonese kingship was strong enough to contrast with the constitutionalism of the Crown of Aragon where, by the end of the reign of Peter IV (1336–87), the exercise of royal power was clearly limited by law and by the establishment of controls and checks on monarchical government. As the momentum of the reconquest slackened from the mid-thirteenth century onwards, the frontier dominated political life to a lesser extent. In accounting for these constitutional divergences, therefore, less attention will be devoted to the theme of the frontier, and much of this chapter will deal with issues which continued to dominate political life during the later medieval period.

The effects of the frontier on constitutional developments, however, were by no means unimportant. It can be argued, for example, that the influence of the frontier on the Castilian–Leonese realms resulted in a socio-constitutional structure which was not feudal. A king who ruled over all his subjects was fundamentally different from a feudal ruler, who was bound to his vassals by contractual ties and limited in his governing by the need to consult and agree with those who participated in the feudal contract. There was a strong tendency in the Crown of Aragon to dwell on the concept of 'vassals' rather than 'subjects', precisely because vassals had a legitimate right to invoke the feudal sanction of resistance against a ruler who, as 'lord', was violating his contractual obligations. Alfonso IV of Aragon (1327–36) explained the essential difference succinctly to his wife, Leonor of Castile: 'Queen, queen, our people are free and are not subjugated like the people of Castile – for they look on us as their lord, and we on them as good vassals and companions.'[38]

There were other and more direct ways in which the frontier affected the development of specific institutions. As the Christian reconquest pushed south, for example, a 'fragmenting' effect became evident when newly incorporated regions gave rise to additional laws of local application. Thus the law code known as the *Liber Iudiciorum*, which the Leonese and Asturians inherited from the Visigoths, was of little importance in a Castile where each frontier region organised itself according to *fueros*, based on a mixture of borrowing, custom and precedent, which were later ratified by the monarchy. This 'patchwork and borrowing' effect was even greater in the Crown of Aragon. Visigothic law, for example, which remained fairly influential in Catalonia, had hardly any effect in Valencia or Mallorca; at the same time, however, the twelfth-century customary laws of the Catalan regions of Tortosa and Lérida were used a century later as the basis for the privileges granted to the town of Mallorca. Similarly, in Aragon proper, although Frankish law was of great importance in shaping the *fuero* of Jaca (1063), which later spread in a most formidable fashion, the customary law of the Teruel region was related to the 'frontier' and 'pastoral' *fueros* of Castilian Cuenca and Extremadura.

In addition to these examples, as will be seen in the rest of this chapter, the presence or absence of other factors alien to the growth of royal power also depended to some extent on the degree to which the frontier affected the various Christian polities.

Royal Authority in Castile, *c.* 1100–1350

THE strength of royal authority in the Castilian–Leonese realms was partly due to a long tradition whereby an intangible authority and religious aura were attached to the notion of kingship. The kings of Asturias were devoted to this 'religion' of monarchy as early as the ninth century. When Alfonso II (791–842) established his court at Oviedo, for example, he stressed religious and institutional continuity with Visigothic Spain by keeping sacred relics, said to be from Toledo, in a special chapel. Moreover, like their Visigothic predecessors, the kings of León and Castile were anointed with holy oil: an early miniature in the antiphony of León cathedral depicts the king prostrated between two bishops and being anointed in a ritual which clearly invested kingship with sacred characteristics. Consequently, although these monarchs were never accredited with the healing powers associated with their French counterparts, the theocratic and sacerdotal aspects of kingship were accentuated.

The existence of the frontier also helped to strengthen royal power. The king was the central figure around whom the reconquest was organised – he initiated the important campaigns and directed the processes of colonisation. Since all lordless land belonged to the king, the reconquest also replenished the fisc, and all who received lands ultimately depended on royal favour. Of greater importance than these factors, however, was the fact that feudalism never developed properly, and so the disintegration of governmental authority, which was evident in Catalonia, never occurred in the Castilian–Leonese realms. The Catalan castellanship (*castlanía*), for example, was a hereditary feudal office; but the Castilian castellan (*alcaide*) was removable at the king's pleasure.

Isolated from the European heart-land from the time of the Muslim conquest down to the early eleventh century, the social and political institutions of Asturias, León and Castile did not develop fully in accordance with that model of feudalism which established itself between the Ebro and the Rhine. It is true that, as elsewhere in Europe, institutions represented the fusion (or confusion) which emerged from the clash between Latin and Germanic concepts and traditions. Such a fusion easily led to the development of certain quasi-feudal features like vassalage, patrimonial concepts of power and authority, and the granting of benefices. To these arguments there can also be added the fact that lordships and immunities grew in importance from the eleventh century onwards while, at the same time, closer contacts with France led to an increase in the trappings of feudalism. Yet feudalism did not thrust deep roots into Castilian soil. The military obligations of nobles, it is true, stemmed not so much from the fact that all subjects owed the king service, as from their commitments as vassals or holders of benefices. But the benefice was not hereditary and its grant was not necessarily accompanied by an act of homage. Moreover, the reconquest militated against the domination of a system whereby nobles performed knightly service in return for landed benefices. There was no shortage of land or of free men who possessed sufficient landed wealth to be able to afford a horse, and since privileges were granted to those free men or *villanos* who provided mounted service, the rulers disposed of cavalry forces which were not organised along feudal lines. Similarly, despite the importation of feudal terminology, governmental institutions were not feudalised, and León–Castile cannot properly be described as a feudal state. The word 'fief' (*feudum*) was used to describe benefices from the twelfth century onwards, but the two separate institutions of benefice and vassalage never fused to produce the fief proper. Above all, there was no fusion of public offices with hereditary benefices or fiefs, feudal relationships did not become essential to the structure of government, and the ruler's theoretical control over officials was not impaired.

Of great importance also was the fact that León–Castile retained its own interpretation of the elements of the feudal veneer which it had adopted. The term 'vassal' was used with increasing frequency during the twelfth and thirteenth centuries, but it did not refer merely to the noble who entered into a dependent and personal relationship to a lord. A peasant could be described as the 'vassal' of a seigneurial lord or monastery, and *all* the inhabitants of the kingdom were also deemed to be the king's 'natural vassals' (*vasallos naturales*). In this latter sense *vasallo* was in effect the equivalent of 'subject', and between the monarch (the *señor natural*) and his vassal-subjects there existed a direct relationship *a natura* which derived from the fact that they were born or lived in the kingdom. Thus the political fabric was not specifically based on feudal relationships of a vassalitical–contractual nature, but on the general relationship between the king and his subjects. During the course of the twelfth and thirteenth centuries the concept inherent in the term *natural* or 'subject' gained ground over the feudal notion of vassal and, although it did not triumph completely, the idea of *naturaleza* came to be widely accepted as defining the most important relationship of the polity. The monarch could command men who were not his personal vassals because they were his *naturales* and he was their *señor natural* – he ruled over all his subjects and lands. Thus we find kings like Ferdinand III and Alfonso X bypassing even the powerful bishops of Galicia in order to make their wishes and commands known directly to those of their subjects who lived within the ecclesiastical lordships.

The relationship between the king and his subjects also had important implications for the fabric of law. For three centuries after the Islamic conquest none of the rulers promulgated laws of a general nature, and customary law, being largely Germanic in inspiration, was regarded as being fundamentally unchangeable. During the twelfth and thirteenth centuries, however, there were two ways in which the monarchs freed themselves from some of the limitations imposed by the various patterns of customary law. In the first place, the role of the Crown in the administration of justice led to an increase in royal control The king administered justice in conjunction with the *curia regis*, and the authoritative status of the court of the *curia* helped to extend princely control over customary law. At a local level, it is true, the judges or *alcaldes* of the various towns and lordships of the realm judged in accordance with regional customs or *fueros*. But the growth of appeals to the *curia* led to an increase in the work of those judges (the *alcaldes de corte*) to whom the judicial functions at court were entrusted, and this in turn stimulated the creation of a larger and more sophisticated central administration.

Secondly, the revival of Roman law in Castile–León, which can be dated to the latter half of the twelfth century, helped to undermine privileges and rights sanctioned by custom and tradition. A new class of men became increasingly influential in the work of government. These were the *letrados* or men of law who, trained at Bologna or in the Spanish universities which appeared during the course of the thirteenth century, acted as the agents of royal attempts to break down the barriers of customary and regional laws. According to Alfonso X (1252–84), for example, there were too many conflicting *fueros* in his realms, justice was lacking, and judgements were rendered which were outrageous. But although Alfonso X was responsible for producing the great law code of the *Siete Partidas*, Ferdinand III had already thought in terms of one single body of law which would transcend the various *fueros* and impose legal uniformity throughout his lands. Nor was the *Siete Partidas* the only law code to be produced during the thirteenth century. The *Fuero Real* or royal *fuero*, for example, was completed in the early 1250s, and although it was never envisaged as applying throughout the kingdom, it was used to impose uniformity in cases of appeals to the royal court. But the *Siete Partidas*, completed in the 1260s, was a greater and more ambitious project in which, in the manner of a vernacular *summa*, Alfonso X systematically compiled and edited a body of law affecting every possible aspect of political and social life. The object of all this work, as stated in the prologue, was to impose the *Siete Partidas* as the one and only *corpus* of law in the kingdom. However, since the code was strongly influenced by Roman law, its imposition to the exclusion of established *fueros* and customs was strongly resisted by towns and nobles alike. Indeed, it was not until the closing years of the reign of Alfonso XI (1310–50) that the code of the *Partidas* was promulgated as the law of the land, and even then its acceptance was subject to the continuing recognition of the validity of urban *fueros* and noble privileges. Nevertheless, although such *fueros* and privileges still had to be respected, and some sections of the *Partidas* stressed traditional views about limitations on royal power, the acceptance of the great code also meant that the absolute authority of the Crown over all subjects and *fueros* could be emphasised. If there was as yet no royal theocracy embodying the principle of legislative sovereignty, the basis for it certainly existed in the *Partidas*, as the following law illustrates:

> An emperor or king can make laws for the people of his dominions, but no one else has the power to make laws with regard to temporal matters except where they do so with their permission. Any laws that are made in any other way cannot be called laws or have the validity of laws, and are not to be regarded as valid at any time.[39]

Such ringing assertions of royal legislative power, of course, did not reflect the realities of the constitutional position of the monarch. In governing the realm, the king was traditionally expected to seek counsel and advice. And here again the frontier was important because circumstances dictated that the king should turn to those whose military role was indispensable for the reconquest – namely, the nobility and the towns.

During the tenth and eleventh centuries the Castilian kings turned for counsel and advice to those who accompanied the court or *curia regis*. In a general sense the king governed and dispensed justice with the *curia*, but some individuals became more influential as royal councillors and, although no attempt was made to institutionalise the royal council until the fourteenth century, the word 'council' was already being used to refer to this select group during the twelfth and thirteenth centuries. In contrast to the *curia ordinaria*, however, a solemn assembly or *curia plena* of the great men of the kingdom was occasionally summoned, and from the early eleventh century the kings of León began to promulgate laws in conjunction with these enlarged *curia* assemblies. In essence the *curia plena* was both consultative and judicial in nature, and this latter function was of great significance because, since the king retained ultimate jurisdiction over many towns as well as over ecclesiastical and lay lordships, the presence of townsmen at the royal court was both natural and advantageous. These judicial and consultative functions help to explain the origins of the representative institutions known as the *cortes*. The *cortes*, as the name implies, was still the king's court; but the deliberative assembly evolved into a representative institution when members of all the estates of society, including townsmen, were summoned. Although townsmen may have been summoned to a *cortes* in Castile in 1187, the first documented *cortes* about which there can be no doubt was held by Alfonso IX in León in 1188. It was attended not only by the king and members of the ecclesiastical and noble hierarchies, but also by duly elected representatives sent by towns (*cum electis civibus ex singulis civitatibus*).

The emergence of these representative assemblies, at a much earlier date than elsewhere in Europe, should be seen as a natural development in which co-operation was beneficial to all concerned. On the one hand, the presence of nobles, clergy and townsmen at court was advantageous to the monarchy since it facilitated the resolution of legal disputes and enabled the king to acquire support for royal policies. But since the men who attended often came with petitions or with demands for better justice, pressure also came from below and brought advantages in the form of royal confirmations of privileges and royal attention to local problems. Such factors were obviously of great importance in promoting the origins of representative institutions, but the development of the *cortes* was also closely related to the problems of the frontier.

The presence of townsmen in representative assemblies at such an early date is not surprising when it is remembered that, by the mid-twelfth century, the frontier had stimulated the rise of powerful municipalities which played a crucial role in warfare and colonisation. Moreover, to towns such as Salamanca, Avila and Toledo, the thirteenth-century reconquest added the rich and large towns of the south, such as Córdoba and Seville. These Castilian towns were independent lords in their own right and, having their own officials and *fueros*, they were dependent on the king alone and could field powerful armies of both cavalry and infantry. Indeed, in no other country in Europe did towns play such an indispensable military role, and the Crown naturally consulted urban representatives on military and financial problems.

The cost of the reconquest campaigns of the twelfth and thirteenth centuries placed an enormous financial burden on the monarchy. Of course huge, if irregular, fortunes could be made from the spoils of battles and sieges. After the battle of Salado (1340), for example, the amount of booty taken out of the kingdom was so great that the value of gold and silver was alleged to have dropped by one-sixth in places as far away as Barcelona, Avignon and Paris. But such windfalls did not compensate for the costs of the many months taken up with laying siege to key positions such as Cuenca (eight months), Seville (sixteen months), Tarifa (five months) and Algeciras (seventeen months). Thus, despite new fiscal expedients, kings found themselves in desperate financial straits when faced with protracted campaigns. Ferdinand III, for example, had to turn in desperation to the Galician towns in order to continue financing the siege of Seville. Over fifty years later Ferdinand IV not only tried to borrow money from the kings of Portugal and England for his siege of Algeciras, but he had to ask the Sevillians to stand surety for loans which he demanded from Genoese merchants. Alfonso XI was literally forced to beg around the towns and merchants of his kingdom in order to raise money for his defence of Gibraltar in 1333. He faced even greater difficulties at Algeciras: not only did he turn to the *cortes* for financial help like other kings before him, but he also obtained 20,000 florins from the papacy and 50,000 from the French monarchy. Yet even these sums were insufficient and, after borrowing further money from the Genoese, the king was forced in the end to give up all his silver plate in order to try and defray his military expenses.

Financial difficulties encouraged monarchs to turn to the *cortes*. As early as 1091 Alfonso VI had sought some form of consent for an extraordinary tax for the war against the Almoravids. During the course of the twelfth century an additional tax, the *petitum*, began to be levied by the monarchy, and since the towns were asked to consent to the tax, the task of treating on this problem eventually devolved on the *cortes*. Yet such subsidies were still insufficient in quantity, and the Crown discovered another profitable source of income in its monopoly over the coinage. Debasement was a tempting expedient for hard-pressed monarchs, but it provoked inflation and caused economic hardship, and the *cortes* attempted to remove temptation by offering the Crown a new tax, the *moneda forera*, as a quid pro quo for non-debasement. This arrangement was first described in the *cortes* of Benavente in 1202 when Alfonso IX of León 'sold' his right to remint the coinage for a period of seven years in return for the *moneda forera*. Subsequent *cortes* in León and Castile were not summoned at regular intervals of seven years, but the *moneda forera* continued to be levied on the same theoretical basis. Despite the increase in income, however, the *petitum* and *moneda forera* revenues remained insufficient to meet royal expenses, and from the mid-thirteenth century onwards monarchs frequently resorted to forced loans and debasements of the coinage. Such policies, as well as the galloping inflation which followed, could hardly fail to cause discontent, and in the late thirteenth century nobles and towns formed *hermandades* or 'brotherhoods' to resist the more arbitrary manifestations of royal fiscality.

These *hermandades*, however, were not linked in any way to the *cortes*, and it would be erroneous to assume that kings and *cortes* were by nature antagonistic to each other or that the development of representative institutions was part of a deliberate attempt to limit the powers of the Crown. The consent of the *cortes*, it is true, was regarded as being necessary for extraordinary taxation, and since it was also generally agreed that the king could only revoke or change laws with the assent of the *cortes*, the latter enjoyed some legislative power. But there is little evidence that the *cortes* deliberately set out to force kings to acknowledge their subordination to the law or to representative institutions. Indeed it could be argued, with some exaggeration, that the *cortes* continued to be rather more like meetings of the *curia plena* than properly constituted representative assemblies with that consciousness of the public character of the polity which would have enabled the development of constitutionalism. Although representatives of towns were summoned to the *cortes*, the *boni homines*, or good men, who attended were drawn from the ranks of those who dominated urban government and who, as we have seen, were often *caballeros villanos* or even *hidalgos*. In fact, during the reign of Ferdinand III, the king and the *cortes* took active steps to ensure both that control in the towns was vested in the class of *caballeros* and that only such men should be chosen to attend the *cortes*. These *caballeros* reinforced the nobility's domination of the *cortes*, and they were not necessarily more representative of the interests of townsmen in general than bishops were of the men living within their lordships. They could appreciate the need for taxes which they themselves did not have to pay and from which they might even derive some benefit. At the *cortes* of Carrión in 1312, for example, the calculations of the representatives (*procuradores*) showed that the Crown could count on 1,600,000 *mrs* from various sources of income. But:

... because they found that the amounts going to the *ricos hombres* and the *caballeros*, and the amounts needed for castles as well as for the maintenance of the king and the offices of his court, came to a total of 9,600,000 *mrs*, they concluded that 8,000,000 *mrs* had to be found. To this end they gave the king five subsidies (*servicios*) which were to be paid by the peasants (*labradores*). . . .

In the event the money voted by the *cortes* and payable by the unrepresented peasantry fell short of its target by 3,000,000 *mrs*, 'and since they could come to no agreement over the sharing out of money because of its scarcity, a fight broke out among all the *hidalgos* in the king's palace and in the queen's apartments. . . .'[40]

The undignified scenes of 1312 occurred during a turbulent royal minority, but they illustrate the extent to which there was a natural identity of interests between the Crown, the nobility and the *cortes* not only in military matters but over fiscal problems as well. The *cortes* did not represent 'constitutionalism' or a 'natural ascending theme' which clashed with a 'descending theocratic' one. Rather, the underlying notion was that of the natural right of nobles and *caballeros* from the towns to co-operate with the king in the government of the realm. In this consultative task procedural matters gave the monarchy a decided advantage. No convention existed that grievances and petitions should be attended to by the monarch before subsidies were provided. The king decided when and if a *cortes* was to be summoned, and if he so wished he disregarded the substance of petitions presented to him. The king did not claim to wield absolute royal power, but the fact that the *cortes* did meet fairly frequently indicates little more than that the Crown found it useful to consult those who mattered and ask them to provide money.

Constitutionalism in the Crown of Aragon, *c.* 1100–1390

By the mid-fourteenth century the outstanding governmental feature of the Crown of Aragon, when compared to Castile or even the rest of Europe, was the impressive system of constitutional equilibrium between the monarchy, on the one hand, and the individual kingdoms and social groupings on the other. The word 'pactism' has been used to describe this constitutional equilibrium which, although reaching its fullest realisation in Catalonia, was equally alive in Aragon and Valencia. The powers of the monarch derived from a contractual relationship between the king and his

people. The king was recognised as ruler on condition that he respected the laws, liberties and customs of his subjects, and it was
only after he had taken an oath to this effect that his subjects
swore allegiance to him. The monarch was bound by the laws and
customs of each state of the federation, and his subjects could
resist him if he did not observe this fundamental principle. These
circumstances led to a belief that a contract had originally created
monarchical power in Aragon proper, that these constitutional
arrangements were to be found in the *fueros* of the legendary kingdom of Sobrarbe, and that the essence of the contractual theory
was contained in the words of the Aragonese oath of allegiance to
the king:

> We who are as good as you and together are more powerful than
> you, make you our king and lord, provided that you observe our
> *fueros* and liberties, and if not, not.

Of course, the exact nature of the balance in the contractual
relationship between the monarch and his peoples was subject to the
incessant changes of practical politics. Yet the fundamental contractual concept was never far from the centre of every political
crisis, and men were accustomed to expressing their aims in terms of
a defence of inalienable liberties and the limitations to be imposed
on royal power.

The path to this constitutionalism was anything but smooth.
Widespread action by the Aragonese nobility in defence of their
interests can be dated back to the late twelfth century, but it was
during the reign of James I (1213–76) that the nobility forced
concessions from the king in the *cortes* of Ejea (1265) and laid the
basis of a powerful league or 'union' which, in the reign of Peter III
(1276–85), almost acquired the characteristics of an official institution of government. It is probable that Peter III's struggle to curb
the nobility and strengthen royal power would have succeeded but
for the events arising from his conquest of Sicily in 1282: the pope
excommunicated the Aragonese king, proclaimed a crusade against
him, freed the nobles from their allegiance, and offered the Crown
to Charles of Valois, son of the king of France. Faced with civil
war and invasion, Peter III sought a way out of his dangerous
situation by summoning *cortes* in both Aragon and Catalonia, and by
capitulating to the demands of his constitutionally minded opponents. In the Aragonese *cortes*, meeting at Zaragoza in 1283, the

nobility and townsmen formally swore to defend their privileges and aid each other in the defence of their interests against the monarchy, and the king had to agree to a *privilegio general*. The language of this constitutional settlement made it clear that, according to his opponents, the king was merely confirming the ancient *fueros* which he had violated. Henceforth the king bound himself to respect the privileges and customs of the nobility and townsmen of Aragon and Valencia, and he agreed to yearly meetings of *cortes* which were to have greater powers.

The Aragonese Union did not extend into Catalonia. Nevertheless, three months later, the *cortes* of Barcelona acted in a similar fashion, and by the constitution *una vegada l'any* the king had to agree to yearly *cortes*, respect for the privileges of the nobility and towns, and no legislation without the consent of the *cortes*.

The decisions taken at the *cortes* of Zaragoza and Barcelona were by no means temporary in nature. Indeed, the unfortunate Alfonso III (1285–91) fell foul of the Aragonese Union, whose members proceeded to invade the kingdom of Valencia, place an embargo on royal revenues and force the monarch to grant even greater concessions in the so-called *privilegio de la unión* of 1287. The monarchy, however, had by no means capitulated completely, and the reign of Peter IV (1336–87) witnessed a savage struggle between the Crown and the nobility who, entrenched within the provisions of the *privilegio de la unión*, proclaimed themselves the guardians of the law. From this struggle the king eventually emerged as the military victor, and in Zaragoza in 1348 he ripped up the privileges of the Union, smashed the seals with a mace, set fire to whatever remained of the documents, and then sarcastically reported to his uncle that 'all this was done amidst great tears which were caused by the thick smoke'. But the king only achieved this revenge after suffering extreme humiliations at the hands of the rebels in Valencia, and although the more extreme demands of the Unionists were set aside, Peter IV's success has been secured by granting concessions to political factions and accepting the permanence of constitutional limitations on monarchical power.

Although necessary, the extremely brief summary of political events which has just been given helps little in accounting for the emergence and development of constitutionalism, and it is to the social basis of the polity that we must now turn. The emergence of contractual notions from an early date in the Crown of Aragon was due to the feudal or quasi-feudal nature of society. In Catalonia the feudal pattern of government became evident when princely powers and offices were subjected to the personal arrangements regarding fiefs. Fiefs became essential links in the structure of government, and their existence and the granting of immunities meant that the ruler's authority was not exercised directly over his subjects. When fiefs and immunities became hereditary, political authority was fragmented to an extraordinary extent. Indeed the Catalan counties, for long administrative areas of Carolingian France, gained their independence precisely because the office of count became hereditary. In such a society the relationships between lords and vassals were not only more important than those between prince and subjects, but they were also regulated by the contractual obligations typical of feudalism. In Aragon, on the other hand, a different point of departure led to contractual relationships between the king and the great nobility which were not unlike those typical of feudalism. Feudal contracts proper were rare prior to the middle of the twelfth century, but since, unlike Castile, lordless land was not automatically regarded as belonging to the royal fisc, monarchical power was severely circumscribed from an early date. The majority of the nobility, of course, did hold some lands from the Crown and this gave rise to contractual obligations which, as far as the nobles were concerned, were usually limited to three days' military service each year. But the lands ruled by some of the great baronial families of Aragon were theirs by right of conquest and inheritance, and since they had not received them from the Crown, they owed the king no military service and governed their allodial 'states' as independent lords. 'Each one of us', they told Alfonso I (1104–34) 'is equal to you, and united we are more powerful.' In general terms, therefore, the socio-political structure of the Crown of Aragon encouraged the nobility to emphasise both their independence from royal control, and the duties and obligations of the ruler towards his vassals.

However, as James I pointed out in the fourth of seven choice items of advice with which he regaled the king of Castile, the power of the nobility could be counterbalanced by that of other social groups:

The fourth was, that if some only were to be kept in his grace, and he could not keep the others, he should keep at least two parties:

the church, and the people and cities of the country. For they are those who God loves more, even, than the nobles and the knights, for the knights revolt sooner against their lord than the others.[41]

For James I the towns constituted the most important of these parties, but they differed in many essentials from those of the kingdom of Castile. From the point of view of administrative autonomy, for example, the towns of the Crown of Aragon were slower in developing than those in Castile. This was especially the case in Catalonia where, prior to the thirteenth century, urban assemblies were subject to the authority of the ruler's territorial officials, such as the *veguer* or *batlle*. Only in the thirteenth century were these urban assemblies replaced by autonomous councils and magistrates. The latter were known variously, according to the locality, as *cónsols*, *pahers* and *jurats*, and they were assisted in their functions by councils which were the essential institutions of the municipalities. In 1265, for example, James I ordered the constitution of a council of one hundred in Barcelona (the *consell de cent*), and it was this council which advised the magistrates or *consellers* who ruled the town.

The emergence of autonomous councils was accompanied by a growing exclusiveness whereby the chief offices in the towns were reserved to the men of higher status in urban society. Barcelona, for example, was dominated by a patrician oligarchy whose members filled the *consell de cent* and provided the *consellers* who ruled the town. But the frontier dominated Catalonia to a much lesser extent than Castile, and the tone of urban society was set by prosperous burgesses and merchants rather than by knights and nobles. Since the fortunes of the Crown of Aragon depended largely on Catalonia, the political importance of the 'merchant republic' of Barcelona is difficult to exaggerate.

The towns, therefore, were not controlled by the nobility or by townsmen in general but by privileged groups, known as *ciutadans honrats* or 'honourable citizens', whose members represented some three per cent of the urban population. The majority of urban inhabitants, the *poble menut*, was completely excluded from governing circles, and the interests of the *ciutadans honrats* often coincided with those of the noble oligarchs who controlled the countryside. But unlike the urban *caballeros* of Castile, the oligarchs of towns like Barcelona and Valencia did not necessarily identify with the nobility, and through time a rationale was created which bestowed its own dignity on the affairs and aspirations of merchants and patricians. This enhancement of the civic virtues of urban oligarchs is to be clearly seen in such writings of Francesc Eiximenis (*c.* 1340–1409) as *Lo Crestià* and the *Regiment de princeps*. The fact that Eiximenis was both a Franciscan and an exponent of pactism makes him an exemplary witness to more than one aspect of the socio-political life of the age.

Eiximenis lived part of his life at court, enjoyed the confidence of Peter IV and travelled widely throughout Europe. But he was most at home in urban society, and his major writings date from that period of his life when he settled in the town of Valencia. At first sight it may appear odd to find a Catalan Franciscan praising the virtues of the merchant life. As elsewhere in Europe, the thirteenth century in Spain witnessed the emergence of the friars as an important apostolate of preaching and poverty in the towns. Indeed the founder of the Dominicans, Domingo de Guzmán, was Spanish, and he stressed poverty as the essential virtue to be practised by his followers in their attempts to combat heresy in southern France. Both the Franciscans and Dominicans regarded themselves as mendicants and, as the conversion of St Francis himself illustrated, they repudiated the merchant life and the commercial aspects of urban society. The emphasis on poverty turned many mendicant thinkers into acute social critics whose writings were characterised by satirical attacks on worldly wealth and hypocrisy. But although they started by rejecting the commercial world and stressing poverty, the friars eventually created a spirituality which, drawing many of its elements from the urban society within which they operated, helped to justify the lives and activities of 'honourable citizens'.

As might be expected, many of the traditional elements in mendicant thought are apparent in Eiximenis's works. For example, his emphasis on Christ's poverty and suffering lead him on to pen strong criticisms of those who make money their God, and even the bishops and clergy are bitterly denounced for their cupidity and immorality. But at the same time he makes it clear that peasants are little better than animals, and he regards the *poble menut* of the towns as being troublesome and rebellious. The merchant, on the other hand, is the salt of the earth, and in a highly eulogistic passage in which he relies on the authority of an imaginary moralist named Filólogus, Eiximenis exalts the place of merchants in society:

He [the moralist] says that merchants should be favoured above all other lay people of the world, because they are the life of the lands in which they live, the treasure of the commonweal, the food of the poor, the mainstay of all good business, and gifted in all kinds of matters. Without merchants, cities fall, princes become tyrants, young people are lost, and the poor lament. . . . He believes without any doubt that Our Lord gives them special grace in life and death because of the great advantages which they bestow on the commonweal and because of the many tribulations they endure on sea and on land. . . .[42]

Quite apart from stressing the eminent respectability of merchants, it will be noted that Eiximenis asserts that they are indispensable in preventing princes from becoming tyrants. In fact, constitutional developments in the Crown of Aragon were closely identified with the specific social bases which we have been examining and from which they sprang, namely the great landed nobility and the oligarchies of 'honourable citizens' in the towns. As we have seen, these constitutional developments gave rise to 'pactist' theories, and these are clearly set out by Eiximenis.

For Eiximenis, political authority was not part of the natural order of things but was created by free men for their own convenience: 'Nature itself made all men equal, because originally there existed no lordship until men themselves elected a lord for their own protection and common good.'[43] This creation of political power was based on agreements between the contracting parties. 'Never', says Eiximenis, 'did people grant absolute authority to anyone save on the basis of certain pacts and laws.' Moreover, such contracts would be weighted against the ruler because 'each community made pacts and conventions with its lords which were principally to the advantage and honour of the community . . . because the community did not elect the lord through love of him, but rather it elected its governor because of love of itself'. Hence it followed that any government which was not based on pactism was tyrannous: 'Those kingdoms and lordships which are ruled by absolute power and by the ruler's own will and without any law or pact with the vassals are tyrannous lordships, or very close to tyranny, and they cannot last for long.'

Eiximenis was not alone in propounding such ideas, and when jurists subsequently elaborated these concepts they provided an impressive constitutional alternative to a royal absolutism bolstered by Roman law. Pactist arguments, of course, did not pass unchallenged, and monarchs ground their 'descending' theses against the 'ascending' millstone. Thus, in a *cortes* speech of 1367, Peter IV asserted that: '. . . there is no power in existence – that is, a principality or lordship – which is not derived from divine ordinance, and therefore anyone who works against [such powers] is working towards the damnation with which he will be punished.'[44]

This view of the prince as the vicar of God, however, could make little headway in states where, unlike León and Castile, the sacramental aura and religion of kingship had a decidedly weak tradition. There is no evidence, for example, that prior to the thirteenth century the Aragonese kings were ceremoniously anointed or crowned. Moreover in Catalonia, which was not even a kingdom, the feudal structure of the polity made it almost impossible for such theocratic concepts to be accepted. For, if practical sovereignty was exercised by the counts of Barcelona from the end of the tenth century onwards, this situation received no juridical sanction until the French Crown gave up its theoretical rights by the treaty of Corbeil in 1258. And even then, as we will see, the ruler of the Crown of Aragon was regarded by many in Catalonia as being simply the feudal count of Barcelona.

If the sacramental nature of kingship was weak, however, theoretical and practical limitations on the powers of the prince could be eroded by the application of Roman law principles. There were two general aspects to this problem. In the first place there was a natural tendency for monarchs to try and introduce order into judicial chaos. In this sense, although the influence of Roman and canon law was already notable by the mid-twelfth century, the reign of James I (1213–76) was particularly important. Famous jurists abounded at court – men, for example, like Raymond of Peñafort, Bishop Vidal de Canellas and Pedro Albert. The educational background of such men was the university of Bologna, the Italian centre of Roman law studies, and this fact is reflected in their work. For example, although the 1247 compilation of the *fueros* of Aragon was mainly a collection of the traditional laws and customs of the country, Bishop Vidal introduced important Roman law modifications into the *fuero* structure. In more general terms, 'common' or Roman law was regarded by lawyers as constituting the best expression of equity and common sense, and as a result it

gradually came to complement regional customs and *fueros* throughout the Crown of Aragon. In many ways such a development was
both practical and natural, and it was this line of argument which
James I utilised when he was accused of using civil and canon law
to infringe the Aragonese *fueros:*

> My answer was that it was true that I had civil and canon lawyers
> in my household, but that I was bound to have such lawyers by
> me: every king's court ought to be accompanied by canon, civil,
> and *fuero* lawyers, for there were law-suits in all those branches.
> I myself, by the grace of God, had three or four kingdoms to my
> share, and law-suits came before me of many diffcrent kinds.
> If I had not with me those who could judge and sentence such
> suits-at-law, it would be a shame to mc and to my court, as
> neither I nor any layman could know all the law-writings there
> are in the world. That they might help me when necessary, I had
> them with me wherever I went, especially on account of my
> different states not being under one *fuero*, or one custom.[45]

These were apparently reasonable arguments with which, as we
have seen, Alfonso X of Castile would have heartily agreed. But there
was another aspect to the problem. For, when men thought that
monarchs were deliberately setting out to build up their power and
destroy the *fueros* and rights upon which the nobles based their
independence of action, conflicts were inevitable. The following
examples from the case of Catalonia illustrate that such conflicts
were at the heart of constitutional issues from the middle of the
twelfth century onwards.

About 1150 a law code, entitled the *Usatges*, was compiled in
Barcelona. It consisted of feudal texts, statements on the powers of
the ruler, and items relating to private and penal law. Although it
was referred to as the *Usatges* 'of Barcelona', it became the law code
of the comital curia and was accepted as the basic text of Catalan
law. However, despite being based on the customs of the country,
the code was the work of the Roman lawyers of Ramón Berenguer
IV's court, and they ensured that the figure of the 'prince', wielding
sovereignty over all the lands and subjects of Catalonia, was introduced alongside the more traditional and familiar figure of the
feudal count of Barcelona with his limited powers and his obligations
to his vassals. From this point onwards, therefore, the *Usatges* would
provide legal ammunition for both sides in the struggles between the

rulers and the nobility. A good example of this is the way in which the counts of Barcelona attempted to take over the ecclesiastical institution of the 'Peace and Truce of God' and use it as a princely weapon of government. One of the new elements introduced in the *Usatges* was an article which attributed the proclamation and execution of the 'Peace and Truce' to the prince, along with the power to issue safe-conducts and mint coinage. Thus in 1173, in Fontdaldara, Alfonso II proclaimed a 'Peace and Truce' which was binding on all his lay and ecclesiastical subjects. But in the view of the nobles such sweeping proclamations of the 'Peace and Truce' needed consent, because they were contrary to the spirit of the *Usatges* and constituted a derogation of the rights of vassals within a feudal structure. Hence, by 1202, the 'prince-count' was forced to accept that he could not issue safe-conducts to the vassals of others without the permission of their lords, that in their relations with the peasantry of their lands the lords were not answerable to the ruler unless they were his feudatories, and that the 'Peace and Truce' was not a princely institution and therefore had no general validity over the lands and people of Catalonia.

The royal concessions of 1202, of course, marked only one incident in the history of the disputes over the nature of the ruler's authority, and well over a century later the lawyers of the court of Peter IV (1336–87) were still invoking Roman law in their attempts to enlarge royal power. Thus Jaume de Montjuich reinterpretated the *Usatges* and the early history of the counts of Barcelona in order to prove that the ruler was not simply the head of the feudal hierarchy, but was a prince who was like an emperor in his principality. Such views were by no means strange in a court which included many other jurists intent on building up the royal supremacy. These men, some of whom were from Rousillon, constituted an important political grouping which contemporaries referred to as '*els rossellonesos*', and it was principally against these councillors that the Unionists of Aragon and Valencia directed their bitterest attacks during the grim struggles of 1347–8.

If constitutionalism eventually triumphed over attempts to enlarge princely power, therefore, this was not because contractual ideas and claims passed unchallenged or because occasional defeats were inflicted on the Crown. On the contrary, the constitutionality of rulers became a reality only when theories were converted into institutions and when political pressure ceased to be occasional and became constant. Of such institutions the *justicia* of Aragon and the various *cortes* of the federation were the most important.

In Aragon there already existed by the early twelfth century an official, known as the *justicia de corte*, whose main task was to co-ordinate the judicial work of the *curia regis*. But when, during the course of the thirteenth century, this official and other jurists of the *curia* began to administer justice in a manner detrimental to traditional and customary privileges, the nobility sprang to the defence of their *fueros*, and in the *cortes* of Ejea of 1265 they forced James I to agree that the *justicia* should henceforth always be a noble. Thus the *justicia* emerged as the guarantor of traditional liberties and privileges, and the nobility pressed for an increase in his powers. All disputes between the nobility and the monarchy (or between individual nobles), and all appeals from the sentences of local judges, fell within the competence of the *justicia*. Subsequently, his powers were enlarged by the *privilegio general* of 1283 and the *privilegio de la unión* of 1287. From 1287, for example, members of the Aragonese nobility and citizens of Zaragoza could be condemned to death only by a judgement of the *justicia* approved by the *cortes*. The *justicia*, therefore, was the champion of the nobility's interests, as enshrined in the *fueros*, and on the morrow of his victory in 1348 Peter IV not only confirmed these *fueros* in the *cortes* but he also guaranteed the position of the *justicia* as the interpreter of the laws of the land. The king and his lieutenant-general had to swear to uphold the *fueros*, and any infringements or *contrafueros*, including those committed by royal officials, fell within the exclusive jurisdiction of the *justicia*. The latter and his two lieutenants, indeed, possessed a special court or tribunal for dealing with such cases, and the king had no power to interfere or to receive appeals. Free from royal control, the *justicia* was responsible only to the *cortes*. It is to this latter institution that we must now turn, for the representative institutions of Aragon, Catalonia and Valencia developed to a degree that was unparalleled anywhere else in Europe.

The first unambiguous references to the participation of towns-men in the various *cortes* of each of the states of the Crown of Aragon all date from the thirteenth century: the *cortes* of Villafranca del Panadés in Catalonia (1218), the *cortes* of Huesca in Aragon (1247), and the *cortes* of Valencia (1283). That these *cortes* enlarged their powers in the course of time was partly due to the control which they gradually established over procedures, membership and regularity of meetings. Both the Catalan and Valencian *cortes* had the normal complement of three estates or *brazos*, but with two estates for the nobility, the Aragonese *cortes* had four *brazos*. In each of these *cortes* matters were complicated for the monarchy by the fact that the estates met separately and deliberated independently. The king, moreover, had little control over membership of the *cortes*. In Aragon proper, for example, the nobility claimed the right to attend even if the king failed to summon them, and any municipality which had once been summoned continued to enjoy the privilege. Of even greater importance was the fact that the monarchy failed to control the election of the representatives or *síndicos* of the towns. Hence the latter were able to maintain their independence from the Crown and could provide their *síndicos* with strict instructions as to their activities in the *cortes*.

In all the *cortes* of the Crown of Aragon the grievances (*greuges*) of the various estates had to be dealt with first before the monarchy obtained supply of taxation. The implications of this were far-reaching. The rulers had to swear before the Aragonese, Catalan and Valencian *cortes* to observe and respect the appropriate laws and *fueros*, and the redress of grievances before supply led to the assumption of legislative power by the *cortes*. This is what lay at the heart of events when, in 1283, Peter III was forced to grant the *privilegio general* in the Aragonese *cortes* and then capitulated to the demands of the Catalan *cortes* meeting in Barcelona. In the latter assembly, for example, it was made clear by article twenty-nine that, if the person of the ruler was treated as a king, this was only because he happened to be king of Aragon, for in Catalonia proper the ruler was not a Roman law sovereign but a mere feudal count. To hammer this point home Peter III was forced to concede that he and his successors would only use the title of count of Barcelona when signing documents relating to Catalonia. Articles nine, eighteen and fifty of this same assembly attributed the general legislative power in Catalonia to the *cortes*, made the ruler dependent on the *cortes* for financial support, and defined the role of the count as 'to concede to his subjects the liberties, immunities and privileges granted to them by his predecessors, and to approve and uphold without violation their practices, uses and good customs'. Thus the *cortes* of 1283 laid down the basis of pactism, and by the end of the thirteenth century the representative institutions of the Crown of Aragon shared sovereignty with the monarchy: the ruler was bound to seek the consent of the *cortes* for legislative, fiscal and executive decisions of great moment. In the Aragonese *cortes* proper, the unanimous consent of all the four *brazos* had to be obtained, for if one of the estates refused to agree to a particular measure, the matter had to be set aside for further deliberation and examination.

To be effective, however, limitations on royal power had to be constant as well as institutionalised. In both Aragon and Catalonia the crisis of 1283 had resulted in agreements that meetings of the *cortes* should be held annually. This ideal of regular yearly meetings was in practice impossible, and in 1301 triennial meetings were stipulated for the Catalan *cortes*. The same principle was established for the *cortes* of Valencia, and six years later, James II and the Aragonese *cortes* agreed to biennial meetings. But the powers of the *cortes* in the Aragonese federation were greatly enhanced by the emergence of a standing committee – the *Diputació* or *Generalitat* – which ensured a continuity of purpose between *cortes* meetings. The Aragonese and Valencian versions of this institution were not set up until 1412 and 1419 respectively, and they never attained quite the same political importance as the Catalan *Generalitat* on which they were modelled.

The origins of the Catalan *Generalitat* can be traced back to the late thirteenth century when the *cortes* appointed delegates to deal with problems left outstanding once the representatives had dispersed. The main task of these delegates was to arrange for the collection of the taxes voted by the *cortes* and ensure that the money was used for the specific purposes for which it had been granted. At first the delegates constituted a temporary committee which was dissolved once it had dealt with outstanding problems. In 1359, however, the temporary committee became a permanent institution which, known as the *Diputació* or *Generalitat*, established its headquarters in Barcelona from 1365 onwards. The membership of this body, as established by the *cortes* of 1365, consisted of seven *diputados*: two clergy, two nobles and three townsmen. Subsequently, however, there were further changes, and it was only in 1413 that the structure of the *Generalitat* was established in a definitive form.

The *cortes* and the *Generalitat*, therefore, were extremely powerful institutions which shared and controlled sovereign power. Yet the *cortes* of the Crown of Aragon were far from being genuinely representative or 'democratic'. For Eiximenis, for example, pactism quite obviously excluded people, such as the peasants, who were hardly better than animals and totally unfitted for any kind of office: 'Such men – *payeses* and rustics who are servile, shameless and lacking in reason – should never be given any place of honour, because all positions and dignities are decried by them . . . , and their life is bestial and demented. . . .'[46] Some two-thirds of the population lacked any sort of representation in the pactist structure of the polity. The *cortes*, in fact, represented only the privileged groups in society and, far from acting as the people's bulwark against royal tyranny, they incarnated the interests of the oligarchs in town and countryside. Thus, since pactism, and its associated notions of consent, representation, and the defence of inalienable rights, was the 'ascending theme' of the select few, it is not surprising that large numbers of the peasantry and *poble menut* would eventually look to the monarchy for support against the tyranny of the pactist oligarchs.

The constitutional developments which have been discussed form an essential part of the background of the later Middle Ages. In many ways the mid-fourteenth century forms a natural turning-point between the central and later medieval period. For example, quite apart from the socio-economic problems which arose after the Black Death, Alfonso XI's victory at the battle of Salado (1340) marked a long halt to the impetus of a reconquest which had already stagnated after the great campaigns of Ferdinand III and James I. Yet, as the constitutional development of the Crown of Aragon demonstrates, there was no sudden transition, and the pactist ideas and institutions which have been described here continued to dominate the political life of Aragon and Catalonia during the later Middle Ages. This element of continuity was not quite as evident in Castile but, as will be seen in the ensuing chapters, in their quest for absolute royal power the later medieval Castilian kings were helped by the 'frontier' basis for monarchical authority which had been established during this period.

PART II

FROM FRONTIER
TOWARDS
EMPIRE,
c. 1350–1500

6. The Politics of Maritime Enterprise and the Formulation of Absolutism

THE later medieval political history of the Iberian peninsula was bedevilled by dynastic crises and civil wars. In Castile, for example, not one of the nine reigns from 1296 to 1504 remained unaffected by either the serious problems posed by a minority or the dangers of a disputed succession. Such issues diverted attention from the traditional task of the reconquest and were obviously of great importance to contemporaries. But they were inextricably bound up with other problems of a profounder nature which contributed to the outbreak, complexity and duration of civil wars – for example, the intervention of foreign powers in Iberian politics, the resistance of powerful noble groupings to the growth of royal power, racial unrest, and economic crisis. In this chapter attention will be focused on those political issues which contributed to the way in which Spain moved ahead of her neighbours in certain fundamental aspects – the decisive lead in maritime enterprise established by the Iberian powers, and the formulation of the most advanced version of absolutism to be found in the whole of later medieval Europe.

The Hundred Years War and Naval Enterprise

FROM 1350 to 1389 European attention was drawn to a protracted struggle being waged for the control of Castile. In the early stages this struggle was primarily a civil war between an authoritarian king, Peter I, and a coalition of nobles, the leadership of which devolved on Peter's bastard half-brother, Henry of Trastámara. But both sides tended to look outside Castile for support, and gradually Spain became another theatre of operations in the Hundred Years War, with the French supporting Henry and his successors, and the English supporting Peter and his heirs.

At first Peter was successful in countering the threats posed by Henry's machinations in France and Aragon. By 1365, however, Henry had been promised effective financial assistance from Aragon, France and the papacy, and at the head of French and English mercenaries he invaded Castile and proclaimed himself king as Henry II (1366). Peter fled to Bayonne and straight into the arms of the Engish: the latter mounted a counter-invasion which resulted in a defeat for the Trastamarans at Nájera (1367) and the re-establishment of Peter in Castile. His triumph was short-lived. By the treaty of Toledo (1368) Charles V fully committed French military support to Henry, who once more invaded Castile and finally defeated and murdered Peter at Montiel (1369).

The first stage in the struggle for Castile, therefore, resulted in a victory for Henry II and inaugurated half a century of close alliance between Castile and France. But the threat to the Trastamaran dynasty had by no means been removed and, for another twenty years, the kings of Castile relied on their ally to an extent which almost made the kingdom a client-state of France. In 1371 John of Gaunt, duke of Lancaster, married Peter's eldest daughter, Constance, and claimed the Castilian throne. In Bayonne a 'Castilian' court was organised for the *emperegilados* (Peter's supporters), the English royal council recognised Lancaster's claim, and diplomatic efforts were made in Portugal, Aragon and Navarre to encircle Castile. Inevitably, the alliance with France became the cornerstone of Trastamaran foreign policy.

In the event, when the crisis came, it manifested itself in Portugal and Galicia. In 1381 Lancaster's brother mounted an abortive campaign in Portugal. In the aftermath of this failure the heiress to the throne of Portugal, Beatriz, was married to John I of Castile (1383). Five months later, Ferdinand I of Portgual died and the Castilian king moved to claim the neighbouring kingdom. But he met unexpected resistance: in April 1384 the Master of Avis was proclaimed king of Portugal, and in the following year the Portuguese, assisted by English archers, inflicted a humiliating defeat on the Castilians at the battle of Aljubarrota.

Aljubarrota presented the Castilians with problems similar to those which had faced the French after their defeat at Poitiers. A programme of governmental reform was set on foot by John I in collaboration with the *cortes*. A sense of unity was desperately needed, for Aljubarrota rekindled enthusiasm for the Lancastrian venture. By July 1386 Lancaster had landed in La Coruña and was concerting military plans with the Portuguese. However, disease crippled the English military effort, the Castilians outmanoeuvred their opponents, and the invasion proved a fiasco. In the negotiations which followed, a marriage between Gaunt's daughter, Catherine of Lancaster, and John I's heir, the future Henry III, was arranged, the Castilians bought off Lancaster's claim to the throne, the truces of Leulingham and Monção (1389) brought the Spanish phase of the Hundred Years War to an end, and the crisis was over.

To a large extent, the events of the period 1350–89 can be explained in terms of noble unrest and dynastic and constitutional issues, but it is also clear that events were often dictated by French and English intervention in peninsular affairs. What were the reasons for this intervention?

Personal and profit motives were obviously important. When Peter I married Blanche of Bourbon, the French had promised an enormous dowry; the fact that this dowry was never paid, and that the king deserted his wife after three days of marriage, only served to strain Franco-Castilian relations. When Peter fled to Bayonne in 1366, he persuaded the Navarrese and the Black Prince to provide military help by promising financial and landed rewards in the kingdom he had lost. Henry was equally quick to offer similar rewards to prospective allies, and it seemed, at times, as if Castile was up for partitioning. As for Gaunt, he obviously had a personal interest in pressing a claim which he only finally surrendered on payment of £100,000, an annual pension of £6600 and the marriage of his daughter to John I's heir.

At a lower level, an important role was played by the mercenary captains and free companies whose activities dominated so much of the later medieval scene. Before the outbreak of the Castilian crisis, unemployed Catalan mercenaries, who had been fighting in North Africa and then in Sicily, were contracted on double pay by Andronicus II to help save Byzantium from the Turks; led by Roger de Flor, the *almogávares* of the Grand Company set sail in 1302 on an expedition which was to end in the establishment of the Catalan duchies of Athens and Neopatras. Later, in the fifteenth century, the Castilians provided soldiers of fortune, such as the famous Rodrigo de Villandrando, who served in the civil wars in France. But now it was the troubles of Castile which attracted the mercenaries. After the peace of Brétigny (1360) the exiled Henry of Trastámara busied himself trying to secure the services of the unemployed free companies. At first he failed through lack of funds; but, with financial backing from the kings of France and Aragon, captains and mercenaries began to gather in Montpellier late in

1365. It was these men – including such famous captains as Bertrand Du Guesclin, Arnoul d'Audrehem and Sir Hugh Calveley – who ensured the success of the invasion of 1366. They expected their pay, a share of booty, and rewards from a grateful 'king'. But many of them would not wish to remain in Castile. Du Guesclin, for example, was eventually given the towns of Soria, Atienza and Almazán; he promptly sold them back to Henry II and returned to France. Moreover, the English captains who participated in the Trastmaran invasion of 1366 were almost immediately recalled by the Black Prince, after Henry's initial successes: the English were aware of French financial backing for the Trastamaran, and the struggle now took on the aspect of an 'official' clash between England and France.

In encouraging and financing the free companies which joined in the 1366 invasion, Charles V was both ridding France of the menace of *routiers* and promoting a *coup d'état* which would provide France with invaluable naval support in the Channel. Castilian dynastic problems provided him with the means of establishing a satellite power and controlling its formidable naval strength. 'Command of the sea' was impossible to achieve in the later medieval period. Moreover, 'official' naval operations and policies must be set within a context of constant 'unofficial' war at sea – piracy flourished and the sea-borne equivalents of the landed mercenaries pillaged commercial shipping. But if complete mastery at sea could not be achieved, it was possible to establish zones of control and, provided the necessary power could be mustered, a strategic naval initiative could be quickly and effectively established each season. All the Iberian powers, except Navarre, owned powerful galley squadrons, but Aragonese naval resources were stretched to the limit in the Mediterranean, and the smaller Portuguese fleet lacked the ruthless spirit of enterprise which the Basque seamen provided for the Castilians. The intervention of the Castilian fleets in the Hundred Years War would not affect the outcome decisively, but it could alter the balance of power at sea and help the fortunes of the French on land.

From the end of the thirteenth century the French and English had made diplomatic efforts to secure the services of Castilian naval power. But the decisive factor was the French move to provide Henry of Trastámara with full support. By the treaty of Toledo (1368), Charles V secured a Castilian naval alliance for French use and, with Du Guesclin intervening militarily on his behalf, Henry was assured of the throne and French protection. For over a quarter of a century, with the Lancastrian threat looming over Castile, the new allies worked closely together – the Trastamarans accepting French advice about the scale of Castilian naval help and the timing of truces with the English adversary. The Franco-Castilian negotiations of the period are filled with arrangements for financing and sending galley squadrons into the Channel and the Atlantic.

The English, for their part, paid dearly for their failure in Castile. True, the treaty of Windsor between Portugal and England (1386) provided some Portuguese naval help for the English, but this was an inadequate counter to the Castilian maritime operations which had already scored some notable successes. In 1372 a Castilian fleet of twenty-three ships linked up with French forces to win a resounding victory over the English at La Rochelle; in 1375 the Castilians attacked and burnt some thirty English ships in the Bay of Bourgneuf. These spectacular victories were not as damaging to the English, however, as has often been thought. They certainly did not establish a Castilian 'command of the sea'. But during the 1370s and 1380s the Castilian galley squadrons kept up a constant marauding pressure on the English coast. The speed and manoeuvrability of the galleys made them ideal not only for naval warfare but also for destructive hit-and-run raids. Of shallow draught, and each carrying some ten men-at-arms and thirty archers as well as a crew of over one hundred men, they could be rowed at speed inshore. Hence several galleys could very quickly beach a sizable raiding expedition. In 1374 the Castilians attacked the Isle of Wight. In 1377 the Castilian admiral, Fernán Sánchez de Tovar, joined up with a French naval force under Jean de Vienne and spent the summer wreaking havoc along the English coast: Rye was attacked and captured, Lewes was burnt, the Isle of Wight was overrun, Plymouth and Hastings were burnt and Portsmouth and Dartmouth suffered at the hands of the raiders. In 1380 the Castilians and French returned again. This time they sacked Winchelsea, and even sailed up the Thames to burn Gravesend. Small wonder that by 1385 the English Crown was licensing some of the coastal towns to pay ransoms for their own safety.

What was life like on the galleys and what sort of men were involved? The magnificent chronicle of *El Victorial* provides some of the answers. The author, Díez de Games, was an eyewitness of the naval expeditions undertaken by his knightly master, Pero Niño, count of Buelna. The range of these expeditions was remarkable. In 1404 complaints about piracy in the Mediterranean led Henry III to order Pero Niño to organise search-and-destroy operations from Seville. There followed expeditions which covered the southern and eastern coasts of Spain, Marseilles, Corsica, Sardinia and the North African coast (including an attack on Tunis). Then, as a result of the rupture of the Anglo-French truce in 1405, Pero Niño (with a marauding flotilla) and Martín Ruiz de Avendaño (with a fleet) were ordered into the Atlantic. The two forces operated independently, and Pero Niño's ships launched the usual sacking raids along various points of the English coast from St Ives to Southampton. The range of these naval operations – from the attack on Tunis to the sack of St Ives – and the spirit and tactics of the men all emerge vividly from *El Victorial*.

And yet by the time of Pero Niño's raids on the English coast, the Spanish phase of the Hundred Years War had ended, and the Castilians and Portuguese, no longer political satellites of the French and English, could freely deploy their naval power for independent maritime expansion.

The truces and treaties of 1389 settled the dynastic issues which had bedevilled the previous quarter of a century. The new dynasties in Portugal and Castile were securely established and had little to fear from each other, or from their former allies and enemies in France and England. With the Lancastrian marriage, Castile moved closer to a *modus vivendi* with England while still maintaining the fiction of alliance with France. Indeed, when the alliance was renewed in 1408, no specific naval contribution was mentioned, and Castile gained the freedom to arrange yearly truces without consulting her French ally. Individual Castilians, of course, could still seek their fortunes in war, and it was at this point that Rodrigo de Villandrando went into French service. Similarly, at sea, the relaxation of 'official' war led to a sharp increase in piracy. The English buccaneers – men like Harry Pay of Poole, John Hawley of Dartmouth and Thomas Norton of Bristol – scoured the Channel in search of merchant prey, and Pero Niño's raids in 1405 were largely reprisal attacks. The sacking of Poole, for example, was a counter to Harry Pay's attack on Gijón. Yet, although the unemployed captains and mercenaries continued to make a living on sea and land, the kings of Castile and Portugal had largely departed from the stage of the Hundred Years War. Annual truces with England meant *de facto* independence from France. Moreover Anglo-Castilian co-operation led to the creation of arbitration machinery which ensured that, from 1410, good relations would not be severely damaged by hostile naval 'incidents'. In theory the alliances still existed, but in practice the Castilians and Portuguese had gained independence of action.

War and trade went hand in hand and, when linked to alterations in the pattern of trade routes, the changes in the international scene at the end of the fourteenth century were of profound significance for all the Iberian powers. About the mid-fourteenth century the power of the Crown of Aragon and its 'commonwealth' seemed hard to rival. Sardinia was conquered in the 1320s, and the Pisans, while retaining a commercial establishment at Cagliari, capitulated and withdrew; the kingdom of Mallorca was annexed in 1343 and its royal family expelled; in the 1370s the duchies of Athens and Neopatras, as well as the island of Sicily, were included in the Aragonese 'commonwealth'. It was a façade of maritime and political expansion which contrasted sharply with the state of affairs in strife-torn Castile. But yet, while Aragon's prosperity was great in the mid-fourteenth century, the change in trade routes impaired her Mediterranean achievements. The conquest of Andalusia had been accompanied by the clearing of the Gibraltar straits by the combined efforts of Genoese, Castilians and Basques. This was a momentous event since it created a direct sea-link between the Mediterranean and Atlantic economies: by the end of the thirteenth century the straits of Gibraltar were regularly traversed by Genoese and Venetian ships going to Flanders and England, and by the Basque shippers who plied a vigorous carrying trade in the Mediterranean. These were to be the most frequented routes in western Europe, and the effect was to push the great commercial arteries southwards, away from Barcelona, and to bring prosperity to the coastal ports of Valencia, Andalusia and Portugal. Catalan interest in expansion, therefore, was partly due to a desire to capture key positions further to the south and east of the Mediterranean, but this inevitably led to clashes with the power of the Genoese sea-borne empire. This struggle favoured the Genoese, for the balance of naval strength was against the Crown of Aragon. Even at the height of its power the Catalan fleet was not as large as that of Genoa, and the latter enjoyed valuable support from Castile and Portugal, some of whose ports were veritable Genoese colonies. Yet, by any account, the maritime ventures of the Crown of Aragon were impressive. The conquest of Mallorca in 1229 fired the interest of the monarchy in building up naval expertise which, apart from resulting in naval victories in all parts of the Mediterranean, also led Catalan and Mallorcan sailors to tackle and solve technical problems. From at least 1272 the Mallorcan sailors used compasses for navigation, and the accurate information on the *portolani* charts provided essential data for short- and medium-distance navigation. But naval victories, such as that over the Genoese at Alghero (1353), did nothing to stem the slow and disastrous Catalan decline. The Catalans were gradually pushed out of Seville, Andalusia and the Canary islands. Across the straits, Ceuta fell to the Portuguese in 1415. In effect, the Catalans were barred from regular access to the north Atlantic, Morocco and the west-African coast. Within the Mediterranean the Genoese inflicted a crushing defeat on the Catalan fleet at Ponza in 1435. Barcelona could not have been more isolated. Between 1445 and 1470 not one Genoese ship on the Atlantic run put in at Barcelona. The latter was, after all, well off the main sea-route and had nothing to offer except naval hostility. Catalan piracy increased from 1390 onwards – thus indicating a failure to compete at a formal level. The short-term profits were huge; in the long run it led to the rupture of important commercial relations with Egypt (1411 and 1445), Tunis (1431) and Flanders (1443).

The Catalan experience stands in sharp contrast to Castilian and Portuguese successes. Civil war and Anglo-French rivalry had dragged the Castilians into the Hundred Years War, but their naval power was brought to bear on a crucial sector of the sea-routes to England, France and Flanders – a sector of vital interest to the Castilian economy. Despite dependence on the French, the Castilian monarchs took every opportunity to obtain trading privileges in return for naval support. The privilege granted in 1364 by Charles V of France to Castilian merchants trading in Normandy, for example, contained forty-three separate sections and substantial benefits of a judicial and fiscal nature. Similar privileges were obtained from the counts of Flanders, and by 1367 the Castilians clearly enjoyed preferential treatment in Bruges. Such privileges were extended in subsequent years – for example, by the French in 1371 – and they were confirmed in the truces which ended the Spanish phase of the Hundred Years War. The Castilian fleet had been used by the French, but Castilian seamen and merchants had established their power and influence in La Rochelle, Brittany, Rouen, Harfleur and Bruges. With their wool, wine, iron, wax, cochineal, mercury, olive oil, soap and fruits they were among the most important exploiters of the Flanders sea-routes.

After the Spanish phase of the Hundred Years War, the continuing growth of the Flanders trade was partly due to Castilian economic expansion and the protectionist policies of the monarchy – for example, Henry III's insistence in 1398 that Castilian goods be transported in Castilian ships. But the political relations between Castile and the other Channel powers also played a crucial role.

The main threat to Castilian interests during the first half of the fifteenth century came from the Hanseatic league. The protectionist measures of Castile's monarchy, the competition of its merchants in Flanders, its monopoly over the wines of La Rochelle, and the piratical acts of its seamen damaged Hansa interests and led the league to hope that they could oust the Castilians in the wake of English military successes over the French. The league was, in fact, in a strong position. The English occupation of Normandy (completed by 1419) entailed the loss of commercial centres such as Harfleur, Rouen and Dieppe, from which the Castilians would be excluded until 1451. Moreover, attacks on the English and Hansa by the Castilians might well lead to a rupture with England's ally, the duke of Burgundy, who controlled Flanders. But John II of Castile acted rapidly and decisively. Ordered to attack the English and Hansa but to avoid confrontation with the Flemings, the Castilian fleet heavily defeated the Hansa at La Rochelle (1419). This secured Castilian supremacy in the Bay of Biscay but led to continuing conflict with the Hansa and considerable tensions with Flanders. With her merchants firmly entrenched in Brittany, Castile now withdrew from even token intervention in Anglo-French warfare and concentrated on isolating the Hansa diplomatically. Within ten years the Flemings made their peace, Castilian privileges in Bruges were fully restored, and Anglo-Castilian trade had been regularised by the almost automatic concession of safe-conducts. The Hansa now had to fight on alone in a ruinous war conducted far from its home bases, and in 1443 they capitulated. At a time when the duke of Burgundy favoured Castilian interests in Flanders, the truce of 1443 excluded the Hansa from competing with Castilians in Spanish ports or in La Rochelle. Castilian domination in the Bay of

Biscay had been secured without forfeiting preferential treatment in Flanders.

From the 1390s onwards, therefore, the old days of firm alliance with France were over, and the Castilian monarchy concentrated on keeping the all-important trading routes open. When the French demanded privileges for their merchants, and when they expressed irritation at the hostility shown by the Basques to the Hanseatic merchants trading in French ports, they encountered unexpected resistance from Castilian diplomats. The granting of privileges to French merchants, it was argued, was not a matter of reciprocity because Castilian privileges in France were the reward for naval help given to the French. Moreover, while it was true that Castilian-Hanseatic rivalry involved French ports, the truce of 1443 was one between independent powers and did not need French approval. In these arguments of the 1450s, the Castilians won acceptance of all their points. But, in fact, ever since the early fifteenth century, the Castilians had been drawing closer to France's rivals. In 1430 Castilian merchants secured privileges in Brittany which, confirmed in 1435 and 1452, provided the basis of an alliance during the reign of the Catholic Kings. Similarly, relations with England were marked by a mutual willingness to sign yearly truces and establish trade on a regular basis. If 'command of the sea' was impossible to achieve, political independence and a policy of careful neutrality, combined with an occasional show of force, ensured that Castile's formidable naval power and merchant interests remained relatively unmolested.

But were not the Andalusian ports and the Mediterranean also important for the Castilians? The straits of Gibraltar constituted a vital strategic zone which, if not properly controlled, could endanger both the arterial routes to Flanders and the military frontier with Muslim Granada. The necessity of controlling the straits and preventing easy communications between Granada and North Africa led Castilian monarchs, from Ferdinand III onwards, to devote attention to building up naval power in the south. The Castilians, therefore, possessed two centres of maritime operations – the north coast for the Bay of Biscay and the Atlantic, and the Andalusian ports for the straits and the Mediterranean. The southern ports, drawing heavily on Genoese and Cantabrian men and expertise, soon proved their worth against Muslim and Portuguese fleets, and during the fifteenth century their squadrons performed the vital task of patrolling the straits during each major frontier campaign – a task which they continued to perform until the final conquest of Granada.

In these southern waters, however, the Castilians were to encounter an old rival. The Portuguese, who were also recovering from the end of the Spanish phase of the Hundred Years War, similarly devoted their energies to maritime expansion. For this task they were initially better fitted than the Castilians. The new dynasty in Portugal owed its security to the great victory at Aljubarrota, but support for the Portuguese 'revolution' was provided by the powerful maritime and commercial interests of Lisbon and Oporto. Thus, in the same year as the Castilians began to prepare for a long war of attrition with the Hansa, the Portuguese crossed the straits and captured Ceuta (1415). There, it is true, they received some naval help from Castile, but the age of discoveries and colonial rivalry had already begun. As early as 1344 the Castilians had laid claim to the Canaries, and by the first decade of the fifteenth century the trade in Guanche slaves from these islands was already flourishing in Seville. As the Portuguese, attracted by the prospect of gold, slaves and spices, launched into their exploration of the west-African coast, they clashed with Castilian interests. Throughout the fifteenth century, the disputes over colonial possessions affected all the diplomatic negotiations between the two powers and even spilled over into clashes in the general Council of the Church which sat intermittently at Basle from 1431 to 1449. The bustling ports of Iberia, with their Castilian, Catalan, Genoese and Portuguese merchants and sailors, had given rise to an age of maritime enterprise and adventure which resulted in the discoveries of the islands of the Atlantic and then America; for it was into this world of naval expertise, politics and adventure that Columbus came peddling his 'Enterprise of the Indies'.

Absolutism in Castile

THE dismal catalogue of civil wars in later medieval Spain inevitably challenged monarchical power and, frequently, the ineffectiveness of kings merely aggravated political dissension. Yet the civil wars also stimulated the formulation of new institutions and new ideas of a constitutional nature. The end result was the establishment of royal absolutism in Castile and the strengthening of 'constitutionalism' in the Crown of Aragon. At times, however, the logic of political events seemed to point to quite different results.

Although in the Crown of Aragon the conflicts of the later medieval period resulted in some strengthening of royal authority, constitutional issues continued to be dominated by the theories and institutions of pactism (above, pp. 104–17). In the struggle against the nobility during the thirteenth and fourteenth centuries, the monarchy had enjoyed some support from the urban patriciates. But from the late fourteenth century the Crown became progressively embroiled in conflicts involving the towns and the peasantry. In the large towns, those without access to political power accused the oligarchs of being responsible for the chaotic state of the municipal finances and economy. In these conflicts the monarchy supported the demands for municipal reform, and in the fifteenth century royal backing was given to new procedures for broadening the basis of urban government. The key town was, of course, Barcelona where the political and economic policies of the oligarchical party of the *Biga* was challenged by the reforming party of the *Busca*. As in other towns, the Crown supported demands for reform, and the solution, virtually imposed by the monarchy in 1455, ended the monopoly of the *Biga*. But the oligarchs did not remain completely powerless within Barcelona, and they retained a powerful voice in the Catalan *cortes* where they found strong allies. Already, by the 1440s, Alfonso V's fiscal demands and his prolonged absence in Italy were causing severe tensions between the Crown and the *cortes*. Moreover, by supporting the demands of the *remensa* peasants (below, pp. 177–8), the monarchy also alienated important sectors of the nobility and church who closed ranks with the urban oligarchs in the *cortes*. The political and social issues, therefore, became subsumed in a constitutional struggle between monarchy and *cortes*. The final step was provided by John II. Succeeding to the Crown of Aragon in 1458, his harsh treatment of his son, the prince of Viana, provided the Catalans with a dynastic issue which symbolised the defence of Catalan privileges. By the early 1460s the death of the prince, the conflicts with the *cortes*, and the crisis over the *remensa* peasants had all become inextricably fused, and the principality was in open revolt against John II. The civil war attracted the attention of Catalonia's neighbours. Louis XI agreed to help John II in exchange for Cerdagne and Rousillon, and the Catalans chose Henry IV of Castile as their prince. The latter was an ineffective protector, and John II, supported by Aragon, Valencia and

Mallorca, gained the upper hand of the Catalans by 1464; but it was only in 1472 that he finally won Barcelona, whose declining fortunes had now been ruined by civil war.

These royal successes certainly represented some degree of growth in monarchical power as well as a relative decline in the fortunes of the powerful nobility and urban oligarchies. But the military triumphs of the monarchy by no means meant that the contractual nature of political power had been swept aside. Pactist ideas survived intact and, as will be seen (below, pp. 161–3), the institutions of pactism were actually strengthened. In Castile, on the other hand, the later medieval period witnessed the emergence of a striking and fully developed doctrine of absolutism.

The formulation of a theory of royal absolutism in Castile came during the reign of John II (1406–54). As we have seen, the code of the *Siete Partidas*, completed in the 1260s and deriving much of its inspiration from Roman law, dealt with such problems as where power was located, who imposed justice, and who had the power to make law. The king, according to the *Partidas*, received his power directly from God and not from the people or from the Church:

> Kings are the vicars of God, each one in his own kingdom, placed over the people in order to maintain them in justice and truth in temporal matters, like the Emperor in his empire. . . . Kings, indeed, have greater powers. For they are not only the rulers of their lands while they live, but they leave them to their successors at their deaths because they hold their lordships by inheritance. Emperors cannot do this because they are elected.[47]

Sovereign kingship, according to the *Partidas*, was the key to the proper functioning of society. The latter was envisaged as a body – the *corpus mysticum* – of which the king was variously described in the *Partidas* as the head, the heart and the soul. Accordingly, the king governed the rest of the body politic and created the laws.

Although the code of the *Siete Partidas* was not accepted as the law of the land until 1348, the reign of Peter I (1350–69) seemed to promise an immense strengthening of royal power. It is possible that the king, like his illustrious predecessor in France, Philip IV, may have been a student of Aegidius Colonna whose *De Regimine Principum* was certainly translated into Castilian round about 1345. Aegidius was a staunch supporter of royal power, and Peter's despotic actions betrayed an extreme disregard for the law and for the deference which was traditionally accorded to the counsel and advice of the great men of the kingdom. But these trends, which seemed to point to the establishment of a strong monarchical power in Castile, failed to develop further during the fourteenth century. The Trastamaran victory in the civil war implied a victory over arbitrary monarchical power, and Henry did offer an alternative and traditional concept of government. As against Peter's ruthless individualism, Henry surrounded himself with powerful relatives and nobles, governed with their help, rewarded them liberally with landed wealth and offices, and heeded the voice of his subjects in the *cortes.* By establishing 'government by collaboration', Henry II won support: after all, his was a concept of government which appealed to traditional principles, and for a century after his death poets continued to sing his praises.

But, lacking a genuine claim to the throne, Henry II had been forced to enunciate principles which were potentially dangerous to royal authority once he had triumphed. Trastamaran propaganda, both during the civil war and Henry II's reign, depicted Peter as a tyrant – a monster who, as the enemy of Christ, trampled on the law and on his subjects. Tyranny might justify rebellion but, in order to justify his own accession to the throne, Henry was also forced to emphasise the elective nature of monarchy. True, Henry was a consummate politician, and he did his best to preserve the fabric of royal authority. He organised rebellion against the 'tyrant', but he did his best to nullify the consequences for monarchy by arguing that God, and not the rebels, had decided the issue. The Trastamaran justification on these points emerges very clearly in the arguments presented to the Black Prince on the eve of the battle of Nájera:

> . . . God took pity on all the subjects of these kingdoms so that they should not suffer this evil [Peter's tyranny] which grew daily. And when nobody was doing anything against him [Peter] in all his lands – save to give him obedience – and while all the people were with him, serving him and helping him to defend these kingdoms, God gave his sentence against him, with the result that he abandoned these kingdoms of his own accord and left. And all the people of the kingdoms of Castile and León were greatly pleased by this, holding that God had pitied them in order to free them from such a harsh and dangerous lord. And all of

them – the prelates, knights, nobles, cities and towns of the kingdoms – came to us of their own accord and chose us to be their king and lord. Therefore we deduce from all these events that this was the work of God. . . .[48]

The implications were clear. Peter was a tyrant, but there had been no rebellion against his royal authority. Instead, while his subjects had been busy obeying the king as good subjects should, God had intervened to secure the tyrant's departure and Henry's election as king. Despite these ingenious arguments, however, God's designs remained obscure, and the practical moral arising from the civil war was that a 'tyrant' could be resisted and an alternative king could be elected. Later, when facing the Lancastrian claims to Castile, John I tried to avoid these issues by quite blatantly asserting that the Trastamaran dynasty had the best hereditary claim to the throne. But the crises of his reign gave rise to further limitations of royal power – this time by the *cortes*. Summoned regularly in order to provide finance and support for the monarchy, the *cortes* found their powers considerably increased and confirmed, especially after the military disaster at Aljubarrota and in the face of Lancastrian invasion. Thus there was a close connection between the events of the Spanish phase of the Hundred Years War and constitutional developments. The overthrow of Peter represented a victory for the traditional view that the king, the great nobility and the *cortes* should collaborate closely in the task of government. During precisely those years when the Lancastrian threat became increasingly dangerous, the powers of the *cortes* grew, reaching their highest point in the 1380s. The king did not enjoy unlimited power: he was bound by the laws of the kingdom. The making of law was a matter for the king and *cortes*, and the latter had some say in the composition of the royal council and in the examination of the accounts of subsidies which they had voted. That the monarchy was to break free from these restrictions in the long run was due to two factors – the negotiated settlement which ended the Lancastrian claims to Castile, and the determination with which John II and his favourite, Alvaro de Luna, set about increasing royal power.

Faced with immense difficulties, John II and Alvaro de Luna deliberately formulated a policy of divine right and absolutist monarchy. What were these difficulties?

Before his death in 1406, Henry III had foreseen the problem of a long minority, and he entrusted the government of the kingdom to his wife, Catherine of Lancaster, to his brother, Ferdinand ('of Antequera') and to the royal council. Ferdinand was to be the dominant personality of the minority. He used his regency to pursue his own family's interests, and his success seriously affected Castilian politics for the rest of the century. In 1412 Ferdinand was elected to succeed the childless Martin I to the Crown of Aragon. However, he still retained his regency in Castile, and until his death in 1416 he concentrated on building up his family's powers in both kingdoms. Two of his sons were to dominate the political scene in Castile. In 1409 Ferdinand secured the mastership of Santiago for his son, the *infante* Henry, who was to be involved in every political disturbance till his death in 1445. His elder brother, the *infante* John, succeeded to the family's vast landed possessions in Castile. Ferdinand also planned a marriage for John which made him king of Navarre in 1425. Subsequently he became John II of Aragon. Until his later years, however, this *infante* remained first and foremost a Castilian noble.

These two brothers were to inherit their father's power in Castile, but the rest of Ferdinand's children were used to consolidate the family's position. The eldest son, Alfonso, succeeded his father and preceded his brother as monarch of the Crown of Aragon. Although mainly interested in Italian politics, he provided Aragonese support for the schemes of his brothers in Castile. Ferdinand's daughter, Mary of Aragon, was to become the wife of John II of Castile; the latter's sister was married off to Ferdinand's son, Alfonso.

All in all Ferdinand of Antequera ensured that the substance of power in Castile was inherited by his sons rather than by his nephew, John II. In 1418, when John II married Mary of Aragon, the future looked gloomy for the young king. The members of the Aragonese party – that is, those Castilians who supported the *infantes* John and Henry – were solidly entrenched in political power and controlled many of the resources of royal patronage.

The assault by the king and Alvaro de Luna on the power of the Aragonese party began in the 1420s and inevitably caused a protracted political crisis. Pensions, privileges and offices were at stake. Many of the nobility supported the *infantes* John and Henry. Moreover the local bases of power of the Aragonese party lay mainly in peripheral areas of the kingdom, to which they could retreat when outmanoeuvred at court or in battle. They also enjoyed refuge and support in the kingdoms of Navarre and Aragon and, consequently, the crisis had international implications as well as being an internal struggle for power. The task of king and favourite was, therefore, threefold. Firstly, they had to expel the Aragonese party from the central basis of power at court. Secondly, they had to wrest from the *infantes* the peripheral areas of the kingdom which served as bases for a counter-attack on the monarchy. Thirdly, they had to build a diplomatic alliance against Aragon. It was a prolonged struggle in which the balance of power was continually changing. As far as Castile was concerned, the domination of the Aragonese party was finally broken in 1445 by the battle of Olmedo. Eight years later, however, Alvaro de Luna himself became the victim of a different court intrigue and was executed by royal command.

That the crisis had ended in a victory for the Crown was due as much to the determination of the royal favourite as to the disunity displayed by the Aragonese party. From the start the royalist party put forward exalted claims concerning the nature of monarchy and its powers. When, for example, some of the nobility criticised royal methods of government in 1439, John II replied:

> The cognizance, judgement, and final decision on this matter, especially since it is of my own making and appertains principally to me, does not belong to anybody else, after God, except myself. All my vassals, subjects, and people, whatever their estate, condition, pre-eminence and dignity, are according to all divine, human, canon, civil, and even natural law, subject, compelled, and bound with all humility, reverence and subjection to my word and deed. They are expressly prohibited and forbidden from detracting or saying anything in any way about these matters; nor are they even to dare talk about it on pain of great and grave punishments according to common law and, especially, according to the laws of my kingdoms which deal with such matters. For, according to these laws, so great is the king's right of power that all the laws and all rights are beneath him, and he holds this position not from men but from God, whose place he holds in temporal matters.[49]

The concept of the king as the head of the *corpus mysticum* and as God's vicar on earth was coupled with a clear attempt to establish absolute royal power. John II justified many of his arbitrary policies and actions by stressing that he acted 'as king and lord, not recognising a superior in temporal matters, and by virtue of my own will, certain knowledge and absolute royal power'. What did this absolute royal power entail? Did it mean that the king was above human law and that he had the power to make laws unilaterally?

The traditional view was that the king was not above the law and could not make laws by himself. The making, revising and annulment of laws was a matter for the king and the *cortes*. John II was largely successful in breaking through these limitations. The formula of the *poder real absoluto* (absolute royal power) was used to make laws which were to be as valid 'as if they had been made in the *cortes*' (*asi como si fuera fecha en cortes*). This marked a great increase of strength in the Crown's position both in political and administrative terms. The royal will could be imposed without restriction, and the cumbersome machinery involved in holding a *cortes* could be partly avoided. The king could make law unilaterally. But nothing better illustrates John II's deliberate policy of absolutism than his use of the *cortes* of Olmedo in 1445.

In 1445 John II and Alvaro de Luna won the decisive battle of Olmedo. With the defeat of the Aragonese party, a strong assertion of the theory of absolute royal power would not have been surprising. Yet it was *before* the battle that the king and his favourite decided to formulate their view of royal power clearly. The *cortes* had already been summoned and, on the eve of battle, the *procuradores* were made to act as the mouthpiece of the king. They condemned the actions of the rebels as being contrary to the political system and the position of the Crown:

> ... some of your subjects and people joined in rebellion, forgetting the natural law by which even the bees have a prince and the cranes follow a leader whom they revere and obey. They also forget the divine law which expressly prohibits and forbids that anyone should dare to touch his king and prince as he is anointed by God. Nor should anyone detract or say anything evil about him, or even think it in his mind. Instead, the king is to be held as God's vicar and honoured as being excellent. No one should dare to resist him, because those who resist the king are seen to resist the ordinance of God to which everyone is bound and tied, not only fearing the wrath of God and the evil and punishment which can affect them as a result of such an action, but also for the tranquillity of their consciences. Those who do the opposite, refusing

to obey their princes and kings, stand accused and are guilty of murder. . . . All of this being set aside, these people have persevered in their stubbornness, saying and pretending that they did so, and are doing so, on account of your majesty's service, and because of some law of your kingdom, which is in the second *Partida*. . . .[50]

The law in the *Partidas* to which the *procuradores* referred gave grounds for arguing that the king should be protected against his own misguided policies, and that it was his subjects' duty to afford such protection. It was an unfortunate choice to make as far as justifying rebellion was considered, and other passages from the *Partidas* were cited in order to provide a weighty refutation of the pretensions of the rebels. In the context of the laws of the *Partidas*, the *procuradores* argued:

. . . it would be abominable, sacrilegious . . . contrary to God, divine law and human law . . . if the king, whose heart is in the hands of God who guides him and inclines him to his wish, the king being his vicar and his lieutenant on earth, . . . the king having all laws and rights under him, and holding his power not from men but from God, whose place he holds in all temporal matters, . . . should be made subject to his vassals and people . . . especially since he recognises no superior in temporal matters save God alone. . . .[51]

Since the king was above the law and held his power directly from God, the concluding petition of the *cortes* was logical:

Therefore . . . we very humbly petition your highness that . . ., interpreting and declaring the said law of the *Partidas* and any others which might in this way be misunderstood, you revoke them by your certain knowledge, your own will, and your absolute royal power.[52]

It would be difficult to find a clearer statement of the doctrine of the divine right of the king and of his absolute authority above the law. It is also striking that these assertions were made by the *cortes*. After all, not only were the *Partidas* the law of the land, not only were the *cortes* failing to provide limitations to royal power, but they were actually confirming the royal absolutism and inciting the king to change any laws which were not to his liking. All this, of course, implied a decline in the power of the *cortes* – a decline which was due to deliberate royal policy, a desire on the part of the *procuradores* for a stronger monarchy, and the fact that the great nobility lost interest in the *cortes* as they realised that, with the growth in royal power, the key to political issues lay at court.

Equally striking, however, is the fact that, although the fortunes of war had not always favoured the monarchy, the nobility repeatedly failed to use political victory in order to impose serious constitutional limitations on the powers of the Crown. To control the king, the royal council had to be controlled; but without constitutional props this control could only be maintained by the ability to exert a continuous threat of political rebellion. The aim of the nobility, however, was not to limit absolutism but to use this absolutism for their own purposes. As we shall see, they had sound economic and financial motives for adopting this point of view (below, pp. 174-82). Hence, to justify rebellion, the nobility did not deny the absolute powers of the monarchy but argued that these powers had been usurped by Alvaro de Luna. In 1440, for example, a long and bitter account of Luna's shortcomings served to justify the actions of some of the great nobility, 'because you, Sire, have wished to submit your royal power, both your absolute power and ordinary power, to your constable'.[53] Nine years later the rebellion of the town of Toledo was similarly justified on the grounds that 'your majesty knows very well that for the last thirty years and more, Alvaro de Luna, your constable, has tyrannically dissipated, devastated, and daily usurps and devastates your kingdom and lordships, usurping to himself the government and rule, and glory and powers of the Crown, which only belong to your highness'.[54]

The inspiration for the exalted conceptions of royal power probably derived from the post-glossators of the fourteenth century. The propagation of these ideas in Castile was the work of *letrados*, but the practical application of a policy of absolutism may well have been due to Alvaro de Luna rather than John II. The execution of the favourite, however, emphasised the fact that this policy had created a royal absolutism. When John II asked for advice on how to proceed against Luna, a *letrado* stated quite bluntly to the king that 'he did not have to account to anyone save God alone'. In the end Luna did not even receive a trial but was executed by royal command, and all possible objections were, as usual, swept aside by the king's *poder real absoluto*.

The fact was that absolutism had been established, and even the disastrous reign of the next king, Henry IV (1454–74), served only to emphasise the point. Time and again noble factions found their plans thwarted by the king's inordinate fondness of using his absolute power. The repeated failure of the nobles' conspiracies led to a serious crisis in 1465. In January of that year the king was forced to accept the most impressive proposals for a reform of government which had been devised during the fifteenth century. This time the programme of the nobility had been carefully elaborated, and it contained measures which did imply the imposition of constitutional limitations on royal power. The very next month, however, Henry IV simply issued an order declaring all the proposals, and his acceptance of them, null and void. The failure of such carefully elaborated plans led some of the nobility to resort to extreme measures. In June they deposed Henry IV in effigy and proclaimed his half-brother, Alfonso, as king. They justified their actions by referring to Henry IV's heinous crimes, and by arguing that the monarchy of Castile was elective. The argument, of course, was not an unfamiliar one. The weak-willed and benevolent Henry IV, however, was hardly a 'tyrant' of the same stamp as Peter the Cruel, and the young Alfonso was a mere puppet in the hands of his masters. In the long run, therefore, the actions of the rebels only served to strengthen the monarchy. The 'election' of Alfonso XII was clearly the work of a faction, and it was evident that it was nothing more than a cynical attempt to legalise the grants and privileges which the electors bestowed on themselves. Alfonso XII was still a boy, his royal powers were not limited, and the nobility used the boy-king's 'own will, certain knowledge, and absolute royal power' for their own purposes. In short, both kings, Henry IV and the pretender Alfonso XII, maintained their absolute royal power until Alfonso died three years later in 1468. The 'elective' experiment, which had not denied the principles of absolutism, was not repeated. The Catholic kings, Ferdinand and Isabella, who have so often been credited with founding the early modern state in Spain, were to receive the power of absolutism intact. They did not have to struggle to gain an acceptance of the theory since these powers were not in dispute. The key political problem consisted in determining who was to enjoy the benefits of wielding the royal powers, and the answer to such a problem inevitably rested with the characters and determination of individual monarchs.

The reign of John II, therefore, marked the establishment of the absolutist position expressed by the legal maxims *quod principi placuit legis habet vigorem* (what pleases the prince has the force of law) and *princeps legibus solutus est* (the prince is free from the limitations of the law). The political vicissitudes of the period should not be allowed to obscure the fact that the theoretical powers of the monarchy grew enormously. Despite the crisis of the second half of the fourteenth century, John II inherited and extended the legacy of Alfonso X and the *Siete Partidas*. If John II's son, Henry IV, failed in practice to live up to the theory of absolutism, his daughter, Isabella, made full use of her inheritance.

7. Institutional Changes and Experiments

COLUMBUS, as we have seen, came peddling his 'Enterprise of the Indies' to a society which had long been accustomed to maritime enterprise and adventure. But we need only look at the powers which he received from the Catholic Kings, Ferdinand and Isabella (1474–1504/16), to realise how indebted the founders of empire also were to those who, over the previous centuries, had elaborated institutions which were capable of being adapted to new challenges and adventures. Columbus's powers as admiral of the Ocean Sea and viceroy of the Indies were solidly based on medieval precedents, and to safeguard his interests he demanded a copy of all the privileges granted to those who had held office as admirals of Castile. He even succeeded, like so many late medieval nobles, in making his offices and powers hereditary, and he obtained permission to found a *mayorazgo* or entailed estate. Those who accompanied or subsequently followed Columbus – the viceroys, *adelantados*, *alcaldes mayores* and officials of the *audiencias* and *corregimientos* – were likewise armed with medieval titles and institutions. Naturally, the new frontier would change the nature of the institutions inherited from the later middle ages, but the number of these which survived into modern Spain and its Empire is very striking. That most famous of Spanish taxes – the *alcabala* – was still in existence in the early nineteenth century. So too was that most typical of Spanish officials, the *corregidor*. And did not the Castilian *audiencias* spread over the face of Spain and the Americas from Santiago to Granada and from Mexico to Santiago de Chile? These institutions and officials were the direct descendants of the late medieval Castilian *alcabalas*, *corregidores* and *audiencias* whose origins lie in those fourteenth-century reforms of government which were carried out during the crises arising out of civil wars and the threat of foreign intervention. Rather than accept the conventional divide between 'medieval' and 'modern', the history of institutions suggests that it is more fruitful to think in terms of a Spanish *ancien régime* period spanning the late medieval and early modern centuries.

The element of continuity with the early modern period is obvious, even if the details are as yet far from clear. But where did the later medieval innovations spring from? There were various 'models' which could be imitated. The *alcabala* tax, for example, owed much to municipal practices and, ultimately, to the Muslim *qabāla* tax of al-Andalus. The office of *maestre racional* in the Crown of Aragon, on the other hand, seems to have been derived from Sicily. The remarkable feature, however, is the number of Iberian innovations in government and administration which seem to have been linked in some way with French practices and patterns. There were, of course, close political connections with France. In many ways later medieval Navarre can be considered as having formed a part of France, and its fiscal accounts during the early fourteenth century were actually audited in the French *chambre des comptes*. Henry of Trastámara lived for some years in France and, until the 1390s, the Trastamaran dynasty in Castile depended on the French for diplomatic and military support. Portugal had less direct contacts with France, but there was certainly a continuous process of 'borrowing' from Castile. Hence, given the extent of French influence, it is hardly surprising to find institutions similar to the financial accounting department of the *chambre des comptes* appearing in Navarre (*cámara de comptos*), Castile (*contaduría de cuentas*) and Portugal (*casa dos contos*). Similarly, John I of Castile had his eye firmly on the French pattern of military administration when he created the offices of marshal and constable in 1382:

> And since we have learnt that in the other Christian kingdoms of this world, and especially in the great and powerful kingdoms, there is a constable, whose office specifically exists for the affairs of wars and arms, and for the governing and good order of soldiers; we, seeing the great wars in which we are involved at present with the king of Portugal and our English enemies . . . make you, the said Don Alfonso, marquis of Villena, our constable. . . .[55]

Shortly after John I's reform, the king of Portugal appointed his first constable, Alvar Pérez de Castro, and the Navarrese followed suit by creating the office of constable in the early fifteenth century.

In appointing his first constable, however, John I emphasised military crisis rather than mere imitation. In this sense the 'anarchy' of the later medieval period was highly productive in that it stimulated institutional developments as much as the reconquest had done in earlier centuries. At all times the threat of foreign invasion or civil war posed problems of military organisation, the need for adequate finances to buy alliances and pay troops, and the need to win support by holding out the promise of governmental and administrative reforms. It is against this background that the institutions described in the following pages should be viewed.

Royal Government in Castile

FOREIGN intervention and civil war meant that the vital problems of government in Castile were military and fiscal. The search for new sources of income was the major preoccupation of the monarchy and led to important fiscal innovations. The thirteenth century had witnessed a growing emphasis on the Crown's right to public taxation, although a good deal of such income needed the consent of the *cortes*. The late medieval fiscal expedient of greatest consequence consisted of the appearance of a new tax (the *alcabala*), and the conversion of this tax into a regular and permanent source of income which did not require the consent of the *cortes*. This was paralleled by the decline of the latter institution into a docile body which obediently voted those taxes which still needed consent, and the creation of financial institutions capable of dealing with the sharp growth in royal income.

In 1342 Alfonso XI, short of money for the war against the Muslims, obtained a new fiscal contribution from some of the towns of his kingdom. This was the *alcabala* tax, and it was granted to the king on a temporary basis for the specific purpose of financing the conquest of Algeciras. Subsequently, however, the Castilian *cortes* were frequently asked to vote *alcabalas*, as well as the other traditional subsidies, in order to provide financial relief for hard-pressed monarchs. Alfonso XI gained further *alcabala* grants, Peter I obtained them both for his wars against Peter IV of Aragon and for his debts to the Black Prince, and the first three Trastamaran kings received them regularly for their military necessities. All these *alcabala* subsidies continued to be controlled by the *cortes*, and they were still regarded as temporary or extraordinary taxes. By the fifteenth century, however, the *alcabala* was no longer within the control of the *cortes* and was being levied every year on a permanent basis. At what precise moment of time this change took place still remains uncertain. John I certainly respected the control of the *cortes* over the tax, and it is probable that, once the Lancastrian threat to Castile ceased to exist, Henry III decided to levy the *alcabala* without consent during the 1390s. Certainly by John II's reign the *cortes* had no say at all in the matter.

In 1342 the contribution to Alfonso XI was probably granted in the form of *alcabalas* because these already existed in some areas as municipal taxes. Thus the *alcabala* was a municipal sales-tax which was absorbed by the Crown. For most of the fourteenth century it was levied at the rate of 5 per cent, but by the fifteenth century it had risen to 10 per cent. It differed from other taxes in that it was theoretically an indirect levy of general application – that is, it was ostensibly collected throughout the kingdom, and the clergy and nobility were not exempted from its operation. Although differing in detail from the French *taille*, which was a tax of repartition and not a sales-tax, the *alcabala* can aptly be compared to the French tax in that it arose from the needs of war, became a permanent imposition and accounted for over 50 per cent of the regular income of the Crown. The importance of the *alcabala* can be seen in the calculations of the Castilian royal budget of 1429. By this time the regular taxes included the *alcabalas*, the *tercias* or royal share of the ecclesiastical tithes, customs duties (*diezmos*), duties levied on the Moorish frontier in times of peace (*diezmo de lo morisco*), the capitation taxes paid by the Jewish and Moorish *aljamas*, taxes on transhumance (*servicio* and *montazgo*), revenues from salines, and a variety of insignificant taxes, such as the *martiniega* and *yantar*, which were the vestiges of seigneurial dues paid to the Crown. The budget of 1429 estimated a total regular income of almost 61,000,000 *mrs* of which 75 per cent derived from the *alcabala* revenues alone. In fact the budget did not take into account the revenues from salines and transhumance, but even when allowance is made for these omissions the importance of the *alcabala* emerges very clearly.

The monarchy, of course, was by no means limited to the regular taxes. If the fourteenth-century kings treated their *cortes* with caution and respect, the opposite was the case by the fifteenth century. With the collapse of the power of the *cortes* (below, pp. 152–5), subsidies were regularly voted in the form of *monedas* and *pedidos*, and the monarchy was free to spend the sums collected as it wished. Ferdinand of Antequera, for example, gained the Aragonese throne with Castilian money: 48,000,000 *mrs* which had been granted by the Castilian *cortes* for the war against Granada, were used by the regent to pay for his 'election expenses' at the Compromise of Caspe.

The pretext of the war against the infidel was also used to obtain money from the Church, while at the same time every effort was made to extract tribute money from Granada. As we have seen, the *tercias* were now regarded as being permanently under royal control. By stressing the war effort against the Moors, the monarchy also obtained subsidies from the clergy, and considerable sums were raised by the sale of indulgences (*cruzada* revenues). When, for example, Eugenius IV in 1443 granted 100,000 florins for the crusade against the Moors, John II used the money for his wars against the rebel nobility. Indeed, if we are to believe the chronicler Alonso de Palencia, Henry IV deliberately misled the papacy in order to obtain new and more comprehensive indulgences. By paying 200 *mrs* for such an indulgence, according to Palencia, an individual 'gained the faculty of withdrawing a specific person from purgatory – a matter which aroused great controversy and which was resolved by stating that, since purgatory was on earth, it fell under the jurisdiction of the pope'. But despite the enormous sums raised by these indulgences, Palencia alleged, not one penny was spent on the war against Granada. Palencia, who loathed Henry IV, could not refrain from exaggerating, and the Castilian monarchy did in fact spend money in exerting sufficient pressure on Granada in order to extract tribute money (*parias*). Thus, while subsidies were obtained from the Church and the *cortes* for war against the Moors, the latter paid *parias* in order to avert war. Truces with the Muslims converted the kingdom of Granada into a vassal-state of Castile and stipulated the amounts of yearly tribute payments; in 1439, for example, the *parias* were fixed at 24,000 golden *doblas* to be paid over the three years of the truce.

The growth in royal fiscality was accompanied by changes in the size and complexity of financial administration. These changes paralleled the decline of royal 'seigneurial' income and the rise in importance of 'public' taxation: the *mayordomo mayor*, formerly the chief financial official, continued to deal with royal household finances, but new officials, known as *contadores mayores* (chief controllers), took charge of all the enlarged financial administration. *Contadores* are first briefly mentioned during the reign of Peter I, but it was only with the advent of the Trastamaran dynasty that the *contadores mayores* made their appearance. By the last decade of the fourteenth century they headed two different financial sections: *contadores mayores de hacienda* supervised the collecting and executive aspects of taxation, and the *contadores mayores de cuentas* headed the accounting section. Below the *contadores mayores* there were other officials, such as *contadores* and *escribanos de rentas*, who were in charge of the registers or *libros* relating to revenues, tax-farms, assigned expenditure and privileges. Although the central financial administration moved with the peripatetic court, in 1436–7 John II decreed the establishment of a house of accounts (*casa de las cuentas*) in Valladolid and at the same time vested the *contadores mayores de cuentas* with extensive jurisdictional powers in financial matters. The latter measure seems to have been put into practice, but the creation of a permanent *casa de las cuentas* in Valladolid proved impossible because of the civil wars of the period.

Most royal taxes were farmed at court to those financiers who made the highest bids and provided sureties for the fulfilment of contracts. The nature and scope of these contracts varied considerably – from the farming of one tax for the whole kingdom for a period of several years, to the farming of a tax, or combination of taxes, in one specific area, such as a diocese. Frequently the larger tax-farmers (*arrendadores mayores*) auctioned smaller areas from their general farms to lesser financiers. The taxes voted by the *cortes* (*monedas, pedidos* and *moneda forera*) were not usually farmed but were levied in much the same way as the French *taille personnelle:* the total amount to be collected was decided upon by the king and his council, and after the approval of the *cortes* had been obtained the total was apportioned to the various regions of the kingdom. At a local level, officials known as *recaudadores* co-ordinated the various ways in which the towns, in their turn, assessed the wealth of areas and individuals within their jurisdictions.

When considered in conjunction with the development of absolutist ideas, the fiscal success of the Castilian monarchy in the later medieval period helps to explain why early modern Spain and its Empire depended to such a large extent on Castile and her resources. As in France, but unlike England and the Crown of Aragon, the financial problems of the Castilian monarchy did not stem from the powers of representative assemblies but from the attempts by pressure groups to control and determine the ways in which royal income was spent.

Increased revenues enabled the Crown to institute military reforms which were designed to help it to cope with the problems of war and civil unrest. These reforms did not lead to the creation of a standing army. Moreover, the Castilian tradition of warfare against the Moors – campaigns of devastation, lightning expeditions and marauding raids – entailed significant differences from French or English patterns of military organisation. The Castilian cavalry had no equivalent to the French mounted battle-unit of the lance which was made up of six men – a man-at-arms, an *écuyer*, archers and pages. In Castile, the term 'lance' could refer to two types of mounted warriors: the heavily armoured knight (*hombre de armas*) used the northern saddle (*silla de brida*), and engaged in mounted shock-combat like his French counterpart; but the ranching economy also produced the lightly armoured *caballero a la jinete* who, like his Moorish opponent, was mounted on a nimble horse, used very short stirrups, and was invaluable in rapid and open-ended warfare. Neither of these knights formed part of a tactical lance-unit, and the *jinetes* were far more numerous. In the final campaigns against Granada (1482–91), for example, there were ten times more *jinetes* than *hombres de armas*, and success depended largely on strategic raids of destruction and systematic siege warfare. Since the Castilians were unaccustomed to set-piece battles, it is hardly surprising that they made such a disastrous showing against the French and English in such engagements during the fourteenth century.

In 1382 John I reorganised the army command structure by creating the office of constable and appointing two marshals. The army itself, however, continued to be composed of surprisingly diverse components. During the fourteenth century the monarchy concentrated on building up forces by means of *acostamientos* or *tierras* which were, in effect, money benefices. In return for a yearly payment, assigned on royal revenues, a knight was supposed to hold himself ready for military service when summoned by the king; when on active service he received wages over and above his regular *tierra* payment. By this system of money benefices, therefore, the monarchy theoretically disposed of an 'army' scattered throughout the kingdom. In the *cortes* of 1432 this army was estimated to be in the region of 10,000 lances, and the budget of 1429 in fact earmarked almost 23 per cent of regular royal income for *tierra* payments for just over 9000 lances. Faced with obvious uncertainties about standards of equipment and fulfilment of *tierra* obligations, successive *cortes* and royal ordinances attempted to deal with these problems by drawing up detailed regulations on such matters as local musters and penalties for failure to obey royal summonses.

Kings did, of course, keep a number of *hombres de armas* and *jinetes* in permanent service, and the court was always accompanied by a small force of royal troops. On campaign this nucleus of an army was strengthened by knights receiving *tierra* payments, mercenaries, the *mesnadas* or retinues of the great nobility, and the urban militias. The latter, the most powerful of which were those nearest the Moorish frontier, consisted of cavalry and infantry. The urban knights, known variously as *caballeros de premia* or *de cuantía*, were defined by their military role or wealth rather than by lineage. As we have seen, the *caballeros villanos* of previous centuries had been able to enjoy noble privileges provided that they performed knightly service and maintained adequate equipment. This had been a matter of choice, but in 1348 Alfonso XI fixed minimum levels of wealth above which the duty to perform such service was made obligatory. These levels of wealth or 'quantities' – hence the term *caballeros de cuantía* – varied from region to region, and the obligation was effectively applied only in the southern towns. The poorer urban inhabitants, for their part, theoretically served as infantry. In practice, however, towns were assigned quotas of the men and provisions which they had to provide for the army, and the cost of meeting these quotas having been shared out at a local level, the money raised was then used to contract men to serve in the militia for a fixed scale of pay.

The retinues or *mesnadas* of the great nobility and the military orders reproduced the structure of the royal army on a smaller scale – that is, they included knights with money benefices, household troops and militia forces from seigneurial towns. The costs of these contingents serving the Crown were partly paid by the nobles, but once the lists of those serving had been submitted to royal financial officials, the king paid a proportion of the wages.

The origins of naval administration date back to the thirteenth century. The first royal fleet was probably that collection of north-coast ships which was pressed into service at the time of the campaigns against Seville (1248). Subsequently, with the help of Genoese expertise, Ferdinand III built up naval strength and Alfonso X laid down detailed naval regulations in the *Siete Partidas*. By the mid-fourteenth century a small but permanent fleet of galleys operated from the naval base at Seville, which was equipped with royal dockyards and provisioning facilities, and the system of money benefices was used, although on a much more reduced scale than in the army, to secure the services of captains and ships from the nor-

thern and southern ports in times of crisis. From the mid-thirteenth
century the Castilian navy had an *almirante mayor de la mar* who commanded the fleet, possessed supreme civil and criminal jurisdiction
at sea and, by means of admiralty courts, exercised some jurisdiction over ports, dockyards and all commercial operations linked
in any way to war, piracy or contraband. The Genoese influence on
Castilian naval development was profound, and a whole series of
admirals were Genoese – Ugo Vento, Benedetto Zaccaria, Egidio
and Ambrosio Bocanegra, and Christopher Columbus. In 1405,
however, the office of admiral of Castile became the hereditary
preserve of the Enríquez family and, thereafter, the admiral's
powers were in practice delegated to lieutenants. At no time does
there appear to have been a serious shortage of such skilled officials
as captains (*cómitres*) or pilots (*naocheros*), but the oarsmen (*remeros*)
for the galleys were sometimes raised from the coastal districts in
much the same way as the infantry of the urban militias – that is,
quotas were assigned to towns, the costs were repartitioned among
the local inhabitants, and *remeros* were contracted to report to naval
officials for duty.

By the late fourteenth century, therefore, the military power of the
crown would appear to be fairly impressive in both size and organisation. In fact, there were serious defects in military organisation, and
the army failed to provide the monarchy with the necessary power
to crush opposition decisively. It was impossible to hand out
thousands of money benefices in single units to individual knights,
and consequently the Crown disbursed them in blocks of units to
great noblemen who, in return, were responsible for providing the
corresponding number of lances. In 1390, for example, the count of
Niebla was allocated 50,000 *mrs* per year in *tierra*, and in 1447 the
admiral held 142,500 *mrs* per year for ninety-five lances. These
tierra payments were usually assigned on royal revenues in the
recipient's lands, and as a result royal and seigneurial military power
tended to fuse in favour of the great nobility. The proper functioning
of the 'royal' army depended on the support of the great nobility,
and this support in turn depended not so much on military pressure –
decisive battles were few and far between – as on the king's ability to
control powerful nobles by a subtle 'guerrilla war' of rewards and
confiscations which was waged through the financial registers of the
royal administration (below, pp. 179–81).

The monarchy's active search for new revenues and more effective military power contrasted with its passive role in reforming justice. Pressure for judicial reforms came from the *cortes* and from litigants who, in the search for better justice, increased the burden of the central administration by initiating more appeals from local courts. The need for the first two Trastamaran kings to win support for the new dynasty and surmount the threat of foreign intervention provided the *cortes* with the opportunity for pressing for reform. In the *cortes* of 1371 a new central judicial court, that of the *audiencia* or *chancillería*, was set up. At first the *audiencia* accompanied the royal court in its endless travels, and there was no clear distinction between its work and that of other institutions and officials with judicial functions. But after further reforms in the *cortes* of 1387 and 1390, the *audiencia* emerged as the highest court of justice with its own seal, a staff of clerks, a *procurador fiscal* to defend the interests of the Crown, a body of judges or *alcaldes*, and a group of supreme judges or *oidores*. The problem of fixing a permanent location for the *audiencia* was more difficult. It was clearly felt that its services should be available both north and south of the central *cordillera*. John I tried to solve this problem by making half of the *oidores* alternate at six-monthly intervals between Medina del Campo and Olmedo, and the other half between Madrid and Alcalá de Henares. In 1390 this complex experiment was given up in favour of locating the *audiencia* in Segovia. John II, however, tried to repeat the experiment of moving the court around, and it was only in 1442 that the *audiencia* found its final location in Valladolid. The problem of 'distributing' the services of the *audiencia* was not properly solved until the Catholic Kings hit on the expedient of establishing additional *audiencias* in Ciudad Real (later, Granada) and Santiago, thus creating a system which could be extended into the New World.

The *cortes* of the fourteenth century played an important part in implementing the judicial, military and financial reforms which have been discussed, and it is clear that they were not merely consultative assemblies but that there were certain matters on which the king needed to obtain consent as well as advice.

In practice, the powers of the *cortes* were most important in the spheres of legislation and taxation. During the fourteenth century the work of legislation was regarded as a task which the king and the *cortes* undertook together. There was no constitutional rule covering the point, but kings did in fact present their laws to the *cortes* for approval and discussion. The explanation for this probably lies in the power of the *cortes* with respect to the revision and annulment of existing laws. The code of the *Partidas* itself indicated that the monarchy's freedom of action was limited, since the laws could not be undone 'without the advice of all the best, most honest, and wisest men of the land'. The *cortes* pressed this point home during the fourteenth century. In 1387, for example, the monarchy formally agreed that the laws of the kingdom could only be changed by new laws made in the *cortes*. In many respects this was tantamount to limiting royal powers in administration as well as legislation, and it confirmed the idea that the king was bound by the laws of the kingdom. Indeed, on several occasions during the fourteenth century, the kings had to agree that royal commands which were contrary to the laws made by the king and the *cortes* should not be obeyed but should be considered as null and void. The king was still not above the law. The consent of the *cortes* was also necessary, as we have seen, for the imposition of certain forms of taxation, and during the second half of the fourteenth century the *procuradores* also managed at times to insist that they should inspect the royal accounts of expenditure, and grant taxes on condition that they were only used for specific purposes.

The powers of the *cortes* in the spheres of legislation and finance, therefore, gave expression to the current of thought contained in the maxim 'what concerns all, ought to be approved by all' (*quod omnes tangit*). The principle was to be carried still further towards the end of the fourteenth century during the reign of John I. Following the disastrous defeat of Castilian arms at the battle of Aljubarrota in 1385, the king acted to allay allegations that he made decisions without consulting the members of his council. In the *cortes* of 1385 a council of twelve members was created consisting of four prelates, four nobles and four men from the third estate. This council was to co-operate in the exercise of some of the royal powers, which meant that a representative body would reside continually at court and participate in the work of government. It was an ideal which the chancellor and poet, Pero López de Ayala, expressed in simple terms:

And let there come to the council with the king,
Prelates, *caballeros*, doctors and *letrados*,
And good men from the towns, for many of them are honourable.
Since these matters affect all, let them all be summoned.[56]

It seemed, therefore, as if the *cortes* would place lasting and practical limits to royal power. But, after the end of the Lancastrian threat to Castile, the conciliar experiment collapsed, and with the systematic assertion of absolutist royal policies the influence of the *cortes* drastically declined. The explanation for this decline lies partly in the control which the Crown exercised over *cortes* procedure. There were no regular meetings, and the summoning of the *cortes* was completely dependent on the will of the king. Once the *cortes* were in session, the Crown and the royal *letrados* controlled the activities of the *procuradores*. In practice, this meant that the latter agreed to taxes and then presented their petitions to the king; and since there was no redress of grievances before supply, the royal replies to the petitions were often vague and evasive.

From the reign of John II the *cortes* also ceased to be representative assemblies in any meaningful sense. The attendance of the first and second estates was limited since the king only summoned those individuals whom he wished should attend; the work of the *cortes* did not directly affect the tax-exempt clergy and nobility, and the latter focused their attention on court politics and lost interest in the *cortes*. Consequently, the participation of the nobility and clergy in the *cortes* tended to be restricted to those who were court officials and members of the royal council, or who happened to be at court when the *cortes* met. Several meetings of the *cortes* in the fifteenth century were little more than assemblies consisting of royal officials and representatives of the third estate.

The representative character of the *procuradores* of the third estate also declined. The 'election' of *procuradores* during the fifteenth century was controlled by the 'closed' town councils or the monarchy. When the urban oligarchs controlled elections they naturally sent two of their own number to the *cortes;* but from the second decade of the century, and especially during Alvaro de Luna's period of power, the Crown sometimes intervened and directly nominated the individuals who were to be *procuradores*. Naturally the king nominated those whom he trusted, and since royal officials were frequently rewarded with offices in urban government, they could be chosen as representatives for the third estate.

Procuradores drawn from the ranks of the patrician oligarchies or from royal office-holders were hardly likely to oppose the monarchy in the *cortes*. Their independence was weakened still further when, from the second decade of the century, the Crown began to pay for their expenses in attending the *cortes*. This dependence on the monarchy was accompanied by a renewed emphasis on social status. Attempts were made to elimiate 'men of small account' from the *cortes*, and the *procuradores* of the third estate were frequently referred to as *caballeros* or *hidalgos* – terms which reflected their noble status within the urban oligarchies.

The 'representative' nature of the third estate was rendered even less of a reality by the fact that for most of the fifteenth century only seventeen towns sent representatives, and even then the king did not always summon all of them for any particular meeting. Moreover, all these towns were on Crown lands since all those situated in noble or ecclesiastical lordships theoretically had their interests represented by members of the first and second estates. In practice, therefore, the *cortes* were small assemblies of some thirty representatives of a limited number of towns who met together with the 'court' – that is, with those nobles, ecclesiastics and *letrados* who were court officials or members of the royal council.

In these circumstances the *cortes* certainly could not provide an effective check on the monarchy. It is true that the king specified that laws formulated by virtue of his absolute royal power should be observed 'as if they had been made in the *cortes*'. Yet this was a minor concession to the once prevalent principle whereby the king and the cortes legislated together. The consent of the *cortes* was still necessary for the imposition of some taxes, but this consent was invariably granted, the petitions of the *procuradores* were given inadequate attention and, as we have seen, the greatest source of royal income, the *alcabala*, escaped the control of the *cortes* from the late fourteenth century onwards. The very weakness of the *cortes* explains the sometimes bewildering changes of attitude displayed by the *procuradores* towards royal policies: since the machinery and procedure of the *cortes* was controlled by the Crown, changes in the balance of power at court were reflected in the *cortes* petitions.

The decline of the *cortes* accelerated the tendency of the great nobility to concentrate on the politics of the royal court in the hope of influencing the process of government. Wherever the king travelled, he was accompanied by important civil servants such as the royal secretaries, *contadores mayores* and chancery officials. These men, helped by their clerks, had an intimate knowledge of the workings of government: they provided the information on which decisions were based and saw to it that orders were drawn up, recorded and expedited. Yet they were only administrators and they hardly played an active part in the struggles between political factions. Despite frequent changes of power at court, many of these civil servants retained their offices and continued with their administrative duties. For example, John II's secretary, Fernán Díaz de Toledo, served the king throughout most of his troubled reign and, relatively speaking, played as important a role in government as the great secretaries of the sixteenth century did in the Spain of Charles V. It was not at the level of the civil servants but rather at that of the royal council that the important political changes of fortune occurred.

Unlike the *cortes*, royal councils functioned regularly, and as a result of reforms and experiments several types of councils came into existence at various points during the later medieval period: a royal council proper, which helped the king to exericse political power, a council of justice, a 'secret' council, and even an embryonic council for the military orders. These experiments pointed the way to the conciliar system of government which was to be so typical of Spain in the early modern period. Indeed, although it is generally argued that the Catholic Kings reformed the royal council in the *cortes* of Toledo of 1480 and made it the corner-stone of their governmental system, they repeated the substance of previous ordinances, which stretched back to the late fourteenth century, and even quoted them almost word for word.

There were sound reasons for the growing importance of councils in central government. The increasing complexities of administration and the burdens of routine work, for example, were met by the creation of *ad hoc* meetings of only a few councillors, or by the creation of rather more formal conciliar variants such as the council of justice. But in matters of political importance, the natural tendency of kings to consult men of their own choice – their 'favourites' – was challenged by attempts to control the monarchy by means of the council. Formalisation of conciliar procedures carried the implication that the council gave proper and collective advice to the king as against the incompetent advice of favourites. But when a king such as John II created hundreds of 'councillors' and accepted or rejected advice arbitrarily, control of the council by the great nobility became an extremely difficult undertaking. Attempts were made by noble factions to specify the membership of the council in detail and to restrict it in size to some ten or fifteen councillors, in order to avoid losing the fruits of political success between powerless honorific councils, on the one hand, and 'inner' councils on the other. This problem of membership was also linked to attempts to curtail royal independence and increase the powers of the council. In 1442, for example, the Aragonese party, being temporarily victorious at court, prohibited the implementation of any royal decisions save those adopted in council and duly recorded in a special register. But these and other similar measures were, in the last analysis, effective only as long as the realities of political power made control of the council feasible. Without a broader basis, such as could have been provided by constitutional arrangements brought forward in the *cortes*, the power of noble factions tended to collapse rapidly and to give way once again to a monarchical rule whereby an 'absolute' king chose his councillors freely.

The key royal officials in regional and territorial administration during the thirteenth century were the *adelantados mayores* and the *merinos mayores*. The former emerged as the more powerful officials during the later middle ages. The geographical circumscriptions of these officials' areas at times overlapped in Castile, León and Galicia, but only *adelantados mayores* were to be found in the sensitive regions along the Moorish frontier, and unlike the *merinos mayores* they wre invested with important military powers. However, there was a tendency for the office to become attached to particular families, and *adelantados mayores* frequently served regional and family interests to the detriment of royal authority. During the fifteenth century, for example, there were long periods of time when, for all practical purposes, the royal administration ceased to operate in a Murcia which was ruled independently by the *adelantados mayores* of the Fajardo family. It is not surprising, therefore, that fifteenth-century monarchs sometimes gave wide powers to specific individuals in order to impose the royal will on territorial officials. For a time in the 1430s, for example, Alvaro de Luna acted as the king's *alter ego* in Andalusia, and the term 'viceroy' actually came into existence during Henry IV's reign: in the midst of the anarchy of the 1460s Pedro Girón stated in his letters that he acted as 'viceroy, appointed and deputed by his highness, for the whole of Andalusia'.[57] These were, however, isolated experiments in territorial administration, and they stand in sharp contrast to the relatively successful way in which the monarchy dealt with analogous problems in the towns.

During the course of the twelfth and thirteenth centuries the 'open' council of citizens (*vecinos*) was superseded by a smaller council made up of *caballeros* and more affluent townsmen. Subsequently the municipal council became a closed corporation which was known variously as the *cabildo, ayuntamiento* and *regimiento*. In the Andalusian towns this development took place on the morrow of the reconquest and there was no tradition of general assemblies of inhabitants. In the central and northern towns, on the other hand, the monarchy had to intervene actively in order to ensure the establishment of closed corporations or *regimientos*. From 1345 onwards, Alfonso XI decreed that in towns such as Burgos, León, Segovia and Madrid the assembly of *vecinos* should be replaced by a fixed body of *hombres buenos* or *regidores* (aldermen). These *regidores* were to be appointed by the Crown, and the magistrates and officials, who had traditionally been elected, were henceforth to be appointed by the *regidores*. Thus officials were no longer elected but appointed by a closed corporation controlled by the king. The number of *regidores* varied from town to town: in many Andalusian towns there were twenty-four, whereas in some of the northern towns there were sometimes as few as eight or ten. Frequently, *regidores* were designated in terms of the number constituting the *cabildo* or *ayuntamiento* – the *regidores* of Seville, for example, were known as *veinticuatros* ('twenty-fours').

Alfonso XI's centralising policy in the towns was probably prompted by a desire to eradicate instability and maladministration, but in the long run the same problems reappeared in a different guise. By the end of the fourteenth century practical control of urban government lay with the *cabildo* oligarchies rather than with the Crown. In theory the *regidores* were appointed by the Crown, but in practice, once an office was vacant, the king confirmed the man designated by the *cabildo*. In this way the office of *regidor* came to be regarded as part of the property of its holder which could be passed on to other members of the family. Moreover, since great social prestige was attached to the position of *regidor*, a clandestine trade in offices developed during the fifteenth century. Indeed, the monarchy itself abused the system by the occasional appointment of extra *regidores*, whose salaries were paid by the *ayuntamientos*, in order to reward deserving royal officials. The result was an inflation of offices: in Seville, for example, there were thirty-five 'twenty-fours' by the mid-fifteenth century. Intermarriage, royal favour, and the sale of offices on a limited scale meant that access to the urban oligarchies was not completely closed to those with money, influence and an appropriate life-style. Consequently, since many *converso* families gained access to the oligarchies, the explosive issue of anti-semitism became firmly linked to the rivalries of political factions and the all too frequent charges of corruption within the *ayunta-mientos* (below, pp. 183–6). The establishment of closed corpora-tions, in short, did not remove the problems of maladministration and instability.

For dealing with urban problems the Crown possessed ideal agents in the royal *corregidores*. Historians often stress the fact that in 1480 the Catholic Kings installed *corregidores* in all the *cabildos* of the principal towns. The *corregidores*, however, first appeared as early as 1348, and even then they formed part of a tradition whereby, from at least the second half of the thirteenth century, royal officials known as *pesquisidores* were sent to restore law and order in the towns. The *corregidores* were in theory dispatched at the invitation of the towns, but in practice the Crown often sent them without any prior consultation. Initially a *corregidor* was appointed on a tem-porary basis, and his salary was paid by the *cabildo*; in practice, he sometimes stayed for several years, and when he left he was often replaced by another *corregidor*. The use of *corregidores* – and they were used fairly extensively by Henry III and John II – aroused hostility in the towns. They were not usually natives of the areas in which they worked, and their intrusion in urban government was backed up by vague and almost limitless powers bestowed on them by the Crown. When his term of office expired, the fifteenth-century *corregidor* was in theory liable to have his activities subjected to a judicial investigation (*residencia*) by the Crown. The *corregidor* and the *residencia* are fitting subjects with which to close this brief survey of Castilian governmental institutions, for like so many other institutions they were to be carried over into the modern period in both Spain and Hispanic America.

Contributions by the Crown of Aragon

IN Castile the development of absolutism was accompanied by major innovations in monarchical institutions, but in the Crown of Aragon the pactist constitutional structure ensured that the royal court was less important as the focal point for change. Reforms were implemented in the royal administration, especially with regard to the problem of 'absentee monarchy', but the major changes took place in the power bases outside the royal court.

In 1344 Peter IV drew up the famous *Ordinacions de cort* which, drawing on earlier reforms, detailed the administrative structure of the royal central administration. Apart from the great household officials, such as the *mayordomo* and the chamberlain, the most important posts were those of the *maestre racional* and the chancellor. The office of *maestre racional* came into existence in the late thirteenth century, and it subsequently became the principal position in a financial administration which included a staff of treasurers and clerks. In 1419 an additional office of *maestre racional* was created specifically for the increasingly important royal patrimonies in the kingdom of Valencia. Below the level of the central administration, Catalonia, Valencia and Aragon each constituted a separate financial administrative unit in which the royal finances were administered by a *battle general*.

Apart from controlling the chancery, the chancellor was also entrusted with presiding over the royal council and heading a special *curia* or *tribunal* which came into existence during the reign of Peter IV as a final court of appeal, and which included officials representing each state of the Aragonese federation.

These reforms in central institutions were overshadowed by innovations in territorial administration which culminated in the appearance of an official – the viceroy – who was to play a leading part in the government of the Spanish Empire. From the mid-thirteenth century the Crown delegated some of its powers in each of the states of the federation to *procuradores* or *gerenti vices*. From the early fourteenth century these limited powers were bestowed on one *procurador general*, whose title changed during the course of the century to that of governor-general and whose powers were in turn exercised by the *gerenti vices* in the various states of the federation. None of these officials acted as 'substitutes' for the monarch, and indeed the governor-general continued to exercise his functions even if the king was not absent. But from the late fourteenth century the problem of royal absenteeism led to the appearance of officials, known as lieutenants-general or viceroys, in Sardinia, Sicily and Mallorca – a pattern which was repeated with respect to Catalonia, Aragon and Valencia as a result of Alfonso V's almost permanent absence in Italy. The lieutenant-general or viceroy was the king's *alter-ego*, and he assumed a full delegation of royal powers during the monarch's absence. Both this office and that of governor-general were usually held by members of the royal family – sometimes, indeed, by one and the same person. But the 'limited' office of governor-general tended to become increasingly honorific, and the viceroyalty emerged as the outstanding office of territorial administration. We have seen that the title of viceroy was occasionally used in Castile during Henry IV's reign, but in the Crown of Aragon it was an established institution, and it served purposes which made it eminently suitable for adaptation in the different context of the Spanish Empire.

The monarch and his lieutenants-general found themselves enmeshed and limited in their freedom of action by the governmental structures and institutions of each of the semi-autonomous states of the Aragonese federation. Despite the royal victories of Peter IV over the nobility, and of John II over the Catalans, these autonomous institutions developed even further, and gained new and important powers. In Aragon proper, for example, Peter IV's victory over the *unión aragonesa* led to an increase in the powers of the *justicia*. The latter, as we have seen, emerged as the champion of the nobility's interests as enshrined in the *fueros* (above, p. 114). He was protected against any kind of intimidation by the monarchy and, by the mid-fifteenth century, his appointment was for life. He was an 'ombudsman' with sufficient powers to protect subjects and the law from abuses by the monarchy.

By the end of the thirteenth century the various *cortes* of the Aragonese federation had already acquired much greater powers than those in Castile (above, pp. 114–16). Both the Crown and the *cortes* could initiate legislation, but the consent of the *cortes* was necessary for all laws, and the grievances of the estates had to be redressed before the voting of financial aid to the Crown. Many of these grievances inevitably concerned the actions of the king or his officials in contravening the customs and laws of each region: for example, they might deal with the violation of privileges and immunities by the governor-general, or the use by the lieutant-general of councillors who were not natives of the state in question. Such grievances were often dealt with quickly and efficiently by the Crown, but occasionally a complicated problem could hold up proceedings for months. Two examples from the *cortes* of Barcelona of

1454–8 will help to illustrate the extent to which real or imaginary grievances could cripple the monarchy's freedom of action.

Among the grievances occupying more than twenty folio pages of the printed record of the *cortes* of Barcelona, the problem of the appointment of Galcerán de Requesens as lieutenant-general of Catalonia in 1453 figures prominently. According to the Catalan *cortes* this appointment was illegal because only a member of the royal family could hold such an exalted office. Alfonso V immediately acknowledged that this grievance was legitimate, and Requesens was reappointed to the more limited office of governor-general. But he had already been lieutenant-general for six months, and the *cortes* claimed that all the acts of his 'rule' were illegal. In fact, the illegality of Requesens's appointment was a pretext for challenging the authority of the Crown on other vital issues, such as the nature of the town government of Barcelona, and the whole dispute formed part of a serious constitutional crisis.

When, in 1453, the king and Requesens helped to oust the oligarchical party of the *Biga* from the town government of Barcelona, the members of the *cortes* were for long bitterly divided on the issue of whether or not to accept the representatives sent to the *cortes* by the new 'popular' regime of the *Busca*. In Catalonia great importance was attached to the fact that the monarchy had no control over the elections of the representatives of the third estate. Since the new council of Barcelona owed its existence to royal backing and intervention, were the representatives sent to the *cortes* not royal officials? Would the presence of these men in the *cortes* not mean that the king was reaching agreements with himself and that pactism no longer existed?

The problem of the legality of Requesens's actions as lieutenant-general, therefore, involved other issues of great importance. As a result the king had to wait one-and-a-half years for the 400,000 florins which the *cortes* had been asked to vote, and even then only an interim compromise was arranged whereby the grant was payable on condition that the monarchy fulfilled certain specific demands.

In between meetings of the *cortes* the king and his officials had to contend with the Catalan *Generalitat* (above, pp. 116–17). The powers of this institution grew substantially after the accession of Ferdinand of Antequera to the throne of the Aragonese federation in 1412: men were not slow to grasp the opportunities provided by the advent of a new dynasty, as well as by the prolonged absences abroad of Ferdinand's successor, Alfonso V. The *Generalitat* already controlled the collection of subsidies granted to the monarchy, and in the 1420s it also established itself as virtually the sole authority charged with the task of ensuring that the laws and liberties of Catalonia were observed and respected. The *Generalitat* interpreted the decisions of the *cortes* and judged disputes between Catalans and royal officials. Both its legal and financial powers implied a strict control over the way in which royal authority was used, and inevitably its bureaucracy grew enormously. From 1413 it maintained its own reserve fund, and for all practical purposes it acted as the treasury of the principality of Catalonia. Since the *cortes* and the *Generalitat* already had the task of collecting the extraordinary taxes, such as the *monedaje* and *bovatge*, they also took over the administration of the customs duties and the *bolla* tax on textiles. In this way, revenues which would have constituted royal taxes in Castile became the income or *generalidades* of the *Generalitat*. Indeed, so sophisticated did this financial administration become that floating debts were set up, and *Generalitat* bonds were issued to buyers whose capital investment yielded them regular payments in the form of a *censo* at a fixed rate of interest.

Pactist institutions, such as the *cortes*, the *Generalitat* and the *justicia* of Aragon, survived into the modern period to give 'united' Spain its unique and uneasy combination of the absolutism of Castile and the constitutionalism of the Crown of Aragon.

Apart from the office of viceroy, only one other institution of major importance was exported to the Castilian part of Spain and its Empire. This was the 'consulate of the sea' (*consulado del mar*). The name was first applied to the association of merchants and shipmasters of Valencia in 1283, but although the Barcelona association or *universidad* did not receive a similar title until 1347, the institution had existed there from the 1250s. The *consulados* of Barcelona and Valencia defended the interests of their members, intervened in judicial matters affecting trade, and created an important and influential body of commercial law.

The later Middle Ages witnessed the spread of the institution to other coastal and inland towns such as Gerona, Perpignan and Tortosa. In Barcelona the birth and existence of the *consulado* was closely linked to the urban oligarchy, whose members appointed the two chief executive officials or *cónsules*. In most cases, however, the members of the *consulados* were free to elect their own officials.

Thus, the *consulado* was an autonomous institution which combined the characteristics of a professional guild of merchants, regulating and encouraging trade, with those of a special tribunal with powers to deal with disputes arising from maritime commerce. From its inception the jurisdiction of the *consulado* extended to the chartering and freighting of ships, maritime insurance, seamen's pay and other related problems. In 1380 the Crown excluded all mercantile–maritime cases from the competence of the royal courts and granted complete jurisdiction to the *consulados*. The tribunals of the *consulados*, staffed by *cónsules*, members, *letrados* and clerks, dispensed rapid and effective justice in accordance with legal customs which, drawn from diverse sources, such as the thirteenth-century 'Customs of the Sea' (*Costums de la mar*), were codified towards the middle of the fourteenth century in the *Llibre del consolat de mar*.

The advantages of the *consulado* system not only ensured its continuity – in Barcelona it lasted down to the early nineteenth century – but also led merchant groups to demand the creation of similar institutions in Castile. In 1494 the wool merchants of the important Burgos guild obtained a *consulado*, and in 1503 the famous 'House of Trade' (*Casa de Contratación*) was set up in Seville for commercial operations with the New World. By the eighteenth century another dozen *consulados* had come into existence. If pactism made little impression on the centralised government and noble-dominated society of Castile, Spain still benefited from the Aragonese federation's long experience in dealing with the problems of monarchical absenteeism and the regulation of mercantile interests.

8. Economic Problems and Social Unrest

Contrasting Economic Fortunes

THE Black Death, which struck Spain in 1348, and the economic recession of the second half of the fourteenth century, affected the states of Iberia in different ways. Like other Mediterranean areas, such as Genoa and Portugal, which were to lead the way in the age of discoveries, Castile recovered fairly quickly from the crisis. In the Crown of Aragon, on the other hand, although Valencia enjoyed a period of economic prosperity in the fifteenth century, the heart of the federation, Catalonia, faltered and declined.

The decline of Catalonia was undoubtedly linked to demographic crisis. From the Black Death down to the end of the fifteenth century, recurring outbreaks of plague resulted in an over-all drop of population. Already betweeen the mid-thirteenth and mid-fourteenth centuries, population growth had been absorbed by emigration into the reconquered areas of Valencia, Mallorca and Murcia, and by Aragonese expansion into Sicily and Sardinia. The total population of Catalonia, which was in the region of 450,000 in 1348, declined by almost 40 per cent to a total of 278,000 in 1497. The decline for Barcelona itself was worse – 50,000 in 1340, 38,000 in 1359, 20,000 in 1477 and 28,500 in 1497. In general terms the population of the Crown of Aragon in the early fifteenth century was less than one million – compared with a Castile of some 5 million and a France of 16 million inhabitants.

In the early fourteenth century the Catalan trading empire was at its height. The route of the islands still pointed to the spices of Alexandria which, purchased with the gold obtained in North Africa from tribute money and the sale of coral, textile and metal artefacts, were then distributed round the Mediterranean. A textile industry in Barcelona found flourishing export markets in Sardinia, Sicily and North Africa. It was an age of vigorous expansion in which, despite papal prohibitions, trade with the infidel not only flourished but was encouraged by the absolutions which could be purchased from a special royal–ecclesiastical tribunal. By the late fourteenth century, however, a decline in trade had set in. Excluded from the Atlantic markets of Europe and Africa, and faced with fierce Genoese competition, Catalan trade was increasingly confined to the western Mediterranean, and was subjected to the dictates of commercial protectionism and political imperialism. The rhythm of the decline in trade varied. In Mallorca, where only four out of a hundred merchant companies survived after 1362, the decline was complete by the end of the fourteenth century. In Catalonia there was a five-fold decline of trade in the port of Barcelona between the mid-fourteenth and mid-fifteenth centuries, but the sharpest period of this decline was after 1425. Only Valencian trade prospered in the fifteenth century, and this was due to a large extent to the fact that the Genoese used the port on the Atlantic run and loaded on cargoes of valuable commodities.

From 1350 the beginnings of economic and demographic decline were accompanied by a financial insecurity which affected the great merchants and bankers of Catalonia. Already, during the reign of Peter the Ceremonius (1336–87), they found investment in urban and royal politics more profitable than investment in trade. Between 1381 and 1383 the major private banks in Barcelona, Gerona and Perpignan collapsed as a result of their commitments to government finance at a time when expansion in population, taxation and trade had ended. After the failure of the powerful Gualbes bank Barcelona lacked any private banks of substance, and as the monarchy and the urban oligarchy drifted further apart, the former turned to Italian financiers for the money it needed. The businessmen and merchants of Barcelona, for their part, solved the worst of their problems by founding the famous deposit bank of the *Taula de Canvi* in 1401. This measure, later imitated in Valencia and Gerona, was related to the need to solve the problems posed by the growth of urban public debts: the municipal taxes of Barcelona, for example, became steadily less profitable and the arrears multiplied. It was a situation which reflected the economic and demographic crisis, and was by no means confined to the municipalities: the revenues of the Catalan *Generalitat*, for example, fell by over 25 per cent in the decade prior to 1425. The *Taula de Canvi* was not a business company but an institution charged with managing the town's public debt and acting as a bank of deposit. Those who invested in it received a fixed interest which, given the manifest insecurity of the economy by the 1420s, proved more attractive than risky investments in trade. The adventurous *entrepreneurs* of a former age were being replaced by *rentiers* whose main desire was to be cautious and immobilise their capital. As *rentiers* they resisted any measures of monetary reform which would threaten the value of their fixed incomes.

The problem of the coinage is important to an understanding of the Catalan economic crisis. In 1346, almost a hundred years after the Florentines first minted their celebrated florin, the gold florin was introduced by Peter IV into his realms. But, whereas the minting of gold coins in Italy corresponded to a favourable trade balance with North Africa and the Levant, the introduction of the Aragonese florin in the mid-fourteenth century came at a time when economic decline was about to set in and a strong balance of payments was impossible because of the stagnation of trade and increased military expenditure. By 1365, therefore, the gold content of the florin had already dropped by 25 per cent, and in the resulting crisis of confidence in the new coin the Catalans turned to the silver *croat* which had symbolised their financial prestige and power in the previous two centuries. The stability of the *croat* was regarded by the oligarchy of Barcelona as being essential for the protection of their *rentier* incomes, and for this reason they bitterly resisted all attempts at devaluation. But, quite apart from the possibly beneficial effects of devaluation on Catalan exports, the crux of the monetary problem was that the silver *croat* was seriously undervalued in terms of gold. Indeed, both the gold florin and the silver *croat* tended to disappear from circulation, and as exports declined more and more gold and silver flowed out of the country. But the problem was more serious for silver because the bimetallic ratio in Catalonia (1:13) was out of step with the rest of Europe (average 1:10·5), and this difference encouraged the flight of silver. During the first half of the fifteenth century attempts to rectify this situation were partially successful, but by mid-century the *croat* and the florin were once again under severe pressure.

In these circumstances the issue of monetary reform assumed serious proportions in Barcelona. To maintain the value of the *croat* and the florin it was necessary to carry out a drastic retrenchment in public and foreign expenditure, or achieve a clear surplus in the balance of trade. Neither of these solutions was possible by 1450. The *Busca*, or popular party, demanded devaluation in the belief that this would halt the outward flow of silver and stimulate a revival in trade. The *Biga*, or oligarchical party, opposed devaluation in order to safeguard their *rentier* income. In the event, when devaluation was finally introduced in 1456, it was too late to have any appreciable effects in halting economic decline. It did, however, contribute to the political crisis which flared up into civil war in 1462. By this time the principality faced economic ruin, and Valencia, which almost doubled its population during the course of the fifteenth century, replaced Barcelona as the financial capital of the Crown of Aragon.

The little evidence that exists for population trends in Castile suggests a relative vitality which contrasted with the depressing experience of Catalonia. Castile, of course, did not escape either the ravages of the Black Death of 1348, or the resulting preoccupations with labour and wage problems which affected the public authorities in most European countries. But despite recurring outbreaks of plague in 1363, 1367 and 1374, losses appear to have been quickly made up, and there was even a moderate expansion of the total population in the century and a half after the Black Death. Unlike the other areas of Europe, the period immediately prior to the plague pandemic in Castile was not one in which landed resources were strained to the limit as population expansion came up against barriers of production. Indeed, the symptoms of such a situation did not manifest themselves until the late fifteenth century. By this time a combination of population expansion and continuing migration to the south meant that towns of the centre and north, such as Burgos (10,000 inhabitants) and Valladolid (25,000), had been out-stripped by southern towns such as Seville (75,000) and Córdoba (35,000). Moreover, the effects of the growth of sheep- and cattle-ranching, which hindered the development of grain production and resulted in a scarcity of cereal-producing land, were particularly felt in Extremadura and western Andalusia, and they help to account for the extensive emigration from these areas to the Indies.

In general terms late medieval Castile continued to be a relatively underpopulated country in which pastoralism predominated. Wool was the most valuable export, and the rapid growth in sheep-farming was stimulated by the advantages of organised trans-humance between summer and winter pastures, by the foreign demand for the wool of the *merino* sheep, by a shortage of manpower, and by the protection and favour which the Crown afforded to the *Mesta* (above, pp. 74–5). By 1480 the total stock had grown to some five million sheep. The principal market was Flanders, although wool was also exported to France and Italy. Burgos, at the centre of the communications network to the ports of the north coast, was the wool capital of Castile. Organised at first as a religious confraternity, the wool exporters of Burgos formed a guild towards the end of the fourteenth century, and within fifty years they had a prior and two consuls whose main tasks were to solve disputes and ensure the efficiency of the export trade. Wool merchants from Toledo, Segovia, Soria, Logroño and other towns further south belonged to the guild, and its officials arranged for shipping contracts, the insurance of cargoes, and the dates of sailing.

Although Castilian sheep were introduced into the New World, the colonial wool industry was limited in scale, and production was for local consumption. The cattle-ranching practices of late medieval Castile, on the other hand, came to dominate large areas of the New World from Mexico to the Argentine *pampas*. Throughout medieval Europe cattle tended either to be one of several elements in a manorial economy geared primarily to crop production, or to be raised on small dairy farms. It is hardly surprising, therefore, that Iberian ranching practices attracted the attention of foreign visitors. 'In Spain and Portugal', according to a German who accompanied Leo of Rozmital to Spain, 'the beasts are not fed in stalls as in other countries, but they mark them with the sign of the owner and leave them in the wilderness.'[58] Thus, real ranching, defined by Bishko as 'the ranging of cattle in considerable numbers over extensive grazing grounds for the primary purpose of large-scale production of beef and hides',[59] was a peculiarly Iberian activity. Ranching was already established by the twelfth century, and like sheep-herding it developed in the grass-lands of New Castile and Extremadura. But it was only in Andalusia that cattle-ranching became a predominating concern in agricultural life. The result was that, although Castilians were increasingly subjected to shortages in supplies of grain, they certainly enjoyed an abundance of meat. Calculating on a basis of 180 meat-days per year, the financial expert Profet el Naçi, whose schemes for economic reforms showed a remarkable statistical accuracy, argued that there was no Castilian household which did not spend an average of at least 5 *mrs* on meat for each such day – thus giving an annual meat consumption which was the equivalent of one cow and eight smaller animals.

Castile, *tierra de bravos toros*, had a special breed of cattle which, being wilder and stronger than other European breeds and of little use for dairy purposes, were invaluable for their beef and tough hides. They flourished, along with unbranded wild cattle, on the open range and in a ranching economy characterised by branding, round-ups, and a mobile control imposed by the horse and the cow-boy or *vaquero*. The latter hired himself out with his horse on a yearly basis, and along with other *vaqueros* he tended the herds under the orders of a foreman or *mayoral*. This background helps to explain the increasing popularity of bullfights. By the later Middle Ages towns such as Seville celebrated any news of importance – for example, a birth in the royal family – with a bullfight. The Bohemian, Leo of Rozmital, and his companions were entertained in this way more than once:

> The Bishop [of Salamanca] showed my lord great honour and sent everything that we needed to the inn. His counts, knights and pages, the mightiest in the town, prepared an entertainment for my lord. They brought wild oxen and hunted them in the market place, sitting on their jenets (very swift horses) and shot the lances which they carried into the oxen, and he who aimed best and shot the most lances was the winner. These so enraged the oxen that they charged the men and struck them. On that day two were carried away as dead men. After the baiting was finished the men attacked each other and shot with their little spears, defend-ing themselves with their shields, or catching them as the heathen are accustomed to do when they fight. In all my days I have never seen more agile horses or men. They ride very short with their knees drawn up to the saddle like the heathen. My lord and I were in a house with certain burghers and looked on. We had beautiful women with us and drank and ate and lived well.[60]

The growth of trade in Castile resulted in a 'colonial' economic structure characterised by the sale abroad of raw materials, the most important of which was wool. Basque iron manufacturers and the Seville soap industry also provided valuable export com-modities, but economic growth did not entail a significant expansion in the production of finished products. Thus, despite the increase in wool production and the fact that cloth manufacturing was the most important Castilian industry, considerable amounts of cloth were imported from England, France and Flanders. Another weak-ness of the economy was the absence of a powerful mercantile class. The merchants of Burgos, it is true, began to expand into all kinds of business from Andalusian olive oil to the running of the royal minting houses, and the northern shippers, organised into their own *hermandad,* were active in all the Atlantic ports and made their presence felt in the Mediterranean. Yet only in a few cases did these merchants and shippers exercise significant political control over the towns of the kingdom, and economic expansion did not secure for them the same kind of socio-political domination which the merchant class of Barcelona enjoyed. The real problem was that the worlds of government, finance and trade were not properly integrated one with another. The Castilian financier, usually a Jew or a *converso,* was not often a merchant except at a local level. The result was that financiers raised capital for the lucrative business of farming royal and municipal taxes, but they did not make extensive use of bills of exchange or deposit and transfer banks. Few Castilian merchants, for their part, moved easily in government circles at either the royal or the urban level. Capital was raised with difficulty, and inter-regional and international transactions were settled by cumbersome methods at the Castilian fairs, the most famous of which was that held at Medina del Campo. The duration of fairs was limited, and this lack of a permanent financial and banking centre could only act as a hindrance to the growth of a strong mercantile class.

A chronic history of monetary instability also did little to help the development of capital and credit operations. After his victory over Peter the Cruel, Henry of Trastámara debased the coinage to such an extent that devaluation of the money of account, the *maravedí,* led to an inflationary spiral in nominal prices. In the 1380s John I again debased the coinage in order to pay for his wars against Lancaster and the Portuguese. In the fifteenth century debasement was particularly frequent from the 1450s and resulted in a state of monetary anarchy. Indeed, in the 1460s private as well as royal mints were operating, and the lure of quick profits inevitably led to such a rate of debasement that the monetary problem was one of the main factors contributing to the anarchy of Henry IV's reign. (See Graph, p. xviii.)

With its raw materials much in demand elsewhere in Europe, such an undercommercialised society was bound to attract the interest of more sophisticated merchant and banking *entrepreneurs.* The economy of Andalusia proved particularly attractive to a wide variety of foreign merchants among whom the Genoese became predominant. Genoese activity in the kingdom of Castile dated from at least the twelfth century, but it was only after the reconquest of the south that it began to play an important role. Based on a special quarter of Seville, the *barrio de Génova*, the Genoese entrenched themselves firmly in such important centres as Cádiz, Puerto de Santa María, Granada and Málaga, and converted the south of the peninsula into a 'colony' of their economic empire. The south had a wide variety of goods to offer foreign markets – olive oil, the wines of Jerez, fruit, tunny fish from the southern *almadrabas*, soap, leather and mercury from the mines of Almadén. But the south also provided a further base in the Genoese westward push from the Mediterranean out towards the Atlantic – a movement which, by deflecting Iberian energies in the same direction and fusing the Italian heritage of commercial endeavour with that of the *conquistadores*, made possible that age of exploration and expansion which culminated in the discovery of the New World. By the second half of the fifteenth century the southern ports of Iberia were already dealing with valuable re-exports from the Atlantic islands and the west-African coast. Early in the century, for example, the Genoese introduced sugar cultivation into the Algarve, and from there it spread to Madeira and the Canary islands before being introduced – by the Genoese again – into the islands of the Caribbean during the sixteenth century. The Canary islands also supplied the *entrepreneurs* of Seville with cochineal, orchil and Guanche slaves. For their part, the Portuguese, pushing along the Atlantic coast of Africa, not only controlled a larger volume of slave traffic but gained direct access to the gold supplies which had previously filtered through to the Iberian and European economies by the trans-Saharan trade routes.

The banking, exchange and trading negotiations in Seville – the economic capital of Andalusia – all centred round the cathedral in the Santa María district. It was here, in the *calle de las Gradas*, that the *lonja* was situated. The *lonja* was the meeting-place of bankers and merchants, and it was typical of Mediterranean areas such as Catalonia, Valencia, Genoa and Venice. The *lonja* of Seville was, in effect, similar to the Rialto of Venice. Each day the merchants met to transact business. Near at hand – mainly in the significantly named *calle de Génova* – the bankers put into effect the transfers necessitated by the deals concluded. The proximity of merchants and bankers in the *lonja* obviously facilitated trade to an enormous extent. It also reflected the fact that most Genoese tended to combine finance and banking with their far-flung trade connections. The

Genoese family of the Centurione, for example, who were extremely
active in Andalusian trade, owned the largest bank in Genoa and
were active in Lisbon. Christopher Columbus was working for the
Centurione of Lisbon in 1478 and was sent by them to purchase
sugar in Madeira.

Of course, the Genoese by no means monopolised economic or
maritime enterprise. Political control of the Indies venture was
vested in the Castilian monarchy, and when Columbus prepared for
his first voyage he was helped by Andalusian and Basque sailors.
As one historian has argued, the Genoese–Castilian relationship can
almost be seen as a *commenda* arrangement: the Genoese supplied
the capital and the sophisticated business techniques, and the
Castilians provided the sailors and men to play the active role in
discovery and the search for 'booty capitalism'. Once Columbus
landed in the New World, so the story goes, he praised God and
enquired urgently after gold.

Social Change and Unrest

ACCORDING to the chronicler Fernán Pérez de Guzmán:

> [Alvaro de Luna] made the king [John II] carry out many and
> great executions, imprisonments, expulsions, confiscations of
> wealth, and deaths. In this task he found substantial support
> because, by sharing out among some what he confiscated from
> others, he had plenty of helpers. For the praiseworthy custom
> of the Castilians has reached such a point, that men will consent
> to the imprisonment and death of a friend or relative in order to
> have a share in the booty.[61]

The chronicler's analysis of a society of rapidly changing fortunes,
whose members engaged in civil strife in order to augment their
incomes by any means possible, was not far off the mark, and despite
variations in regional economic trends it is a picture which holds
true for later medieval Spain as a whole. It was an age of rapid social
mobility and one in which some men tried to offset a crisis in their
incomes by struggling for alternative sources of wealth. What were
the factors causing social change and unrest?

There can be no doubt that war itself was a powerful agent for
social change at all levels. Between 1300 and 1480, for example, the
Castilian aristocracy was transformed by the disappearance of the

oldest and most powerful noble families and the advent of new dynasties such as the Velascos, Ayalas, Pachecos, Mendozas and Manriques. Doubtless this transformation was due partly to the fact that some families simply died out, but in many cases the rise and fall of these noble families was determined by the fortunes of war and politics – for example, the ruthless persecutions by Peter the Cruel, the rewards and confiscations resulting from Henry II's victory in 1369, the making and breaking of the great families of Castile by John II and Alvaro de Luna, and the changing fortunes of the civil wars of Henry IV's reign.

When the great Alvaro de Luna himself was ruined by court intrigues and executed in 1453, his downfall became an object-lesson in the vagaries of fortune, and it provided wonderful material for poets and moralists. But, for Fernán Pérez de Guzmán, Luna's fate was by no means unique: 'Many other great and middling men were ruined. For Castile finds it easier to acquire new wealth than to retain wealth already acquired. Often she destroys those whom she herself has raised up.'[62] In fact, what was true of the great nobility was also true of lesser men. Rodrigo de Villandrando, a poor *hidalgo*, gained fame, wealth and titles by his career as a mercenary in the civil wars of France and Castile. Even more striking was the case of the Catalan peasant leader, Francesc Verntallat, who rose from being a mere freeholder to the status of viscount, and whose forebears came to be numbered by a contemporary amongst the companions of Charlemagne. These success stories, however, were outnumbered by the histories of those who came to an obscure end in the feuds and disputes which continually plagued Galicia, the Basque country and northern Catalonia and frequently affected the rest of the peninsula. What fortunes might have awaited the mercenary captain, García Méndez de Badajoz, if a mob in Burgos had not trapped and lynched him to death in 1467?

The root cause of much social unrest lay in the crisis of incomes which affected noble and ecclesiastical lords. As we have seen, Castile had already suffered in previous centuries from an abundance of land and a lack of manpower. Sheep-farming and ranching, of course, moderated the worst effects of such a situation. But demesne exploitation had never been widespread, and by the twelfth century some lords were already changing from a regime of peasant services or wage labour to a systematic leasing out of demesne lands. Even before the Black Death, monasteries such as

Silos and Cardeña were in such a precarious financial position that they had to mortgage their lands in order to cover their losses. The effects of the Black Death were less severe in Castile than elsewhere, but the result was to confirm the trend whereby lords tried to salvage some of their income by granting favourable leases in return for fixed rents. In Catalonia, a similar switch to demesne leasing and fixed incomes was aggravated by the absence of large-scale ranching and pastoralism as alternative forms of exploitation. In Castile, on the other hand, sharp rises in the nominal price movement eroded fixed incomes.

How did lay and ecclesiastical lords react to such a situation? Inevitably, as demesne income and rents dwindled, there was a greater emphasis on seigneurial dues and jurisdiction. This emphasis varied from region to region and took various forms. In Castile, seigneurial revenues tended to be inelastic and subject to diminishing returns. For example, during the period of chronic price inflation running from 1454 to 1466, the seigneurial dues of Pedro de Avila. derived from his lands at Villafranca and Las Navas, actually declined in nominal as well as real value, while the royal tax of the *tercias* in the same areas almost tripled in value. But the fixed income from fairly insignificant dues could be increased if the size of lordships could be enlarged to include more people. Thus, while the important element in royal grants of lordship had originally been the land, the later medieval emphasis was on lordship over people. Lordship, in short, often consisted of a diffuse collection of rights and immunities over widely scattered areas. Indeed, in some remarkable cases the Crown even created lordships over a specified number of 'vassals' first, and once the latter had been located the land on which they lived was incorporated into the grant. In 1453, for example, John II granted 300 vassals to the count of Medinaceli, and a royal official was sent to locate them in the area round Atienza; subsequently, a lordship was created over these 300 vassals and, thereafter, they paid their seigneurial dues to the count of Medinaceli. In general terms, therefore, there was no emphasis on exploitation of landed resources. Instead, a crisis in income could be offset by the acquisition of further lordships and the attached multiplicity of small dues paid by the seigneurial population. The demand for enlarged and new lordships was matched by the evident necessity of the Trastamaran kings to buy political support, and the advent of the new noble dynasties of the later medieval period was accompanied by an almost complete change in the control of lordships.

Only a few privileged or powerful noble families could hope to obtain royal grants to enlarge their lordships substantially and permit the founding of entailed estates (*mayorazgos*). Not surprisingly, therefore, a 'seigneurial reaction' was in evidence at a local level. Occasionally this took the form of a ruthless exploitation of lordship inhabitants. In 1466, for example, the count of Béjar arbitrarily levied contributions on his lands amounting to a total of 633,000 *mrs*. More frequently, however, the nobility usurped the wealth and lands of the towns and monasteries. The number of deserted villages in the lands round Salamanca and Palencia, for example, reflected the depredations of nobles, such as Gómez de Benavides, rather than the effects of the Black Death. Monastic wealth was particularly susceptible to usurpations which were given theoretical justification by *encomiendas* – that is, agreements whereby a noble 'protected' a monastery in return for a share in monastic income. In the 1380s a royal commission discovered that almost all Castilian monasteries were suffering from the imposition of *encomiendas* and that even the king's bastard brother was involved in the protection system.

The scale of seigneurial depredations and the extent of the resulting social unrest varied. Generally speaking, the areas which suffered most were those where alternative sources of income were lacking, where the monarchy was at its weakest both as guardian of the peace and as distributor of pensions and financial rewards, and where the lesser nobility were much thicker on the ground and the size of their lordships was much smaller than elsewhere. A mixture of some or all of these factors helps to explain the constant state of agitation and anarchy which affected northern Catalonia, the Basque provinces and Galicia.

The endless oppressions and acts of banditry perpetrated by the Galician lords on the unfortunate inhabitants of the countryside surrounding their strongholds finally provoked a widespread rebellion in the years 1467–70. The Galician *hermandino* movement was led by some of the lesser nobility but drew its strength from the oppressed population of the countryside and some of the towns. To the cry of 'Long live the king and death to the *caballeros*!', over one hundred noble strongholds were destroyed and their lords forced to flee from Galicia. The triumph of the *hermandinos*, however, was short-lived, and by the end of 1469 the seigneurial forces had broken the rebellion.

The *remensa* movement in Catalonia was of a more complex nature. Towards the close of the thirteenth century, the Catalan *payeses* were already suffering from legislation which restricted their freedom of movement and made them subject to seigneurial exactions of an arbitrary nature which were known as the *malos usos* or 'evil customs'. The most important of these was the *remensa* payment: the 'serf-peasant' had to give this to his lord in order to obtain that redemption from his status which would give him the freedom to leave his land. But the immediate consequences of the Black Death favoured the peasantry, and down to the 1380s the lords had to offer favourable leases in order to attract tenants. Consequently, when the lords attempted, towards the end of the fourteenth century, to remedy their financial situation by insisting on an exaction of all their old rights, the economic position of the various social groupings had altered. The economic situation, indeed, was as important as the continuing grievances about the legal issues related to servile status, and the *remensa* movement must be placed within its proper socio-economic and geographical context.

Widespread peasant unrest was confined to Old Catalonia (east of the Llobregat), and in particular to the areas between Gerona and Vich. The seigneurial structure of this region was quite different from that in southern Catalonia. The southern areas – and especially the lands along the Ebro valley – were characterised by the existence of a peasantry who were exempt from the degradation associated with serfs, although they were not proprietors in their own right, and they worked the land within the framework of great lordships and the concentration of seigneurial power in relatively few hands. In the north-east, on the other hand, the lesser nobility were much more numerous, the lordships were much smaller, and seigneurial power often consisted of little more than the jurisdiction over a village or the lands round a rural stronghold. It was in these areas, where lords and lordships were very numerous, that the crisis in incomes was most acute. But these were also areas where there was a high proportion of peasant freeholders, and the juxtaposition of free and servile tenures stimulated rural unrest. Indeed, the areas of *remensa* agitation were precisely those with most free tenures, while in those regions where freeholders were lacking, for example to the west of the Llobregat, peasant unrest was minimal.

Rural unrest in Old Catalonia, therefore, was not simply a matter of poor serfs reacting to seigneurial oppressions. On the contrary, a frequent cause of unrest was the attempt by the lords to make relatively prosperous peasants pay extra seigneurial dues for the deserted farmsteads which they had acquired in the aftermath of the fourteenth-century mortalities. There were, in fact, two 'wings' to the *remensa* movement. The conservative group of relatively affluent peasants, although willing to pay seigneurial dues and rents, aimed at obtaining the suppression of the *malos usos* and the confirmation of their free status. The revolutionary faction of poor *payeses*, on the other hand, demanded full and free ownership of their lands and the abolition of all seigneurial dues. Continual unrest in the countryside finally came to a head towards the middle of the fifteenth century, and subsequently the issues became inextricably involved in the civil war of 1462–72 between the Catalan *Generalitat*, which supported the lords, and the monarchy, whose agents and lawyers had for long favoured the demands of the peasantry. The remarkable alliance between the monarchy and the *remensa* movement can be partly explained by the agreement of the peasantry in 1448 to pay 100,000 florins to the Crown for the abolition of the *malos usos*. Yet prior to this agreement, the Crown and its agents had already roundly condemned the evils of the *remensa* condition, which Queen María de Luna described as 'execrable and abominable servilities', 'evil and detestable customs', 'the most oppressive and vile state and condition suffered in any part of the world by men bound by the yoke of serfdom', and 'the shame of the Catalan nation'.[63]

In 1455 Alfonso V suspended the *malos usos* and declared the *remensa* peasantry free. But royal victory in the civil war that ensued was ultimately achieved with the help of many of the Catalan nobility, and as a result it was not until 1486, after further peasant unrest, that the demands of the conservative wing of the *remensa* movement were met by Ferdinand the Catholic's *Sentencia* of Guadalupe.

In their search for alternative sources of income, the Iberian nobility did not devote their attention exclusively to agrarian rents and seigneurial dues. Many Castilian noble families, for example, displayed their interest in *rentier* income by acquiring shares in the Seville soap industry, and the Catalan nobility showed a marked preference for investing in *Generalitat* bonds or the *Taula de Canvi*. Few nobles seem to have been involved in strictly commercial activity. Some Catalan noble families owned ships, and the trade of Castile's northern and southern coasts attracted the attention of such great families as the Velascos, counts of Haro, and the Guzmanes, dukes of Medina Sidonia. In the latter case, for example, the ducal officials of the second half of the fifteenth century dealt directly with foreign merchants, administered the ducal tunny fisheries and prepared the duke's ships for their voyages abroad. But in the vast majority of cases it is clear that the great nobility of Castile controlled the heights of the economy and lived off the profits of economic activities in which they seldom became directly involved: the counts of Haro acquired the customs duties of the north-coast trade, the marquis of Villena controlled the sheep-routes into Murcia, the Acuña family held the chief office in the *Mesta*, the count of Medinaceli's regional salt monopoly alone was worth some 80,000 *mrs* per year in the 1430s, a century of fierce competition ended with the Enríquez establishing a virtual monopoly of shares in the soap industry, and the counts of Benavente controlled the fairs at Villalón. Many other similar examples could be cited, and there can be little doubt that these forms of rather parasitical economic activity provided alternative and valuable sources of income for the nobility. The most profitable financial opportunities in Castile, however, were related to the royal revenues, and it was the Crown which attracted the enduring attention of the great nobility.

At a time when the agrarian and seigneurial incomes of many of the nobility were in decline, the monarchy successfully increased royal income by the imposition of new taxes (above, pp. 145–7). This increase was not always sufficient to match expenditure in times of crisis (for example, during the period of the Trastamaran civil war and Lancastrian intervention), and kings showed a marked preference for escaping from financial commitments by debasing the coinage. (See Graph, p. xviii.) Debasement and inflation, moreover, did not usually have detrimental effects on the Crown finances because, since the taxes were farmed, the prices of tax-farms moved in sympathy with other prices. The monarchy, in short, was not burdened with the problems of a fixed income, and constitutional and political issues provided opportunities for aristocratic attempts to obtain 'shares' in the royal fiscal monopoly.

There were several ways in which political pressure could give the nobles a share in the Crown's wealth. Yearly assignments of stipulated sums of royal income could be granted by the king as privileges (*mercedes*). The recipient of a *merced* usually held it either for life (*de por vida*) or in perpetuity (*juro*). *Mantenimientos* ('maintenances') were special yearly payments which the king gave to individuals of outstanding political or social importance. *Tierra* payments, as we have seen, were yearly assignments of cash which theoretically entitled the Crown to the service of a corresponding number of lances (above, pp. 149–51). *Raciones* and *quitaciones* were salary payments to office-holders.

How much royal income was expended on these items? The budget of 1429 shows that, of the total regular income of the Crown, over 25 per cent was earmarked for *mercedes*, almost 8 per cent was set aside for *mantenimientos*, over 20 per cent was assigned to *tierra* payments, and *raciones* and *quitaciones* accounted for 15 per cent. Most of this money, amounting to over 60 per cent of royal expenditure, went to the nobility. But this was by no means the whole story, because the Crown also provided 'indirect' wealth for the nobility in the form of appointments in the Church, the towns and the military orders.

The sums which the Crown handed out in all these various ways seldom imposed specific obligations on the recipients. This was most obvious in the case of *mercedes*, but even the salaries of many of the great nobles were paid for the holding of purely nominal offices. The count of Medellín, for example, even went so far as to include his post of 'chief butler to the king' in the entailed estate which he founded in 1462.

How much money did individual members of the great nobility obtain from the Crown? The amounts varied considerably but were in most cases very high. In 1447, for example, the count of Alba held almost 1,000,000 *mrs* from the Crown, while Rodrigo de Villandrando held 360,000 *mrs*. The really powerful men in the land, such as Alvaro de Luna and the *infante* John, could hold as much as seven or eight million *mrs* in the royal registers – without, of course, taking into account the profits from offices such as the mastership of the Order of Santiago. Such huge sums more than compensated for declines in seigneurial income or any crisis in agrarian rents. Thus, to take an outstanding example, of the *infante* John's total estimated annual income in Castile in 1444, only 5 per cent was derived from seigneurial revenues while over 90 per cent was provided in one form or another by the Crown.

But what about the middle or lower ranks of the nobility? There were many who failed to obtain those grants from the Crown which would compensate for their declining incomes. Thus in northern Catalonia, where only a few benefited from the holding of royal offices, many nobles tried to make careers for themselves in the law or the Church. The Gerona tonsure registers, for example, contain many cases of two or more noble brothers being tonsured at the same time. In Castile, on the other hand, the patronage structure of the 'court' did not impede the redistribution of wealth to levels below that of the great nobility. In fact, the situation was similar to that which Claude de Seyssel (1450–1520) described in France:

> The princes of the blood and other great lords, who all receive some position and favour from the king, support many other nobles, and so on down the scale: the counts, barons and other powerful and rich nobles support some of the lesser nobility, each one according to his resources.[64]

Tierra payments for large quotas of lances, for example, were redistributed by the great lords to their noble clients; and *juros*, which could not be re-alienated to the Church or to foreigners, could otherwise be freely renounced, exchanged or sold. Patron–client groupings were built up on the existence or expectancy of such rewards. The allegiance of the Sandoval family to the cause of the *infante* John in the 1420's for example, was secured by the *infante's* renunciation of several thousand florins, held from the Crown as a *juro*, to Diego Gómez de Sandoval.

The spoils of the royal fiscal system acted both as incentives and as rewards for the political activity of the complex and ever-changing groupings of nobles. Strong kings could use patronage to ensure co-operation and to reward faithful service; weak kings used patronage in an attempt to bribe political opposition out of existence. The king, after all, was the greatest patron in the kingdom, and the financial privileges and revenues granted to the great noble families were listed in patronage registers (*libros de asientos*) which revealed alternative courses of royal action – in the form of further rewards or confiscations – at a glance. The great nobility, for their part, rarely opposed the royal system of taxation in the *cortes*. Instead, they preferred to await the rewards of their political machinations. For, as Fernán Pérez de Guzmán put it, the Castilian nobility, 'will consent to the imprisonment and death of a friend or relative in order to have a share in the booty'.

The web of patronage and alliances allowed the great nobility of Castile to drag the towns into their political movements. However, in both the Crown of Aragon and Castile there were other and more serious factors promoting urban unrest. Conflict between the urban masses (the *vulgares* or *pueblo menudo*), who were excluded from power, and the oligarchs, who were becoming increasingly aristocratic, was endemic, and it often fused with the growing intolerance which resulted in anti-semitic pogroms.

It was in Catalonia, and especially in Barcelona, that the demands for a broadening of the base of urban government had the profoundest effects. In the Aragonese federation generally, the first half of the fifteenth century brought royal support for reforms in municipal government in such widely scattered towns as Mallorca, Zaragoza, Castellón and Vich. These reforms were achieved without grave disorders, but in Barcelona, where demands for urban reform went back as far as the revolt of the artisans under Berenguer Oller in 1285, royal support for similar measures provoked open conflict in the 1450s between the two parties of the *Busca* and the *Biga*. Who did these parties represent, what were their objectives, and what repercussions did the struggle have on Catalan politics generally?

The *Biga* was the party of the ruling oligarchy in Barcelona – that is, the group of men, described as *ciutadans honrats*, who belonged to families which had controlled government since the late thirteenth century. They were on good terms with the aristocracy and oligarchs in other towns, and having largely renounced an active mercantile role, they lived on the incomes from their investments in bonds and the rents from their landed estates. The Dezplá and Gualbes families, for example, owned country estates in the areas around Barcelona. The *Biga* faction was also supported by some tradesmen, artisans and, above all, by the powerful town lawyers whose knowledge was placed at the disposal of a party which stood for the defence of the existing laws and constitutions. The salient characteristic of the oligarchy was its stand against any attempt by the monarchy, or the *Busca* party, to act contrary to the town's privileges, and in this resistance they were aided by the *Generalitat* and the oligarchies in other Catalan towns.

The *Busca* party found its support among the artisans, workmen and shopkeepers who were excluded from the important municipal offices. Nevertheless some substantial citizens and merchants, disillusioned with the *Biga* oligarchy, gave valuable assistance to the

Busca party and helped it, in the early 1450s, to form a 'syndicate' of the people. For example, it was Ramón Gerau, a merchant and leader of the syndicate, who most eloquently proclaimed the need for reforms in a city whose economic fortunes were on the decline.

In theory, the supreme governing body in Barcelona was the *consell de cent*, which contained some *Busca* members, although the majority consisted of *Biga* supporters. In practice, however, the *consell de cent* was only a deliberative assembly, and effective power was wielded by a small executive council which was controlled and advised by the *Biga* leadership. Most of the *Busca* grievances arose from this 'subversion' of the constitution: the *Biga* leadership was blamed for the city's disastrous financial position, a monetary policy which drained silver out of Catalonia, an unfair distribution of heavy taxes, corruption in the distribution of the most important offices in urban government, and the complete disregard of any royal measures favourable to the *Busca* cause. In 1453 the combined pressure of the 'syndicate' and the Crown finally unseated the oligarchy and the *Busca* attained power in Barcelona.

The changes in Barcelona's government in 1453 were followed by monetary reform (1454), the royal decree suspending the *malos usos* (1455), and the reform of municipal government in Gerona (1457). All these measures marked the end of a long period of royal negotiations with the landowners and urban oligarchs, and they strengthened the alliance between the Crown and the lower orders of Catalan society. The key to Catalan politics, however, continued to be the situation in Barcelona: serious divisions between the moderates and extremists of the *Busca* party proved fatal, and after seven years the *Biga* succeeded in attracting the support of the *Busca* moderates, regained power, and led the city and principality into the ruinous civil war against John II.

The events of the 1450s in Barcelona were remarkable in that the issues merged with the constitutional and *remensa* struggles, and finally led to civil war. But instances of conflict between the populace and the oligarchies were not at all uncommon in Spanish towns in general. Indeed, in Barcelona itself serious disturbances in 1391 brought to the fore the usual grievances about taxation and financial maladministration, and for a short time men of the lower orders took part in the governing processes of the city. But the events of 1391 in Barcelona formed part of a much larger anti-semitic movement which swept across the face of Spain, and it is this growing tide of racial intolerance which we must now examine.

What factors explain the growth of anti-semitism and the frequent pogroms which replaced the relative tolerance of previous centuries? There can be no doubt that Henry of Trastámara had deliberately mounted a propaganda offensive against the allegedly pro-Jewish policies of Peter I, and that in the ensuing civil war the Jewish communities (aljamas) suffered severely. Yet the Trastamaran kings, including Henry II, relied on the abilities of Jews and conversos as much as Peter the Cruel had done. However, despite royal protection of these minorities, the violent outbursts of anti-semitism continued. The 1391 pogrom. beginning in Seville on 6 June, quickly engulfed numerous other Andalusian towns. (See Map 5.) From these it spread in several directions, reaching Toledo on 18 June, Valencia on 9 July, and Mallorca, Barcelona, Gerona, Logroño, Lérida, Jaca and Perpignan during the first fortnight of August. From 1449 onwards a whole series of anti-semitic movements once again disturbed the life of many towns and culminated in the pogrom of 1473 which, beginning in Córdoba, led to massacres in many of the Andalusian towns.

Undoubtedly religious factors were important in causing these disturbances. It was, after all, a fanatical archdeacon, Ferrán Martínez, whose preachings sparked off the 1391 uprising in Seville, and the old idea of the collective responsibility of the Jews for the crucifixion of Christ survived strongly. The pogrom of 1391, however, proved a turning-point in that fear of persecution led to mass conversions in the large towns. In Seville, for example, the synagogues were converted into churches, and the Jewish quarter as such virtually disappeared. John II's secretary, Fernán Díaz de Toledo, himself a converso, argued that baptism 'makes the baptised a new man, cleanses him, cancels any obligation of atonement, and eliminates blame and sin. . . .' But the conversos, although Christians, continued to be the victims of mob furies, and this fact may be partly explained in terms of the wide spectrum of beliefs which existed among the Jewish and converso groups. Both Jews and conversos, for example, suffered from the hatred and bitterness directed against them by those among their own numbers who were genuine and fanatical converts to Christianity. Others, of course, became Christians under duress and retained their former beliefs. Finally, many among the Jewish and converso élites were fundamentally irreligious, and scorning both Jewish and Christian beliefs they asserted that 'we live and die like the beasts'. This complexity of religious attitudes not only provoked Christian hostility but led to serious tensions amongst the *conversos*.

The apparent wealth and social success of Jews and *conversos* also aroused acute resentment. In reality, the majority of Jews in the towns were artisans or shopkeepers, and Jews were excluded from the urban oligarchies and almost all offices in the royal administration. Some gained positions of great influence because of their learning and skills. Alfonso X, for example, welcomed them at court, and in the towns and the households of the nobility they enjoyed an almost official status as physicians. From the thirteenth century, however, an even greater social and economic gulf separated a small minority of financiers and administrators from the majority of Jews. These Jewish financiers were deeply involved in the urban, seigneurial and royal fiscal administrations. Most of them lived in the towns, but the very extent to which they farmed the royal revenues made the richest of them acceptable at court.

Legally, the Jew was barred from almost all offices and professions in Church and State, but the reasons for this limitation were religious and not racial. The paradoxical result of the 1391 pogrom, therefore, was that the Jews who became *conversos* found the legal impediments removed, and their success in gaining entry into public offices was so marked that contemporaries inevitably began to talk about widespread corruption and conspiracies. *Converso* families infiltrated the patrician oligarchies of many Castilian towns. Burgos and Segovia, for example, were controlled by *converso* families; in Córdoba they were accused of disposing of all public offices; and in Toledo their expulsion from office became the chief aim of some political factions. The entry of *conversos* into urban government was matched by their successes in the Church and the royal administration. For example, the *converso* families who controlled Burgos – the Santa María, Maluendas and Cartagenas – also produced bishops of Burgos, Coria and Plasencia. The Arias family, who for long controlled affairs in Segovia, could count on the support of Diego Arias de Avila, *contador mayor* and royal secretary, whose son was made bishop of Segovia. In fact *converso* assimilation into Christian society was so successful, that by the middle of the fifteenth century, the royal secretary, Fernán Díaz de Toledo, could convincingly demonstrate the existence of a degree of intermarriage which implied that almost all the nobility had *converso* relatives and ancestors.

The wealth and success of a substantial number of Jews and *conversos*, therefore, helps to explain why they, rather than the Mudejars, were the victims of pogroms. But we must also bear in mind that popular unrest was related to economic conditions.

Inevitably, perhaps, the evidence shows that the combined elements of bad harvests, chronic shortages of grain, plague, and price inflation formed an essential background to urban unrest. From 1400 to 1445, for example, the nominal price movement in Castile remained fairly stable and these were years which were relatively free from serious urban unrest. From 1445 onwards, however, there was a high degree of price inflation which reached serious proportions by the 1460s and 1470s. At the same time, subsistence crises occurred more frequently and culminated in the widespread crisis of 1469–73 when the prices of grain and other foodstuffs, especially in Andalusia, reached catastrophic heights. These were years of endemic urban unrest which led up to the pogroms of 1473.

The economic background helps to explain why unrest was predominantly, but not exclusively, anti-semitic in nature. Small hunger riots might merely take the form of a house-to-house search for bread, but popular agitation usually involved more complex and specific grievances. As nominal prices rose so did the price of tax-farms, and this resulted in an obvious increase in taxes for which, of course, Jews and *conversos* were held responsible. The pogrom of 1449 in Toledo, for example, was sparked off by an additional and heavy tax levied by the Crown. The tax-farmer was a *converso*, Alonso Cota, and his house was the first target of the enraged populace. But Cota, like so many other *conversos*, was something more than a mere tax-farmer: he was a merchant and treasurer of the town council – in other words, he was one of a 'subversive' group who raised prices and, by controlling municipal government, condoned the unfair distribution of royal taxation as well as profiting from local mal-administration. The attempts to exclude *conversos* permanently from office in such towns as Toledo and Córdoba, therefore, were the logical consequences of the 'moral' objectives of urban uprisings.

In the long run the later medieval persecutions of Jews and *conversos*, especially in Castile, had profound effects on the Spanish polity. In the first place, although the successes of the *conversos* after

1391 emphasised the fluidity and 'openness' of society, it is clear that the anti-*converso* movements of the second half of the fifteenth century became progressively racial in nature. Since *conversos* were Christians, they could not be barred from urban, ecclesiastical or royal offices on religious grounds. Consequently, purity of blood (*limpieza de sangre*) became the criterion for advancement, and the obsession over the issue was one of the major factors in the development of the more 'closed' social structure with caste-like features which characterised the early modern period.

A second important consequence arose from the way in which popular agitation became linked to the disputes between the monarchy and the nobility. The late medieval kings condemned the persecutions of the Jews and *conversos*, and acted as best they could to prevent the worst excesses. But in Toledo in 1449, a nobleman, Pero Sarmiento, intervened and redirected the popular fury into a movement against the monarchy. Thereafter, popular unrest came to be increasingly used as a weapon against royal government, and the Crown's hold on both the towns and the populace was seriously endangered. The monarchy regained the initiative, however, when it set up the Inquisition in 1478, for the urban populace now witnessed the official persecution of many of those who had previously been the targets of popular insurrection. The Inquisition was, in a different sense, a 'popular' institution and Isabella the Catholic was a 'popular' monarch.

9. Society, Religion and Culture

THE late medieval Gothic cathedrals at Palencia, Oviedo, Burgos, Seville, Barcelona, Tortosa and Palma, and the large number of frontier ballads recounting epic encounters with the Moors of Granada, are eloquent testimony to that continuity of the 'eternal' Christian and frontier values which would manifest themselves yet again in the Gothic churches of the New World and in the deeds of the *conquistadores*. The impressive cathedrals, however, cannot obscure the serious economic and religious problems which affected the Church. If some churchmen were preoccupied with reform many more feared the machinations of heretics, and the establishment of the Inquisition in 1478 was to mark the official transition from an 'open' to a 'closed' society.

Reform, Religious Sentiment, Heresy, the Inquisition

IN general terms the crisis in incomes, examined in the previous chapter, also endangered the finances of ecclesiastical institutions, but whereas royal gifts of lordships and revenues saved many of the nobility from financial disaster, the same was not true for the Church. There were, of course, obvious exceptions. The monastery of Guadalupe, for example, not only prospered from its ranching activities but also benefited from the largesse of the Trastamaran kings and some of the great nobility. In general, however, the great age of landed donations to the Church had gone for ever, and if a few bishops were politically powerful enough to join in the scramble for royal revenues, the Church as a whole was not. The parish clergy suffered most, expecially in areas such as the Basque country where both the churches and the tithes were often regarded as the property of lay patrons. And, as we have seen, even the great monasteries were subjected to the ruthless exploitation of noble 'protectors'. In the fourteenth century the largest monasteries, such as Santo Domingo de Silos and San Millán de la Cogolla, found it difficult to balance their income, and many of the smaller houses were ruined. In 1392, for example, the Benedictine monastery at Budiño had no roof and the only usable buildings were huts of straw.

In addition to these economic difficulties, the Church was faced with serious religious and political problems. In his *Rimado de Palacio* the chancellor of Castile, Pero López de Ayala (1332–1407), gloomily reflected on the Great Schism, which had divided Christendom since 1378, and penned a blistering attack on the clergy's immorality and ignorance. Nor did an even greater degree of royal control over the Church, arising from the Schism and its aftermath, provide a solution to problems of ecclesiastical reform, for as Ayala noted in his *Rimado*, the king was subjected to the incessant pressures of a nobility who regarded benefices in much the same light as royal financial privileges.

Given these circumstances, it is not difficult to find evidence of ecclesiastical immorality or ignorance, and dozens of examples relating to all sections of the clergy – from the warrior-archbishop of Toledo, Alonso Carrillo, down to the Basque and Navarrese priests whose style of life so shocked Cardinal Margarit in 1478 – could be cited to illustrate the point. But there are difficulties and dangers in constructing simple interpretations in terms of decadence and corruption. The ambiguities of religious life are well illustrated by the fourteenth-century *Book of Good Love* (*Libro de Buen Amor*) whose author, Juan Ruiz, was archpriest of Hita. This masterpiece, cast in an autobiographical form, abounds with hilarious and obscene adventures. Yet the archpriest also includes sincere religious lyrics, mainly addressed to the Virgin, a satire on clerical concubinage, and episodes designed to imply the futility of sensual love. Thus the *Book of Good Love* is about the love of God as well as love of the flesh, and we must accept the sincerity of the religious sentiments.

Similarly, while accepting the evidence of pluralism, absenteeism and immorality in general, it is also necessary to emphasise those positive features of religious life which constituted what Marcel Bataillon has called pre-Counter-Reformation trends. There was, indeed, no lack of men working towards reform. Observant movements, for example, revitalised houses in the Benedictine, Cistercian, Franciscan and Dominican orders. These movements, at times fiercely resisted, were supported by kings who were anxious to break foreign ties and centralise dependence on observant centres in Spain. Help was also forthcoming from bishops, and the general calibre of the hierarchy began to improve steadily from the late fourteenth century onwards.

The mixture of spiritual fervour and practical ability, which was

increasingly evident in some aspects of religious life, is well illustrated by the example of the Jeronymites. The Order of St Jerome,
starting off in the monastery of San Bartolomé de Lupiana in 1370,
expanded rapidly to a total of twenty houses by the end of the
fourteenth century. The most famous of these was the monastery of
Guadalupe which, being in need of reform, was incorporated into
the Order of St Jerome in 1389. This isolated monastery even rivalled
Compostela as a pilgrimage centre, and the German, Tetzel, whose
comments on the Castilian clergy and the anarchy at Compostela
were most unfavourable, heaped praise on the rich but pious monks
of Guadalupe. The Jeronymites, in fact, viewed wealth and power
not as causes of corruption but as aids to the proper functioning of
charity and religion. In the late 1420s Juan de Serrano, who was
twice prior of Guadalupe, skilfully defended this new and positive
view in reply to papal demands for a greater asceticism in the
order. Jeronymite religious fervour, argued Serrano, was not by
nature ascetic, and was combined with positive worldly virtues;
wealth and power enhanced piety and the ability to perform good
works. These views, perhaps, pointed forward to subsequent developments in Erasmist Spain, but they also coincided with the period of
greatest impact by the *conversos* on society and religion, and the
suspicion of crypto-Judaism retarded the further development of
this aspect of Jeronymite spirituality.

The Jeronymite order was part of that body of clergy which constituted the 'official' Church, but the formulation of religious values
had long ceased to be a clerical monopoly. Royal courts and towns
surpassed the monasteries in social and political importance, paper
replaced parchment, and the lay view of life betrayed the same preoccupation with this world as characterised Guadalupe monasticism.

Literary treatment of such themes as 'death', 'fortune' and
'avarice' suggests at first sight a continuation of conventional
religious beliefs. In the age of the Black Death these traditional
beliefs seem to be reflected not only in Ayala's gloomy *Rimado de
Palacio* but in the 'Dances of Death', the *Ubi sunt?* theme so prevalent
in the poetry of the period, the popular 'wheel of fortune' theme with
its reminders of the disasters that can befall even the greatest of
men, the frequent condemnations of vanity and avarice, and the
growth in demand for requiem masses, altar paintings and funerary
chapels. All these suggest that the laity subscribed to the belief that
life is an illusion and that the Christian should turn his back on the

vanities of this world, reflect on death and be concerned with the progress of his soul to heaven. These points were best expressed by Jorge Manrique in his famous poem *Coplas por la muerte de su padre:*

> Who doubts that estates and wealth suddenly leave us? Let us expect no constancy from them, because they belong to a lady who changes. For wealth belongs to Fortune, who turns her rapid wheel, and she cannot be of constant mind, nor remain stable nor decide on one thing. . . . So many splendid dukes, so many marquises and counts and gentlemen as we saw, all so mighty, tell me, Death, where do you hide or take them to?[65]

All these manifestations of religious sentiment, however, display a decisive shift of perspective in lay society and, since most of them date from the fifteenth century, it is difficult to relate any of them to the direct consequences of the Black Death. What they reveal is an intense preoccupation with worldly life mingled with an awareness of the inevitability of death. The 'Dance of Death' theme, for example, implies that events are finally controlled not by God but by Death, and far from being welcomed as the liberator of the soul, Death is detested because he brings to an end 'the joy of living'. Consequently, if we are not quite faced with the 'we live and die like the beasts' philosophy which supposedly characterised the beliefs of many Jews and *conversos,* a strong case can be argued for the existence of an epicureanism which helps to explain the extravagance and luxury of courtly life, and the elegant eroticism which lies behind the idealised love-poems of the anthologies known as *cancioneros.* Even in Manrique's *Coplas* the emphasis on the transitory nature of this world cannot hide the nostalgic pain of sweetly remembered pleasures:

> What has become of the ladies, of their head-dresses, their dresses and their scents? What has become of the flames of the fires of lovers? What of all that inventive playing, and of the harmonious music that they performed? What has become of that dancing, and of the fine dresses they wore?[66]

The fleeting nature of life was a matter for regret, and there was little pretence of welcoming Death in joyful anticipation of an after-life. Even the funeral practices of the period contained extreme manifestations of grief, which were heightened by the hiring of professional female mourners (*plañideras*) whose miserable excesses sometimes disturbed the public authorities. The acts of the town council of Jerez for April 1455, for example, record that:

> ... inasmuch as it has become known that at the funeral of Juan Catalán which took place yesterday, Tuesday, the women who accompanied his body to the monastery of Santo Domingo of this town made many noises of grief in a shameful manner and contrary to the ruling of the Holy Church, and inasmuch as this is a survival from the period of the Gentiles, but now, by the grace of God, we are in his Holy Catholic faith . . . , it was ordered that henceforth no person or persons attending funerals should make lamentations of this kind in the streets and urban districts on pain of a fine of three hundred *mrs*.[67]

In their preoccupation with worldly affairs men reacted differently to the threat of futility posed by Fortune and Death. Some took practical steps. The death of Juan Catalán, for example, would undoubtedly be viewed by some contemporaries as only one of the many ills stemming from the eclipse of the sun which had occurred the previous month, and the professor of astrology at Salamanca, Diego de Torres, produced a treatise which provided the necessary cures for facing up to the consequences of this event. But the most important reaction was the anxiety among those in the upper reaches of society to ensure that their lives should in some way earn a fame that would survive death. Already evident in the writing of Alfonso X's nephew, Juan Manuel (1282–1348), this desire to live on in the memories of men became increasingly important and was manifested in magnificent funeral sculptures. This preoccupation with worldly fame, of course, was closely connected to such factors as the increase in literacy and the growing importance of the urban and courtly nobility. At a more popular level, men turned to new or developing forms of piety, and combined religious and secular activities in organisations which existed on the margins of the 'official' Church.

All over Spain the Virgin and the major saints gained ground at the expense of cults dedicated to local saints. Ever since the thirteenth century the literary and religious preoccupation with the Virgin Mary had increased sharply while, with the declining impetus of the reconquest, interest in Santiago had slackened. Here again the monastery of Guadalupe serves as a good example. The origins of the shrine date back to a point, around 1330, when a cowboy from

Cáceres is supposed to have seen a vision of the Virgin on the banks of the Guadalupe river. The subsequent discovery of an image of the Virgin and the establishment of a church led, as we have seen, to the incorporation of the shrine into a Jeronymite monastery in 1389. Long before this date, however, the cult had already spread far and wide. It was this Virgin, for example, that Alfonso XI invoked in 1340 at the battle of Salado, and as early as 1365 we find a peasant woman from Arcos de la Frontera, over two hundred miles away, bequeathing two *mrs* to Santa María de Guadalupe.

The rapid growth in the number of confraternities, however, shows that popular religion, linked to the cult of saints, existed outside the confines of the 'official' Church. Faced with the insecurity of urban life, men turned to these artificial 'families' of voluntary fraternity which, unlike the politically motivated leagues or *hermandades*, provided the individual with a meaningful framework encompassing all aspects of religious and social life. The emphasis of these confraternities was on the pious enactment of ceremonies in honour of God, the Virgin and the saints, and on providing for the afterlife of members by arranging honourable funerals and requiem masses. Economic resources, usually in the form of lands and houses, were owned and administered by the confraternities to ensure a sufficiency of wealth for the fulfilment of these religious obligations. The absence of a member from an important confraternity occasion was severely punished, as was unseemly behaviour by those attending the religious ceremonies.

A few confraternities centred their cults on monastic establishments and accepted the active involvement of the regular clergy, but in general they were largely autonomous and existed outside the parochial structure of the Church. In Cáceres and Jerez, for example, most of the confraternities had their own churches or oratories and their own chaplains. Seldom were the confraternities involved in the ceremonies of the parish, and priests were only admitted as members on fulfilment of the same conditions laid down for the laity. The suspicion that the secular clergy inspired little confidence in the populace is reinforced by other evidence. For example, those who endowed anniversaries or chaplaincies often specifically excluded priests from benefiting from them and even provided for the annulment of their foundations if the secular clergy should in any way interfere with them.

The confraternities laid down rules for membership which often had the effect of excluding the very poor and reinforcing a natural tendency for those of a similar occupation to belong to the same organisation. In Cáceres, for example, the *cofradía* of Santa Olalla, founded in 1467, required that all members should be co-proprietors of the grazing lands of Aldeyuela, and that on entry they should pay the modest sum of 50 *mrs* and half a pound of wax. None of the members, therefore, were poor or destitute and all of them had some interest in stock-raising. Yet while approximately half of the founding members were nobles, there were even some shoemakers among the remainder.

The example of the *cofradía* of Santa Olalla shows that the religious aspects had a natural appeal for men of varying social status, but quite apart from financial factors, confraternities could be exclusive in other ways. The members often tended to be drawn from succeeding generations of the same families living in the same districts of the same town. Above all, the religion and piety, which attracted both shoemakers and members of the lesser nobility, might also become dangerously affected by that hatred for the *conversos* which, as we have seen, was so characteristic a feature of life in some of the Castilian towns. Popular religion and popular unrest, of course, constituted an explosive mixture, and as the chronicler Garci Sánchez relates, Henry IV seems to have been one of the few to realise the gravity of the problem:

> While in Toledo during this month of April [1465], King Henry enforced friendship on the members of two confraternities – one of *conversos* and one of Old Christians – who were full of hatred for each other. The king united them into one confraternity, and he himself joined along with the other members in order to bring peace among them. And he made them swear that they would be as one and, in order to help with certain problems which they had to tackle in order to be united, he gave the confraternity (which had been created by fusing the former two) a *juro* of 10,000 *mrs* in perpetuity.[68]

This attempt to solve tensions at street level was unsuccessful, and two years later the *converso* districts of Toledo once more witnessed frightful carnage. Nor was Toledo exceptional, as the events in Córdoba which sparked off the widespread pogrom of 1473 illustrate. The immediate cause of the troubles lay in the deliberate creation of a Marian confraternity – that of the *Caridad* – which specifically excluded *conversos*. In March 1473 a public procession organised by the confraternity wound its way through the streets of Córdoba; feelings were running high, and as the procession passed through the street of the smiths, a blacksmith, Alonso Rodríguez, yelled out that urine had been thrown at the effigy of the Virgin from a *converso* house. At the head of the mobs, Rodríguez set about the grim business of burning and killing.

In an atmosphere charged with popular religious fury, heresy could flourish, and there was more than a hint of millenarianism in the uprisings which shook Toledo in 1449. But for the first serious manifestations of heresy we must move to the Basque country, and in particular to the Duranguesado. These were areas where the fabric of Christian life was weak, and Bishop Alonso de Cartagena, whose diocese adjoined the Basque country, had no hesitation in emphasising that neo-paganism was an essential element of the Durango movement. They were also areas which had close trading links with the Low Countries, and it may well be that heretical ideas, as well as wool, travelled the Flanders route. For, whatever the background of the movement, there is little doubt that the Durango heresy was yet another manifestation of the movement of the Free Spirit.

Beginning around 1425, the rapid growth of the Free Spirit heresy in Durango owed much to the preachings of the Franciscan Alonso de Mella, brother of the bishop of Zamora, and gained widespread support among the peasants and artisans. The main characteristics of the heresy were the communal sharing of wealth, the repudiation of marriage, the rejection of sexual moral norms as a sign of spiritual emancipation, the repetition of the characteristic cry of *¡'Aleluya y caridad!'* (echoing the Beghards' 'Bread for God's sake!'), the denial of the real presence of Christ in the sacrament, and the belief that the age of the Holy Spirit had already arrived. In the 1440s the authorities intervened to crush the movement, Alonso de Mella fled to Granada, and a number of heretics were burned in Valladolid and Santo Domingo de la Calzada.

It is impossible to determine whether there were any direct connections between the movement in Durango and the events in Toledo in 1449, but although the Toledo uprising was primarily anti-*converso* in nature, there were several remarkable similarities. Once again 'marginal' men were involved, for with the important exception of the nobleman Pero Sarmiento and two cathedral canons, the nobility and beneficed clergy seem to have played no part in the uprising. It is possible that some Franciscans were involved in the rebellion, but the overwhelming majority were urban workers and artisans, many of whom were peasants who had migrated to the town over the preceding years. The rebels' 'prophet' was Marcos García de Mora, a *letrado* who was known pejoratively to his enemies as *el bachiller* Marquillos. Marquillos, who was himself from a peasant family and was advised sarcastically by the *converso* royal secretary Fernán Díaz to return to his plough, proclaimed that he had been called by God to Toledo in order to confound the *conversos* and their satanic activities. Needless to say, his actions and the excesses committed by his followers were all justified as being part of a mission whose leader, Marquillos, was guided by the Holy Spirit. Bishop Alonso de Cartagena who, as we have seen, emphasised the neo-pagan background of the Durango heresy, compared Marquillos and his followers with the Hussites. It was an exaggerated comparison, and the fact that the bishop was a *converso* should be borne in mind. But there can be no doubt that a spirit of religious exaltation reigned over the uprising of 1449 and that Marquillos, who was subsequently hanged, fitted in very well with the millenarian tradition of 'prophets'.

Years later, in the 1480s, the *converso* chronicler Diego de Valera, whose brother had been one of those sent by John II to investigate the Durango heresy, reflected on the outcome of these events and 'erroneous opinions'. The Durango heresy, Valera implied, had survived John II's actions and still found some adherents at the time when he was writing. But there were also those who subscribed to the belief that there was nothing more to life than birth and death. This belief, as we have seen, was commonly attributed to many insincere *conversos* who had been assimilated into influential positions in Christian society. By the time Valera was writing, however, the Inquisition had already come into existence, and Church and State would henceforth clamp down firmly both on the Old Christians and *conversos* in the upper reaches of society who were not above suspicion, and on those among the urban populace who would take the law into their own hands in a spirit of religious exaltation.

The setting up of the Inquisition in 1478 marked the official transition from a pluralistic and heterodox society to a rigid and closed society bent on enforcing orthodoxy. In 1449 powerful *conversos*, such as the royal secretary Fernán Díaz de Toledo and Bishop Alonso de Cartagena, could openly write in defence of the *conversos* and against the absurd accusations of the Toledan insurgents. Fernán Díaz, indeed, even poked fun at some of the Old Christians, invited Marquillos to return to his peasant labours, and provided a wealth of information to show the extent to which the *conversos* had been assimilated into Christian society. After 1478 *conversos* could never again write openly in this vein, because the setting up of the Inquisition fulfilled that popular ideal of summary justice which was capable of bringing down those in the highest positions of Church and State.

Ballads, Tiles and the Frontier

WE have seen that the very success of the *conversos* and their rapid assimilation into Christian society helped to provoke popular anti-semitic movements in the towns, and that the religious and political issues arising from this situation led to the setting up of the Inquisition. But what was the situation with respect to the Mudejars and Moors of the peninsula ?

The ballads known as *romances fronterizos* bear witness to the survival of frontier military values in later medieval Spain. Although they reveal an admiration of Moorish chivalry and wealth, the deeds they recount are those of bold frontier nobles who were apparently conscious of the religious and 'manifest' destiny which pitted them in combat against the Moors. Moreover, since the Castilian monarchs hardly figure in the ballads, and since the latter flourished among the illiterate or semi-literate sectors of society, it is tempting to conclude that the spirit of the frontier was retained by the 'people' or 'folk' at a time when weak kings turned their back on Castile's destiny and plunged the country into ruinous civil wars. However, the evidence reveals that such an assumption does little justice to the complexity of the realities.

As we have seen, the Castilian monarchy was presented with threats of foreign intervention from England, France, Aragon and Portugal (above, Chapter 6). The Moorish frontier, therefore, was only one element in a complex political pattern, and since Castilian royal policy attempted to prevent encirclement and the opening up of new fronts, it is hardly surprising that during the period 1350–1460 there were eighty-five years of peace and only twenty-five of 'official' war with the kingdom of Granada. The Castilian Crown, however, also derived substantial benefits from the *parias* paid by

Granada, and a combination of diplomatic and military pressure was needed to ensure a succession of truces with favourable economic terms. It is against this background that the apparently 'independent' adventures of the frontier nobility must be set. In fact, with one exception all the frontier ballads relate incidents which took place during periods of 'official' war, and we know that in some cases the 'independent' frontier hero was carrying out the designs of the monarchy. The ballad *Alora la bien cercada*, for example, relates how a frontier governor, Diego de Ribera, besieged the Moorish stronghold of Alora and was treacherously killed by a Moorish archer during a parley. These details are confirmed by the chronicles, and the resulting impression is that another frontier lord has been removed from the scene after taking the military initiative. However, the financial accounts of Seville reveal that in March 1434 the governor was ordered by John II to mount a campaign into the areas round Alora, the Crown co-ordinated the military preparations, and royal officials accompanied the troops in order to hold the necessary musters and pay the soldiers.

The frontier ballads flourished as oral literature and must have been constantly sung and recreated by poet-singers, but the evidence does not suggest that they were the preserve of the 'folk' or the 'common people'. On the contrary, the ballads did not reflect the peaceful preoccupations of illiterate society in general but the military values of the *caballeros*, and they were probably composed by minstrels in the service of nobles and governors on the frontier.

As against the armed conflict depicted in the ballads, there is a wealth of evidence to suggest that peaceful relations were the main preoccupation and objective of the communities on both sides of the frontier. A substantial number of 'hinge' men mediated between the two cultures. When truces were negotiated both sides arranged for the appointment of special judges, the *alcaldes entre cristianos y moros*, whose task it was to deal with frontier incidents. These judges, however, were seldon effective in dealing with the ordinary 'police' problems, and these were dealt with by *rastreros* or scouts, appointed by the local municipalities, whose task it was to investigate complaints along with their colleagues from other areas. While the *rastreros* investigated frontier incidents, the job of officials known as *alfaqueques* was to seek out and ransom or exchange captives. The *alfaqueques* were immune from frontier hostility and travelled extensively in the performance of their duties. Christian *alfaqueques*, for example, made frequent trips to the city of Granada to discuss problems with the Moorish authorities.

The cases which *rastreros* and *alfaqueques* had to deal with were not always clear-cut frontier problems. There was, in any case, no such thing as a clear geographical frontier, as the following complaint sent by the Moorish authorities of Cambil to Christian Jaén illustrates:

... A Moor coming from Granada to Cambil lost his direction near Torre el Galín, left the way and took a path which he thought would take him to Cambil, but he ended up in [Christian] Huelma where he is being held by the *alcaide* of Huelma. The *alcaide* of Cambil, Mahomad Lentín, has written to the *alcaide* of Huelma about this so that the said Moor may be returned, but he has not received a reply. Now, inasmuch as Christians going to Huelma very often get lost and end up in Cambil, and the *alcaides* of Cambil do not arrest them but provide Moors to show them the way to Huelma, the authorities of Huelma should behave likewise. If this particular Moor got lost, the *alcaide* of Huelma should have shown him the way – for this, after all, is what neighbours are for.[69]

In the *Book of Good Love* the Archpriest uses the proverb 'to mistake a path for the proper road, like an Andalusian' in order to indicate the confusion and complexity of a love intrigue, but the interesting point about the complaint of the Moors of Cambil is that it emphasises the concept of 'neighbourliness' as the proper way of dealing with the proverbial ease with which people strayed across the frontier.

Even more complications arose from the fact that there was also a frequent blurring of the mental and religious frontiers. The sanctuary of San Ginés de la Jara near Christian Cartagena, for example, was venerated by both Christians and Moors, and there are documented cases of Moors crossing the frontier to visit the sanctuary. More problematical were the frequent cases of the *tornadizos* – that is, those Moors or Christians who crossed the frontier, changed their religion and refused to return home. The Moorish authorities at Colomera, for example, profusely apologised to the Christian officials of Jaén for failing to return a shepherd, Pedro, who: 'has become a Moor and we, being vexed by this, requested him to return with his companions but he did not wish to do so. Therefore, send his mother and relatives here to Colomera in order to persuade him to

return with them, and we will let him go.'[70] Cases like this made the
task of the *alfaqueques* extremely difficult, especially since the
'religious' motives of the *tornadizos* were often dubious. Here, for
example, are the Moorish comments on one of the cases being dealt
with by *alfaqueques*:

> We reply that this woman who is alleged to be a Christian is not
> really of the same type as the others who are being discussed at
> present. She, as is well known to be the truth, came over [the
> frontier] of her own accord and, after staying in this city of
> Granada as a Moorish woman, Martín de Lara the *alfaqueque*
> came and spoke with her alone, but she remained as she was, a
> Moorish woman. And afterwards she married, and was for long
> in the house of the *alcalde mayor* of the Moors; but thereafter she
> fled from her husband's house with her Mudejar lover and was
> caught and imprisoned. Thus, seeing how matters stand and how
> these things happened, you can see whether it is proper to
> petition for a woman of this sort.[71]

Despite the military emphasis of the ballads, therefore, the
evidence suggests that during periods of peace the Moors and
Christians coexisted fairly amicably, and that cultural and religious
boundaries were not always sharply delineated. Moreover, in the
Christian towns and countryside the Mudejars continued to live
peacefully, and unlike the Jews and *conversos* they were not subjected
to popular furies or pogroms. The reason for this absence of hostility
probably lies in the fact that, over the generations, Mudejar
labourers and artisans continued to apply their specialised knowledge to crafts which, although of great practical value to society,
were not socially prestigious. It is therefore worth contrasting the
oral literature of the ballads with another semi-literate tradition such
as that of the potters and tilemakers.

The illiteracy of many of the potters is attested by the spelling
errors in the kufic lettering of words of salutation, such as 'pardon'
and 'blessing', which they carefully painted over the surface of such
objects as vases and which, in a sense, were their equivalent of the
formulistic diction of the ballads. In the kingdom of Granada the
work of these craftsmen betrayed Persian influences up to about the
middle of the fourteenth century, but Gothic designs subsequently
became very noticeable, and in the scenes of daily life depicted on
tiles and pottery there even appeared figures of people dressed in

European costume. Part of the explanation for this phenomenon lies in the itinerant habits of craftsmen on both sides of the frontier and, as one might expect, the appearance of Gothic in the kingdom of Granada was matched by the influence of Muslim designs in Christian Spain. In Christian Valencia, for example, the centres staffed by Mudejar craftsmen became so famous from the second half of the fourteenth century that their potters and tilemakers were commissioned to work as far afield as Avignon, Bourges, Poitiers and Naples. Moreover, since Granadan ceramics were freely imported into Valencia during the fourteenth century, the descriptive inventories of the period are understandably confused as to where particular wares were manufactured – to such an extent, indeed, that it is clear that the Valencian craftsmen began by faithfully copying the Granadan decorative styles. As far as the craftsmen themselves are concerned, the surviving contracts are full of Moorish names down to the early fifteenth century, but then the Christianised names of succeeding generations tend to predominate. From the early fourteenth century down to the 1530s, for example, the Murcí family specialised in the production of tiles, but whereas the earliest brothers bore the unmistakably Moorish names of Abdelaçiz and Abrāhīm Almurcí, their descendents bore the surname of Murcí and Christian names such as Juan, Pedro and Jaime. Inevitably, this slow process of change was accompanied by the introduction of new designs and shapes which departed from the styles originally borrowed from across the frontier.

From a more general point of view, the fact that the Mudejars virtually monopolised the crafts associated with building and ornamentation meant that they left their imprint on buildings all over Christian Spain. In the Crown of Aragon, for example, members of the Murcí family were at various times contracted to work on such projects as the royal palace at Valencia and the castle of Gaeta near Naples. In the kingdom of Castile the Mudejar style influenced all kinds of buildings from the monastery of Guadalupe to the synagogue of *El Tránsito* which Peter the Cruel's treasurer, Samuel Leví, erected in Toledo.

Processes of acculturation and assimilation of styles, therefore, were not confined to potters and tilemakers, and the mixture of Gothic and Muslim designs became more marked on both sides of the frontier from about the mid-fourteenth century onwards. The explanation for this phenomenon lies not so much in the itinerant habits of craftsmen as in the long period of peace between Castile and Granada which lasted from *c.* 1350 to 1406. These years constituted the period of the civil war and the Lancastrian threat of invasion, and in the south they were marked not by confrontations between Christians and Moors but by trans-frontier alliances and periods of peaceful coexistence. Indeed, one of the earliest frontier ballads, *Cercada tiene a Baeza,* relates the siege of the Trastamaran stronghold of Baeza in 1368 by the combined forces of Peter the Cruel and Mahomet V of Granada. Consequently, if we take into account the continual trans-frontier movements of allies, ambassadors, merchants, *alfaqueques* and craftsmen, it is not surprising that the fusion of Christian and Muslim influences even affected the courts of the rulers. It was during the late fourteenth century, for example, that the astonishing paintings in the domes of the *Sala de los Reyes* in the Alhambra palace of Granada were executed. These contain scenes in which Christian and Moorish nobles and ladies are depicted in such chivalrous pursuits as fighting, hunting and playing chess. But the style is Franco-Gothic, and since the artist is unknown, there is no way of ascertaining whether he was a Muslim or a Christian. The counterpart to these Franco-Gothic paintings of the Granadan court is the palace (*alcázar*) begun by Peter the Cruel in Seville. Craftsmen, sent by the ruler of Granada, worked on this building, and besides providing the makings of a genuine Moorish palace they left behind the usual inscriptions invoking the blessings of Allah for the Lord Sultan – that is, Peter the Cruel. But it was with the reign of Henry IV of Castile that the extent of 'heathen' practices and customs at the royal court began seriously to disturb the state of opinion among the nobility.

Henry IV's Islamophil tendencies revealed themselves to the nobility during his early campaigns against the kingdom of Granada. Large armies were raised, but the king repeatedly refused to commit his troops to battle, withheld permission for raids of destruction, and whiled away the time in ineffectual skirmishes or in admiring the presents and minstrels with which his Moorish enemies regaled him. Although the communities of places like Cambil and Jaén were good neighbours in peacetime, the *caballeros* of these areas – the home of the *romances fronterizos* – knew that frontier warfare was a grim business, and the futility of Henry IV's war games shocked and irritated them. Here, for example, is Valera's description of one of the royal sallies from Jaén:

In this manner the king and queen arrived with these troops to a position so close to Cambil that it seemed as if they wanted to combat the fortress, and the Moors, seeing the troops arriving in this manner manned the parapets. The queen asked for a bow, and when the king gave it to her ready for action, she fired a few arrows at the Moors. After this game was finished the king returned to Jaén where those *caballeros* who knew how to make war and were accustomed to it, laughed scornfully and said that this kind of war did more damage to the Christians than to the Moors. Others said: 'There's no doubt about it. This war is certainly like that which the Cid used to wage in his day.'[72]

After the southern campaigns were over, the style of life at the royal court became even more bizarre. The very frontier ballads, which portrayed the military values of the *caballeros*, became popular in court circles, while at the same time the king, dressing and eating like a Moor, surrounded himself with a large Moorish guard whose members he rewarded with lands and money. Mudejar artisans were acceptable and, indeed, indispensable to Castilian society. But the creation of an Islamophil court was another matter, and Henry IV's enemies repeatedly accused him of all sorts of heathenish, heretical and unnatural vices, and even when due allowance is made for the venomous exaggerations of such men as the chronicler Palencia, there can be no doubt that there was a good deal of substance in the allegations. Philippe de Commynes, for example, states that when Henry IV and Louis XI met in 1463, the Castilian king was accompanied by a guard of 300 cavalry who were mainly Moors from Granada with a few Negroes thrown in for good measure. Those who accompanied Leo of Rozmital in his journeys through Castile in 1466 had no reason to besmirch the reputation of Henry IV, and they amply confirmed some of the more serious allegations. When they visited the royal court they found it full of 'heathen' whom they identified as 'Saracens'. Henry IV himself, they reported, 'eats and drinks and is clothed and worships in the heathen manner and is an enemy of Christians', and when they were received at court 'he and the Queen sat side by side on the ground'. What was true of the royal court, of course, was not necessarily true of the rest of the kingdom, and the travellers described the contrasts. In Salamanca, for example, they were impressed by the Christian texture of life, but when travelling north from Toledo they passed through lands from which Henry IV 'had driven out the Christians and settled the heathen in their place'. In this area the travellers took a keen interest in Muslim religious practices, were treated with great respect, and reported that they were safer than in Christian areas.

As we have seen, the *converso* problem was largely an urban phenomenon, and popular unrest formed the essential background to the creation of the Inquisition. The Moorish problem, on the other hand, manifested itself not in the towns and countryside in general, but in the court of Henry IV in particular. The reaction did not take the form of popular unrest but of demands by the nobility that the Moors should be ejected from the court, and that the traditional task of reconquest should once again be undertaken seriously. These demands were clearly set out, for example, in the programme of the rebel nobility which was drafted in the year prior to Rozmital's visit to the royal court. The grievance at the head of the massive list of complaints about the king's misdemeanours concerned the Moors of the royal court. On this point a commission which was set up to decide on the elimination of abuses declared:

> . . . we order that within fifty days the king is to throw out and separate from his person, company, household and court all the said Moors who, either on horse or on foot, serve in his guard; and we order that he is not to bring them or others back again to serve in his house and guard, either at present or at any future time. We order and declare that those among these Moors who are Mudejars are to depart within the specified time to the *morerías*, houses and places where they belong, that henceforth the king is not to give any of them salaries, wages, privileges, gifts or military pay, and that they are not to accept these things from the king or from anybody else on his behalf. With respect to the Moors who are from the kingdom of Granada and other places, we order and declare that, if these Moors are free, they are to leave the kingdoms and lordships of the king within the specified time and are not to remain or to return to them, and if they are the king's slaves they are to be sent to the Moorish frontiers so that they can be exchanged for those Christians who are held captive. . . .[73]

These decisions, supported by a demand for an immediate and effective war against Granada, were never put into effect because Henry IV repudiated the work of the commission. The nobility, of course, were still engaged in their endless quest for larger shares in the profits of royal fiscality, but just as the urban mobs combined looting with anti-semitism, so also did the nobility combine their search for financial windfalls with demands for a moral reform of the court and the revival of the reconquest. This revival of the crusading spirit came with the Catholic Kings, and many felt that it was an endeavour which united the monarchy and nobility in a common cause.

In 1478 the Inquisition was established. In 1492 the Catholic Kings conquered Granada. In the same year they forced the Jews to choose between baptism and exile. In 1502 the Muslims of Granada were given the same choice. Peaceful coexistence had officially come to an end, and the closed and orthodox society was being formally established. But the monarchy had never been so popular with both the majority of the nobility and the populace in the towns.

Courts, Scholars and Humanists

DURING the later Middle Ages the minority of literate people grew progressively larger, technical improvements facilitated cultural communication, vernacular literature gained in strength, and Spain's links with the outside world multiplied. The most obvious sign of expansion was the increase in the production and copying of literary works. In part this increase reflected a greater demand, but production in turn encouraged literacy and was facilitated by technical innovations – the availability and cheapness of paper, the manufacture of spectacles, and the establishment of printing in the 1470s.

The primacy of the vernaculars in literature did not, of course, imply the creation of barriers to foreign influence. On the contrary this period, as we have seen, witnessed Spain's active intervention in both the Atlantic and Mediterranean spheres of European politics, and this was accompanied by a complex and bewildering combination of cultural influences. The chronicler Fernando del Pulgar remarked that never had so many Castilian knights gone out into the four quarters of Christendom in search of adventure. Many writers travelled widely outside Spain. The chronicler and poet Pero López de Ayala spent many years of his life on diplomatic missions abroad, the Valencian author of *Tirant lo blanc* travelled to Portugal and England, and the chronicler Diego de Valera visited France, Burgundy, England, Germany, Bohemia and Denmark. The interest in foreign lands increased the demand for travel books. Marco Polo's account of his journey to China and Sir John Mandeville's *Travels* were translated, and in the narrative of his embassy to Tamburlaine, the Castilian Ruy González de Clavijo provided a meticulous description of his travels to Samarkand and back. On the other hand, quite apart from the knights and mercenaries who poured into the peninsula during the civil wars, dozens of examples could be given of the influx of foreign writers and artists. Some, like Jan Van Eyck, paid only fleeting visits. Others, like the German architect John of Cologne, settled permanently and prospered, or like the Florentine artist Daniello Delli, died in miserable circumstances after years of fruitful activity.

As in previous centuries, both native and foreign artists and writers gravitated to the monasteries, churches, towns and courts which provided them with a living. The chronicle of Miguel Lucas de Iranzo, for example, contains fascinating descriptions of the tournaments, plays and entertainments which constituted the cultural life of the constable's court at Jaén. But these centres of patronage could not now compete with the extraordinary flowering of political and cultural interest which focused on the royal court, and this fact alone explains much about the varying developments of cultural life in Castile and the Crown of Aragon.

In Castile the obsessive interest of political factions in maintaining or gaining influence at court is clearly reflected in the literary works of the period. This is particularly the case in the fine collection of chronicles whose authors, almost without exception, concentrated on the events of the court, either because they were the appointed and salaried chroniclers of the monarchy, or because they attached themselves to particular factions. The greatest and most prolific of these chroniclers was Pero López de Ayala (1332–1407) who skilfully defended his desertion of Peter the Cruel and his subsequent support of the Trastamaran cause. Ayala, however, also left an unforgettable and grim picture of Trastamaran court life in his poem *Rimado de Palacio*. The king, according to Ayala, is continually tortured by the gaze of so many eyes that he cannot lift a spoonful of food to his mouth without three hundred people noting the fact, and subjected to the endless demands and advice of councillors and nobles he is like a dumb bull suffering from the goads of the picador's *garrocha*.

From Ayala's time onwards the men of letters began to participate much more actively in the political arena. In many cases this participation took the form of attacks on personalities or of anonymous satires. The marquis of Santillana, for example, savagely attacked Alvaro de Luna in several of his poems, particularly in his *Doctrinal de privados*, and the anonymous *Coplas del provincial* revealed the existence of gross immorality in the court of Henry IV. But there was also a new tendency – especially among the humanists connected with the court – for writers to turn away from satire and advocate specific political programmes. One of the greatest of these men was the secretary for Latin letters, Juan de Mena, who in 1444 presented John II with a long poem, *Laberinto de Fortuna*, which was an extremely sophisticated piece of political propaganda designed to win support for Alvaro de Luna's policies. Similarly, in his *Claros varones de Castilla*, the chronicler Fernando del Pulgar attempted to heal the divisions of the past in order to win for the Catholic Kings the undivided loyalty that was essential for their programme of conquering Granada.

Some of these literary-political creations were no doubt prompted by the sense of order and purpose inspired by the policies of Alvaro de Luna and the Catholic Kings, and the absence of these qualities in Henry IV may well explain why that unfortunate monarch was so mercilessly vilified by another humanist and royal secretary for Latin letters, Alonso de Palencia (c. 1423–92). But we must also remember that literary men were just as interested as the nobility in the rewards of royal patronage. Monarchs, for their part, courted the chroniclers, humanists and poets, and it is no accident that so many of them held offices in the royal administration. The importance of these offices and salaries in determining political attitudes is clearly revealed by the case of the chronicler Diego Enríquez del Castillo. Castillo was the only chronicler to support Henry IV against his opponents, including Isabella. After Henry IV's death and the accession of Isabella, however, Castillo wrote to the queen and complained about her refusal to continue paying the salary of 37,000 mrs which he had formerly received as official chronicler to the Crown. Isabella, he argued, should pay him his salary, and he would then provide her with the same literary support as he had accorded Henry IV; but if she refused, he was not bound to serve her like a slave, and he would find another patron.

The importance of courtly patronage greatly influenced the development of sophisticated literature. This is particularly clear in the contrasting fortunes of Castilian and Catalan literatures. In Castile, Alfonso X had consciously developed the use of the written vernacular at the royal court, and by the fifteenth century even cultivated lyric poetry, which had been for long the preserve of Galician-Portuguese, was composed in Castilian. The key institution at both the Castilian and Aragonese courts was the chancery. In the Crown of Aragon administrative reforms led to the emergence of a group of secretaries whose taste for classical culture was clearly reflected in their writings in the Catalan vernacular. Reaching the height of their influence in the reign of John I (1387–95), these men aimed at enlarging royal power at the expense of pactist institutions. The outstanding figure of this Catalan pre-Renaissance was the royal secretary Bernat Metge. Like the Castilian chancellor, Ayala, Metge was anxious to justify his political actions, and his *Lo somni* (1399) illustrates once again the degree to which the men of letters were tied to court politics. This flowering of Catalan literature, however, was adversely affected by the accession of Ferdinand of Antequera to the throne of the Aragonese federation in 1412. Castilian not only became the spoken language of the court, but writers also began to use it as an alternative to Catalan. When the royal houses of Castile and Aragon were united in 1474, sophisticated Catalan literature was deprived of courtly patronage to an even greater extent and went into a long decline. Thus, although popular literature continued to flourish, the contrasting fortunes of the royal courts help to explain both the flowering of Castilian letters in the late medieval and early modern period, and the long period of decadence in Catalan literature which lasted down to the nineteenth century.

The role of the royal court as the centre of patronage raises important questions about the nature of intellectual endeavour and the extent to which it was shaped by foreign influences. Undoubtedly, chivalric values were heavily imprinted on the courtly style of life. When Jorge Manrique looked back on the court of John II, it was the jousts, tournaments, crests, dances, dresses, standards and flags which he recalled to mind. Manrique's memory did not play him tricks. The chronicles are full of descriptions of chivalric 'happenings' arranged by and for the court. Chivalrous adventures were taken seriously by contemporaries, and Iberian knights actually did set out to perform deeds in places as far apart as England and Bohemia. The Valencian knight Joanot Martorell, for example, involved himself in 'heroic' feuds and exploits which took him for some time to the court of Henry VI of England, and it was partly because of these experiences that his novel of chivalry, *Tirant lo blanc*, departed from the unbelievable and recounted the adventures of the knight Tirant in a wholly realistic manner.

The inspiration for the increasing number of romances of chivalry (and for almost all ideas related to war in general) derived from France. Moreover, although Italian influences became more important at roughly the same time as the Spanish phase of the Hundred Years War ended, Spaniards continued to look northwards during the fifteenth century to France, Burgundy and Flanders. The great Alvaro de Luna, for example, had Honoré Bonet's *Tree of Battles* translated into Castilian, and he lies at rest along with his wife in tombs sculpted in the Flemish style. Throughout the fifteenth century the majority of new influences and ideas, particularly in the plastic arts, continued to come from northern Europe rather than Italy.

But what place did learning hold in the scale of chivalric values which set the tone of society? Did the noble warrior or courtier consider it necessary to combine the practice of arms with the study of letters? Traditionally and ideally, a noble was expected to measure his words, live by the sword, give good counsel, maintain loyalty to the king and have a firm faith in God. This at least was the way that Díez de Games saw it, and in his *Victorial* he argued that learning was not important: 'He who has to learn and use the arts of *caballería* should not spend much time in a school of letters.' On the other hand, the picture given by such writers as Fernán Pérez de Guzmán and Fernando del Pulgar is different. The count of Haro, for example, was not only praised by Pulgar for possessing all the traditional virtues but also because 'he learned to read Latin and devoted time to studying chronicles and the past'. An even better example is Pulgar's portrait of the marquis of Santillana who is presented as the perfect noble and prototype of the courtier precisely because he combined learning with military success. It is a combination that we find in the plastic arts as well, as can be seen in that tomb in Sigüenza cathedral which depicts Martín Vásquez de Acuña, suitably clad in military attire, propped up on one elbow reading a book. Does this not call to mind the famous portrait by Justus of Ghent in which the Italian renaissance prince, Federigo da Montefeltro, is shown sitting down, clad in armour, and reading in his study?

There is indeed an echo of the Renaissance in the activities of such men as Santillana. But, as Russell has cogently argued, only a handful of magnates combined learning and chivalry, and the limited scale of noble patronage meant that humanism developed fitfully and slowly. In this respect the Spain of Santillana was similar to the England of John Tiptoft, earl of Worcester, rather than the Italy of the renaissance commune or court. It is true, of course, that the beginnings of humanism – defined as a revival of classical studies – can be dated back to the late fourteenth century in Catalonia and the first half of the fifteenth century in Castile. There is also no doubt that nobles like Santillana and Enrique de Villena were aware that a study of Latin and Greek authors could be of great value. Moreover, both John II of Castile and Alfonso V of Aragon were patrons of humanist scholars, and Spanish writers in general were increasingly influenced by Italian literature. The scholar who had studied in Italy was sure of a welcome at the Castilian court. After studying in Salamanca and in Italy, for example, Juan de Mena was received into John II's court and given the post of secretary of Latin letters. But the significance of such examples should not be exaggerated. The Italian humanists at Alfonso V's court in Naples seem to have had singularly little influence on Spanish scholars. Moreover, although fresh allegorical structures, Italian in origin and influence, invaded peninsular literature, the mere piling up of quotations from classical sources and the inadequate translations of classical authors – carried out for men who, like Santillana, were ignorant of Latin – reveal that humanist scholarship in Spain was superficial in quality. Towards the end of the sixteenth century Fernando de Herrera was to argue that the Spaniards had been forced to give precedence to arms over letters because of their crusade against the infidel. There was some point to his argument, and it was only in the sixteenth century, when the Italian Renaissance itself had already moved from a civic to a courtly setting, that the new scholarship and values could be fully absorbed by a Spanish society which had become increasingly more princely and aristocratic in nature.

Conclusion

IN 1530 an obscure, illiterate and illegitimate adventurer from the lean lands of Extremadura set out from Panama with some 200 men and thirty horses for the conquest of Peru. Three years later Francisco Pizarro had mastered the Inca capital of Cuzco and was in possession of enormous quantities of gold and silver, including the gold with which the captive Inca ruler, Atahualpa, had filled a room in a vain attempt to secure his liberty. The royal fifth was sent to Castile, the rest of the booty was shared out, and Pizzaro was made a marquis in 1535.

Is there not an element of *déjà vu* in this and other similar episodes in the history of the *conquistadores*?

> Great were the rejoicings there when the Cid won Valencia and entered the city. Those who had been on foot now became *caballeros*. And the gold and the silver, who can count it?[74]

There was, in fact, a strong element of continuity between 'medieval' Spain and 'early modern' Spain and its Empire. The lust for gold was as strong as it had ever been and the *conquistadores* continued to invoke the help of Santiago in battle.

Of course, sixteenth-century Spaniards in both Europe and the New World were faced with religious and geographical frontiers which differed greatly not only from those of previous centuries but also from one area to another. Inevitably, therefore, attitudes and institutions were continually adapted in the light of changing circumstances: the *conquistadores* went in search of gold, but it was silver that came to dominate the European economy; cattle-ranching and sheep-farming in the New World developed on a different scale than in Spain; the means whereby Amerindian labour was recruited to meet the traditional problem of a crisis of manpower were essentially new and different; quite apart from other factors, distance alone determined that the viceroys, *audiencia* officials, *corregidores*, *alcaldes* and *contadores* of the New World would acquire roles and powers different from those of their counterparts in Castile.

Changes and adaptations, however, do not alter the fact that in dealing with new frontiers and challenges, the Spaniards perforce drew – and drew heavily – on that stock of experiences which they had accumulated during the course of the medieval centuries. This was, after all, the declared policy of the monarchy: 'Inasmuch as the Kingdoms of Castile and of the Indies are under one Crown, the laws and the manner of government of the one should conform as nearly as possible to those of the other.' The emphasis, of course, was on Castilian institutions rather than on those of a 'united' Spain. Indeed, under the façade of unity, continuity was even more obvious in a different way. In the Catalan *cortes* of 1480–1 Ferdinand the Catholic specifically recognised and confirmed all the late medieval institutions of pactism. 'Where the foundations were being laid in Castile for absolute royal power', writes Professor Elliott, 'in Catalonia the old mediaeval contractual State was scrupulously restored. Whether this was really the form of government best suited to the needs of a new age was apparently not considered.'

Bibliographies

Abbreviations

A.A.	*Al-Andalus*
A.E.M.	*Anuario de Estudios Medievales*
A.E.S.C.	*Annales: Économies, Sociétés, Civilisations*
A.H.D.E.	*Anuario de Historia de Derecho Español*
A.H.R.	*American Historical Review*
B.A.E.	Biblioteca de Autores Españoles
B.H.S.	*Bulletin of Hispanic Studies*
C.H.A.	*Congreso de la Historia de Aragón*
C.H.E.	*Cuadernos de Historia de España*
Cuadernos	*Cuadernos de Historia: Anexos a la revista Hispania*
E.H.R.	*English Historical Review*
H.A.H.R.	*Hispanic American Historical Review*
J.W.H.	*Journal of World History*
M.A.	*Moyen Age*
M.C.V.	*Mélanges de la Casa de Velásquez*
M.L.R.	*Modern Language Review*
P.P.	*Past and Present*
R.A.B.M.	*Revista de Archivos, Bibliotecas y Museos*
R.H.	*Revue Historique*

Introductory Note

In a book such as this a detailed bibliography would be out of place. A list of further reading in English includes several recent works of a high level of scholarship as well as older or more popular books. Several large gaps remain but the diligent student can cover most of the ground by resorting to some of the works in the select bibliography of works in languages other than English.

To make cross-reference by author or editor easier, both bibliographies have been subdivided on the following plan:

1. ORIENTATION AND GENERAL WORKS
2. SOURCES
3. POLITICAL AND INSTITUTIONAL HISTORY
4. SOCIAL AND ECONOMIC HISTORY
5. RELIGION, THE CHURCH AND CIVILISATION

Sections 3, 4 and 5 are in turn each subdivided into:

(*a*) General   (*b*) Down to *c*. 1300   (*c*) From *c*. 1300 to *c*. 1500

A SELECT BIBLIOGRAPHY OF WORKS IN ENGLISH

1. ORIENTATION AND GENERAL WORKS

A short introduction to the various archival repositories and schools of historical erudition – both medieval and modern – is provided by J. M. Jover, 'Panorama of Current Spanish Historiography', *J.W.H.*, VI (1961) 1023–38. A great deal of discussion has been expended on the great debate on the nature of Spanish history and things Spanish. Américo Castro's ideas, emphasising the importance of the Muslim and Jewish contributions to the formation of the Spanish nature and character, can be followed up in his *The Structure of Spanish History* (Princeton, 1954) and *The Spaniards. An Introduction to their History* (Berkeley, 1971). Castro's thesis was submitted to a searching and revealing examination by Claudio Sánchez-Albornoz in *España, un enigma histórico*, 2 vols (Buenos Aires, 1957) and it is a pity that this side of the debate was not given the English translation it deserved. A flavour of the master at work, however, is available in C. Sánchez-Albornoz, 'The Frontier and Castilian Liberties', in *The New World Looks at its History*, ed. A. R. Lewis and T. F. McGann (Austin, 1963) pp. 25–46. The clash between Castro and Sánchez-Albornoz has stimulated interesting reformulations of interpretation and methodology of which a good example is T. F. Glick and O. Pi-Sunyer, 'Acculturation as An Explanatory Concept in Spanish History', *Comparative Studies in Society and History*, XI (1969) 136–54.

Both J. Vicens Vives, *Approaches to the History of Spain* (Berkeley, 1970) and P. Vilar, *Spain. A Brief History* (Oxford, 1967) devote brief but stimulating sections to the medieval period. Although it is showing its age, R. B. Merriman, *The Rise of the Spanish Empire*, vol. 1: *The Middle Ages* (New York, 1918; reprinted 1962) remains invaluable. G. Jackson, *The Making of Medieval Spain* (London, 1972) contains magnificent illustrations but the text is brief and, in parts, disappointing. *Spain. A Companion to Spanish Studies*, ed. P. E. Russell (London, 1973) gives the medieval period its full share of attention and is particularly useful for cultural aspects. *From Reconquest to Empire: the Iberian Background to Latin American History*, ed. H. B. Johnson (New York, 1970) gathers together various extracts and translations from works illustrating the mainly medieval background to Spanish expansion in America.

A useful bibliographical essay is C. J. Bishko, 'The Iberian Background to Latin American History', *H.A.H.R.*, XXXVI (1956) 50–80. There are no really good historical atlases. The maps on the medieval period in J. Vicens Vives, *Atlas de historia de España*, 6th ed. (Barcelona, 1969) are on the whole clearly laid out. A. Ubieto Arteta, *Atlas histórico. Como se formó España*, 2nd ed. (Valencia, 1970) is confined to the medieval period but, although some of the ideas are excellent, the quality of the mapping is very disappointing.

2. SOURCES

The most exciting chronicle in translation is Gutierre Díez de Games, *El Victorial. A Chronicle of the Deeds of Don Pedro Niño*, trans. Joan Evans (London, 1928) which recounts Castilian naval exploits in the Mediterranean and Atlantic. Earlier chronicles for the Crown of Aragon are *The Chronicle of James I of Aragon*, trans. J. Forster, 2 vols (London, 1888) and *The Chronicle of Muntaner*, trans. Lady Goodenough, 2 vols (London: Hakluyt Society, 1920–1).

Two massive works which are invaluable in all sorts of ways for Christian and Muslim Spain respectively are *Las Siete Partidas*, trans. and ed. S. P. Scott, C. S. Lobingier, J. Vance (Chicago, 1931) and Ibn Khaldûn, *The Muqaddimah. An Introduction to History*, trans. F. Rosenthal, 3 vols (London and New York, 1958).

Much translation has been prompted by an interest in either literary works or travellers' descriptions. The *Poem of the Cid*, trans. L. B. Simpson, 6th ed. (Berkeley, 1970) is particularly useful when used in conjunction with the English introduction to the edition by Colin Smith (B2) and the book by R. Menéndez Pidal (A3–*b*). Two other recent translations of classics are Juan Ruiz, *Libro de Buen Amor*, ed. with an English paraphrase by R. S. Willis (Princeton, 1971) and Rojas's *La Celestina* under the title of *The Spanish Bawd*, trans. J. M. Cohen (London, 1964). On rather different lines there is *The Jewish Poets of Spain, 900–1250*, trans. D. Goldstein, rev.

ed. (London, 1971); the fine book by A. J. Arberry, *Moorish Poetry. A Translation of 'The Pennants', An Anthology Compiled in 1243 by the Andalusian Ibn Sa'id* (Cambridge, 1953); and the early modern (but fascinating) *El Abencerraje*, trans. and ed. F. López Estrada and J. E. Keller (Chapel Hill, 1964). For travel books see: Ruy González de Clavijo, *Narrative of the Embassy of Ruy González de Clavijo to the Court of Timour at Samarcand (1403–6)*, trans. and ed. C. R. Markham (London: Hakluyt Society, 1859); Pero Tafur, *Travels and Adventures, 1435–1439*, trans. and ed. M. Letts (London, 1926); and *The Travels of Leo of Rozmital*, trans. and ed. M. Letts (Cambridge: Hakluyt Society, 1957).

3. POLITICAL AND INSTITUTIONAL HISTORY

(a) *General*

Merriman's book (A1) should be supplemented by the two good and succinct chapters by R. B. Tate and R. Hitchcock in Russell (A1). H. J. Chaytor, *A History of Aragon and Catalonia* (London, 1933) remains useful. W. Montgomery Watt, *A History of Islamic Spain* (Edinburgh, 1965) is the best general survey on an area which is also covered by S. M. Imamuddin, *A Political History of Muslim Spain* (Dacca, 1961).

(b) *Down to c. 1300*

There is no work in English for this period as a whole but several studies fill out the picture given by the general books listed above. A. R. Lewis, *The Development of Southern French and Catalan Society, 718–1050* (Austin, 1965) deals at length with government and institutions; in J. L. Schneidman, *The Rise of the Aragonese-Catalan Empire, 1200–1350*, 2 vols (New York, 1970) domestic as well as foreign politics are discussed; A. J. Forey, *The Templars in the Corona de Aragón* (London, 1973) is a detailed study which contains, amongst much else, useful information on administration and land management.

For León and Castile, R. Menéndez Pidal, *The Cid and his Spain* (London, 1934) remains invaluable. On various aspects of Castilian–Leonese institutions see J. O'Callaghan, 'The Beginnings of the Cortes of León–Castile', *A.H.R.*, LXXIV (1968–9) 1503–37; *idem*, 'The Affiliation of the Order of Calatrava with the Order of Cîteaux', *Analecta Sacra Ordinis Cisterciensis*, XV (1959) 161–93 and XVI (1960) 3–59, which covers far more ground than the title suggests; E. S. Procter, 'The Towns of León and Castile as Suitors before the King's Court in the Thirteenth Century', *E.H.R.*, LXXIV (1959) 1–22; *idem*, 'The Judicial Use of *Pesquisa* in León and Castile, 1157–1369', *E.H.R.*, Supplement 2 (1966); *idem*, *The Castilian Chancery during the Reign of Alfonso X (1252–1284)* (Oxford, 1934), J. F. Powers, 'The Origins and Development of Municipal Military Service in the Leonese and Castilian Reconquest, 800–1250', *Traditio*, XXVI (1970) 91–112.

(c) *From c. 1300 to c. 1500*

Spain in the Fifteenth Century, 1369–1516, ed. R. Highfield (London, 1972) contains extremely useful translations from studies by Spanish historians, of which those by Suárez Fernández, Torres Fontes and Font y Rius are particularly relevant for political and institutional history. A superb study of political, diplomatic and naval aspects of the Spanish phase of the Hundred Years War is P. E. Russell, *The English Intervention in Spain and Portugal in the Time of Edward III and Richard II* (Oxford, 1955). C. F. Richmond, 'The War at Sea' in *The Hundred Years War*, ed. K. Fowler (London, 1971) pp. 71–121; J. Robson, 'The Catalan Fleet and Moorish Sea-power (1337–1344)', *E.H.R.*, LXXIV (1959) 386–408; and Díez de Games's chronicle (A2) all throw some valuable light on warfare at sea and Iberian naval power.

For fifteenth-century political history there is the admirable introduction in English to Hernando del Pulgar, *Claros varones de Castilla*, ed. R. B. Tate (Oxford, 1971). See also R. B. Tate, 'An Apology for Monarchy. A Study of An Unpublished Fifteenth-century Castilian Historical Pamphlet', *Romance Philology*, xv (1961) 111–23; J. O'Callaghan, 'Don Pedro Girón, Master of the Order of Calatrava', *Hispania*, xxi (1961) 342–90; J. A. Maravall, 'The Origins of the Modern State', *J.W.H.*, vi (1961) 789–808. For the reign of the Catholic Kings there is J. H. Mariéjol, *The Spain of Ferdinand and Isabella*, trans. and ed. B. Keen (New Jersey, 1961) in which the editor's commentaries bring Mariéjol's work up to date. J. H. Elliott, *Imperial Spain, 1469–1716* (London, 1963) and J. H. Parry, *The Spanish Seaborne Empire* (London, 1966) are the best books covering the transition into the modern period.

4. SOCIAL AND ECONOMIC HISTORY

(a) General

The essential textbook is J. Vicens Vives and J. Nadal Oller, *An Economic History of Spain* (Princeton, 1969). Extremely useful interpretations which try and seize on the essential features of the social structure are E. Lourie, 'A Society Organized for War: Medieval Spain', *P.P.*, no. 35 (1966) 54–76 and the studies by C. Sánchez-Albornoz, and Glick and Pi-Sunyer (A1). C. Verlinden, 'The Rise of Spanish Trade in the Middle Ages', *Economic History Review*, x (1960) 44–59 is still useful.

T. F. Glick, *Irrigation and Society in Medieval Valencia* (Cambridge, Mass., 1970) is superbly conceived and, though rather disappointing on society, is extremely enlightening on the irrigation techniques of the *huerta* environment. R. S. Smith, *The Spanish Guild Merchant. A History of the Consulado (1250–1700)* (Durham, 1940) opens up a field of investigation which scholars have been slow in following up.

The Spanish Jews have attracted more studies than their Muslim counterparts. The best work is Y. Baer, *A History of the Jews in Christian Spain*, 2 vols (Philadelphia, 1966), but see also A. A. Neumann, *The Jews in Spain: their social, political and cultural life during the middle ages*, 2 vols (Philadelphia, 1944) and *The Sephardi Heritage*, ed. R. D. Barnett, vol. 1: *The Jews in Spain and Portugal Before and After the Expulsion of 1492* (London, 1971). S. M. Imamuddin, *Some Aspects of the Socio-economic and Cultural History of Muslim Spain, 711–1492* (Leiden, 1965) is less promising than its title suggests.

(b) Down to c. 1300

This period is discussed in some detail in the general studies – notably, Vicens Vives, Lourie and Sánchez-Albornoz (A1; A4–a). There are two outstanding studies on Valencia by R. I. Burns: *Islam under the Crusaders. Colonial Survival in the Thirteenth-century Kingdom of Valencia* (Princeton, 1973) and *The Crusader Kingdom of Valencia. Reconstruction on a Thirteenth-century Frontier*, 2 vols (Cambridge, Mass., 1967). The rise of the herding and ranching economies is treated in exciting fashion in C. J. Bishko, 'The Castilian as Plainsman: the medieval ranching frontier in La Mancha and Extremadura' in *The New World Looks at its History*, ed. A. R. Lewis and T. F. McGann (Austin, 1963) pp. 47–69 and *idem*, 'The Peninsular Background of Latin American Cattle Ranching', *H.A.H.R.*, xxxii (1952) 491–515. An article by R. S. Lopez, which I have only seen in its Spanish version in *A.E.M.*, iv (1967) 3–11, is to be found in English as 'The Origins of the Merino Sheep', *Joshua Starr Memorial Volume* (New York, 1953).

(c) From c. 1300 to c. 1500

J. Klein, *The Mesta. A Study in Spanish Economic History (1273–1836)* (Cambridge, Mass., 1920) remains indispensable but some of its conclusions need modification in the light of Bishko's studies (A4–*b*). For the 'partnership' between Hispanic expansion and Italian entrepreneurial initiative see C. Verlinden, 'Italian Influences in Iberian Colonization', *H.A.H.R.*, XXXIII (1953) 199–211, and R. Pike, *Enterprise and Adventure. The Genoese in Seville and the Opening of the New World* (New York, 1966).

J. R. L. Highfield, 'The Catholic Kings and the Titled Nobility of Castile' in *Europe in the Late Middle Ages*, ed. J. Hale, R. Highfield and B. Smalley (London, 1965) pp. 358–85 is an exploration in greater depth of some of the more general points in Highfield (A3–*c*), Vicens Vives (A4–*a*) and Tate's introduction to Pulgar (A3–*c*).

The later medieval Jews and *conversos* are well covered in English. B. Netanyahu, *The Marranos of Spain from the Late Fourteenth to the Early Sixteenth Century* (New York, 1966) provides a source of new ideas to complement Baer (A4–*a*) and, by forcefully arguing that the *conversos* were not crypto-Jews and that their outstanding characteristic was successful assimilation, raises – but does not attempt to solve – the problem of explaining their persecution and the setting up of the Inquisition. The causes and consequences of popular unrest and anti-semitism are covered by P. Wolff, 'The 1391 Pogrom in Spain. Social Crisis or Not?', *P.P.*, no. 50 (1971) 4–18, which appears in much the same form in chapter 5 of M. Mollat and P. Wolff, *The Popular Revolutions of the Late Middle Ages* (London, 1973). A. MacKay, 'Popular Movements and Pogroms in Fifteenth-century Castile', *P.P.*, no. 55 (1972) 33–67 examines the social and economic background of popular unrest in the period up to the Inquisition, at which point H. Kamen, *The Spanish Inquisition* (London, 1965) becomes essential reading. See also the essays on *conversos* by A. Domínguez Ortiz and F. Márquez Villanueva in *Collected Studies in Honour of Américo Castro's Eightieth Year*, ed. M. P. Hornik (Oxford, 1965) and the essay by F. Cantera Burgos in Highfield (A3–*c*).

E. J. Hamilton, *Money, Prices and Wages in Valencia, Aragon and Navarre (1351–1500)* (Cambridge, Mass., 1936) is the only serious study of its kind on medieval Spain.

5. RELIGION, THE CHURCH AND CIVILISATION

(a) General

There is nothing general for the English reader to cover the Church and religion during the medieval period. An admirable survey of literature is provided by A. D. Deyermond, *The Middle Ages* (London and New York, 1971). Chapters 6, 7, 11 and 12 of Russell (A1) cover literature, the visual arts and music. The first chapter of A. Terry, *Catalan Literature* (London and New York, 1972) goes down to the Renaissance. The emphasis of W. Montgomery Watt (A3–*a*) is on the cultural history of Muslim Spain and T. Burckhardt, *Moorish Culture in Spain* (London, 1972) is wide-ranging and well illustrated. See also Otis H. Green, *Spain and the Western Tradition. The Castilian Mind in Literature from El Cid to Calderón*, 4 vols (Madison and Milwaukee, 1963–6); *idem, The Literary Mind of Medieval and Renaissance Spain* (Lexington, 1970); Bernard Bevan, *History of Spanish Architecture* (London, 1939); J. Lassaigne, *Spanish Painting from the Catalan Frescoes to El Greco* (Geneva, 1962); and Bradley Smith, *Spain. A History in Art* (London, 1966).

(b) Down to c. 1300

Although the number of studies in English on religion or the Church remains disappointingly small, the immensely readable book by P. Linehan, *The Spanish Church and the Papacy in the Thirteenth Century* (Cambridge, 1971) and the information on ecclesiastical organisation in Valencia in Burns (A4–*b*) go far to redress the balance. See also C. J. Bishko, 'The Cluniac Priories of Galicia and Portugal: their

Acquisition and Administration, 1075–1230', *Studia Monastica*, VII (1965) 305–56 and D. Lomax, 'Don Ramón, Bishop of Palencia (1148–84)', *Homenaje a Jaime Vicens Vives* (Barcelona, 1965) vol. I, pp. 279–91.

In addition to general works, notably Deyermond (A5–*a*), aspects of literary developments in Christian Spain are covered in the admirable introduction by the editor in *Poema de mio Cid*, ed. Colin Smith (Oxford, 1972); R. Menéndez Pidal (A3–*b*); J. E. Keller, *Gonzalo de Berceo* (New York, 1972); *idem, Alfonso X, El Sabio* (New York, 1967); and E. S. Procter, *Alfonso X of Castile. Patron of Literature and Learning* (Oxford, 1951).

A. Bonet Correa, *Arte Pre-Románico Asturiano* (Barcelona, 1967) is superbly illustrated and carries an English translation of the text.

J. M. Millás Vallicrosa, 'Arab and Hebrew Contributions to Spanish Culture', *J.W.H.*, VI (1961) 732–51 admirably surveys problems which are treated in a more diffuse fashion in Baer (A4–*a*), Barnett (A4–*a*), Watt (A5–*a*) and Burckhardt (A5–*a*).

Although I have tried to present a clear picture of the importance of the *muwashshahas* and *kharjas*, it is obvious that the intricacies which they raise have not been conducive to generally accepted conclusions. A lively work which favours the thesis of Spanish influences on troubadour poetry is R. Briffault, *The Troubadours* (Bloomington, 1965). See also J. T. Monroe, 'The Muwashsshatat' in *Collected Studies in Honour of Américo Castro's Eightieth Year*, ed. M. P. Hornik (Oxford, 1965) pp. 335–72, and the trenchant comments of R. Hitchcock, 'Some Doubts about the Reconstruction of *Kharjas*', *B.H.S.*, L (1973) 109–19, in which reconstruction techniques are likened to those used for solving crosswords.

(c) From c. *1300 to* c. *1500*

Inevitably interest has centred on the tensions between Christians, Jews and *conversos*, and these are discussed by the various studies already cited (A4–*a, c*). There is nothing in English on the heretics of Durango. For more positive aspects relating to individuals or reform see R. H. Trame, *Rodrigo Sánchez de Arévalo, 1404–1470: Spanish Diplomat and Champion of the Papacy* (Washington, 1958); R. B. Tate, *Joan Margarit I Pau, Cardinal-Bishop of Gerona* (Manchester, 1955); V. Beltrán de Heredia, 'The Beginnings of Dominican Reform in Castile', in Highfield (A3–*c*); and A. A. Sicroff, 'The Jeronymite Monastery of Guadalupe in Fourteenth- and Fifteenth-century Spain' in *Collected Studies in Honour of Américo Castro's Eightieth Year*, ed. M. P. Hornik (Oxford, 1965) pp. 397–422.

On ballads see: W. J. Entwistle, *European Balladry* (Oxford, 1939); *idem*, 'The *Romancero del Rey Don Pedro* in Ayala and the *Cuarta Crónica General*', *M.L.R.*, XXV (1930) 306–26; C. C. Smith, *Spanish Ballads* (Oxford, 1964); D. W. Foster, *The Early Spanish Ballad* (New York, 1971); A. MacKay, 'The Ballad and the Frontier in Late Medieval Spain', *B.H.S.*, LIII (1976). For potters and their artefacts see A. W. Frothingham, *Lustreware of Spain* (New York, 1951).

For some of the men of letters who lived in the shadow of the court see R. B. Tate, 'López de Ayala, Humanist Historian?', *Hispanic Review*, XXV (1957) 157–74; D. W. Foster, *The Marqués de Santillana* (New York, 1971); *Letter of the Marquis of Santillana to Don Peter, Constable of Portugal*, ed. A. R. Pastor and E. Prestage (Oxford, 1927); and A. Krause, *Jorge Manrique and the Cult of Death in the Cuatrocientos* (Berkeley, 1937).

The best studies on fifteenth-century humanism are in English: the section by the editor in Russell (A1) pp. 237–42; *idem*, 'Arms versus Letters: Towards a Definition of Spanish Fifteenth-century Humanism', in *Aspects of the Renaissance: A Symposium*, ed. A. R. Lewis (Austin and London, 1967) pp. 47–58; and N. G. Round, 'Renaissance Culture and its Opponents in Fifteenth-century Castile',

M.L.R., LVII (1962) 204–15. As well as stressing the continuing dominance of the romances of chivalry in Renaissance Spain, K. Whinnom, *Spanish Literary Historiography: Three Forms of Distortion* (Exeter, 1967) makes some salutary comments on the thinly veiled erotic and obscene aspects of *cancionero* verse. The '*converso* predicament' and its effect on the development of Spanish culture is, of course, a highly complex and emotive problem. N. G. Round, 'Politics, Style and Group Attitudes in the *Instrucción del Relator*', *B.H.S.*, XLVI (1969) 289–319 throws valuable light on the attitudes of the *conversos*. S. Gilman, *The Spain of Fernando de Rojas* (Princeton, 1972) studies the *Celestina* in terms of 'the *converso* predicament', but although the book is unquestionably interesting it has to be used with extreme caution; see, for example, the review by K. Whinnom in *B.H.S.*, LII (1975) 158–61.

B. SELECT BIBLIOGRAPHY OF WORKS IN OTHER LANGUAGES

I. ORIENTATION AND GENERAL WORKS

By far the best recent bibliographical surveys are: C-E. Dufourcq and J. Gautier-Dalché, 'Histoire de l'Espagne au Moyen Age. Publications des années 1948–1969', *R.H.*, CCXLV (1971) 127–68 and 443–82; *idem*, 'Les Royaumes chrétiens en Espagne au temps de la "Reconquista" d'après les recherches récentes', *R.H.*, CCXLVIII (1972) 367–402; *idem*, 'Economies, sociétés et institutions de l'Espagne chrétienne du Moyen Age', *M.A.*, LXXIX (1973) 73–122 and 285–319. See also J. M. Lacarra, 'Orientation des études d'histoire urbaine en Espagne entre 1940 et 1957', *M.A.*, LXIV (1958) 317–39. *Indice Histórico Español* is an invaluable periodical which first appeared in 1953 and which gives brief notes on books and articles dealing with all aspects of Spanish history. For earlier material there is the rather cumbersome work by B. Sánchez Alonso, *Fuentes de la historia española e hispano-americana*, 3 vols, 3rd ed. (Madrid, 1952).

The best one-volume survey of medieval Spain is, despite its occasionally complex style, J. A. García de Cortazar, *La época medieval* (Madrid, 1973). By far the best projected work of more than one volume is L. García de Valdeavellano, *Historia de España. De los orígenes a la baja edad media*, 4th ed. (Madrid, 1968) of which only the first part (in two volumes) has appeared. This covers the period down to 1212, contains an admirable survey of the sources and bibliography, and skilfully combines all the historical threads into a chronological–analytical pattern of great clarity. Claudio Sánchez–Albornoz, *España. Un enigma histórico*, 2 vols (Buenos Aires, 1957) is a dazzling interpretative survey but the author has several axes to grind and, as an introduction, the work lacks the serenity and comprehensiveness of Valdeavellano's work. L. Suárez Fernández, *Historia de España. Edad Media* (Madrid, 1970) covers the period 711–1504 but is heavily biased towards a rather overwhelming political chronology. Much the same can be said of the volumes of the massive *Historia de España*, ed. R. Menéndez Pidal, although vol. XIV: *España cristiana: crisis de la reconquista, luchas civiles* (Madrid, 1966) and vol. XV: *Los Trastámaras de Castilla y Aragón en el siglo XV* (Madrid, 1964) are of a much better quality than some of the other volumes (the prologue to vol. XIV by Ramón d'Abadal is an outstanding and wide-ranging survey of the society, economy and government of Catalonia). The first two volumes of F. Soldevila, *Historia de España* (Barcelona, 1952) cover the medieval period and have the unusual merit of looking at Spanish history from a Catalan or 'Crown of Aragon' vantage point.

The best general work for social and economic history is *Historia social y económica de España y América*, ed. J. Vicens Vives, vol. I: *Colonizaciones, feudalismo, América primitiva* (Barcelona, 1957) and vol. II: *Patriciado urbano, Reyes Católicos, Descubrimiento* (Barcelona, 1957). L. García de Valdeavellano, *Curso de historia de las instituciones españolas. De los orígenes al final de la edad media*, 2nd ed. (Madrid, 1970) is an excellent survey of institutions and government. J. A. Maravall, *El concepto de España en la edad media*, 2nd ed. (Madrid, 1964) focuses attention on awareness of 'Spain' in literate and courtly circles, and in *Estudios de historia del pensamiento social* (Madrid, 1967) several of the same author's studies on medieval Spanish political and social thought are brought together in one useful volume.

For Muslim Spain there is the indispensable work by E. Lévi-Provençal, *Histoire de l'Espagne musulmane*, 3 vols, new ed. (Paris and Leiden, 1950–3). This work only goes down as far as 1031 but a measure of its quality is the fact that the Spanish translation constitutes the relevant volumes of the *Historia de España*, ed. R. Menéndez Pidal. A brief but good introduction which covers the whole period is J. Vernet, *Los musulmanes españoles* (Barcelona, 1961). See also E. Lévi-Provençal, *Islam d'Occident. Études d'histoire médiévale* (Paris, 1948).

For the kingdom of Castile there is the short survey by J. Valdeón Baruque, *El reino de Castilla en la edad media* (Bilbao, 1968).

There are two indispensable works of reference: *Diccionario de historia de España*, ed. Germán Bleiberg, 3 vols, 2nd ed. (Madrid, 1968) and *Diccionario de historia eclesiástica de España*, ed. Q. Aldea, T. Marín and J. Vives, 3 vols (Madrid, 1972).

2. SOURCES

It is quite impossible to give an adequate summary of the published sources in such a bibliography. For an exhaustive and admirable survey see Valdeavellano's, *Historia de España* (B1), vol. I, pp. 42–104, which lists the great collections, archival catalogues, narrative sources, biographical and genealogical works, autobiographical sources, law codes, cartularies and other ecclesiastical material. Valdeavellano's survey should be supplemented by the works listed in the articles by Dufourcq and Gautier-Dalché (B1).

An old but useful edition of law codes, from the *Liber Iudicum* to the *Novísima Recopilación*, is *Los códigos españoles concordados y anotados*, 12 vols, 2nd ed. (Madrid, 1872–3). For the acts of the *cortes* see the relevant volumes of *Cortes de los antiguos reinos de León y de Castilla*, published by the Real Academia de la Historia (Madrid, 1861–1903) and *Cortes de los antiguos reinos de Aragón y de Valencia y principado de Cataluña*, published by the Real Academia de la Historia (Madrid, 1896–1922).

An immense amount of source material relating to *repartimientos, fueros*, cartularies, and municipal ordinances has been published. Model examples are: Julio González, *Repartimiento de Sevilla*, 2 vols (Madrid, 1951); J. Maldonado and E. Sáez, *El fuero de Coria* (Madrid, 1949); L. Sánchez Belda, *Cartulario de Santo Toribio de Liébana* (Madrid, 1948); *Colección diplomática de Sepúlveda*, ed. E. Sáez (Segovia, 1956).

The *Poema de mio Cid*, ed. Colin Smith (Oxford, 1972) and the *Primera Crónica General de España*, ed. R. Menéndez Pidal, 2 vols (Madrid, 1955) are indispensable for both literary and historical studies. Medieval chronicles have not been edited in one systematic collection. The volumes of *Textos Medievales*, ed. A. Ubieto Arteta constitute a useful and still growing collection of Muslim and Christian sources which mainly covers the early and central middle ages and includes facsimiles of earlier printed editions. The *Colección de Crónicas Españolas*, ed. J. de Mata Carriazo, 9 vols (Madrid, 1940–6) contains many of the later medieval chronicles and maintains a high standard of scholarship. These two collections of chronicle material, however, by no means cover the whole field and while, on the one hand, there are chronicle editions of the highest standard, such as Tate's edition of Pulgar (A3–c), a great chronicler like Pero López de Ayala can only be read in the dismal edition of the 'Biblioteca de Autores Españoles'. For the communal struggles in Sahagún and Compostela see *Las crónicas anónimas de Sahagún*, ed. J. Puyol (Madrid, 1920) and *Historia Compostelana*, ed. Manuel Suárez and José Campelo (Santiago de Compostela, 1950).

Finally it should be remembered that a lot of documentary material is printed in article form or in appendices to books – for example, E. Lévi-Provençal, 'Les "Mémoires" de 'Abd Allāh, dernier roi zīride de Grenade', *A.A.*, III (1935) and IV (1936), and the two volumes of documents in Julio González, *El reino de Castilla en la época de Alfonso VIII*, 3 vols (Madrid, 1960).

3. POLITICAL AND INSTITUTIONAL HISTORY
(a) General
In addition to the works already cited (B1) see: J. M. Font y Rius, *Instituciones medievales españolas* (Madrid, 1949); idem, 'El desarollo general del derecho en los territorios de la Corona de Aragón', *VII C.H.A.*, vol. I (Barcelona, 1962) pp. 289–326; A. García Gallo, *Manual de historia del derecho español*, 2 vols (Madrid, 1967); J. Lalinde Abadía, *Iniciación histórica al derecho español* (Barcelona, 1970).

L. García de Valdeavellano, 'Las instituciones feudales en España', in the Spanish translation of F. L. Ganshof, *El Feudalismo* (Barcelona, 1963) pp. 229–305, is the best survey of a peculiarly complicated problem. C. Sánchez-Albornoz, *Estudios sobre las instituciones medievales españolas* (Mexico, 1965) contains detailed and searching studies on such subjects as the *behetrías*, feudalism and lordships. A. Sinués Ruiz, *El Merino* (Zaragoza, 1954) is a good study of an official whose powers were at their greatest during the central middle ages. J. Goñi Gaztambide, *Historia de la bula de la cruzada en España* (Vitoria, 1958) is useful for aspects of the reconquest, Church–State relations, and the royal finances.

(b) Down to c. 1300
A. Barbero and M. Vigil, 'Sobre los orígenes sociales de la reconquista: Cántabros y Vascones desde fines del Imperio Romano hasta la invasión musulmana', *Boletín de la Real Academia de la Historia*, CLVI (1965) 271–339, provides alternative interpretations about the nature of early 'resistance' in the northern areas and the origins of the reconquest.

For studies of specific periods, areas and reigns see: Ramón d'Abadal, *Catalunya carolingia*, 4 vols (Barcelona, 1926–55); idem, *Els primers comtes catalans* (Barcelona, 1958); S. Sobrequés Vidal, *Els grans comtes de Barcelona* (Barcelona, 1961); J. M. Lacarra, *Vida de Alfonso el Batallador* (Zaragoza, 1971); idem, 'Alfonso II el Casto, rey de Aragón y conde de Barcelona', *VII C.H.A.*, vol. I (Barcelona, 1962) pp. 95–120; F. Soldevila, *Vida de Jaume el Conqueridor* (Barcelona, 1958); idem, *Jaume I. Pere el Gran* (Barcelona, 1955); idem, *Pere el Gran*, 4 vols (Barcelona, 1950–62); J. E. Martínez Ferrando, *Jaime II de Aragón*, 2 vols (Barcelona, 1948); J. Pérez de Urbel, *El condado de Castilla. Los trescientos años en que se hizo Castilla*, 3 vols, 2nd ed. (Madrid, 1969); J. González, *El reino de Castilla en la época de Alfonso VIII*, 3 vols (Madrid, 1960); idem, *Alfonso IX*, 2 vols (Madrid, 1944); A. Ballesteros, *Alfonso X el Sabio* (Madrid and Barcelona, 1963); Mercedes Gaibrois, *Historia del reinado de Sancho IV de Castilla*, 3 vols (Madrid, 1922–9).

The basic work for reconquest and repopulation is *La reconquista española y la repoblación del país*, ed. J. M. Lacarra (Zaragoza, 1951). C. Sánchez-Albornoz, *Despoblación y repoblación del valle del Duero* (Buenos Aires, 1966) is a good defence of the author's 'depopulation' theory. J. M. Lacarra, 'Aspectos económicos de la sumisión de los reinos de taifas (1010–1102)', *Homenaje a Jaime Vicens Vives* (Barcelona, 1965) vol. I, pp. 255–77, is an exciting article which stresses factors which are also studied in H. Grassoti, 'Para la historia del botín y de las parias en León y

Castilla', *C.H.E.*, xxxix–xl (1964) 43–132. *A.A.*, xii (1947) contains two good articles on aspects of the reconquest of Toledo and Zaragoza: R. Menéndez Pidal and E. García Gómez, 'El conde mozárabe Sisnando Davídiz y la política de Alfonso VI con los Taifas'; J. M. Lacarra, 'La conquista de Zaragoza por Alfonso I'. For the subsequent history of repopulation and *repartimiento* down to the thirteenth century see: R. Pastor de Togneri, 'Poblamiento, frontera y estructura agraria en Castilla la Nueva (1085–1230)', *C.H.E.*, xlvii–viii (1968) 171–255; J. E. Martínez Ferrando, 'Estado actual de los estudios sobre la repoblación en los territorios de la Corona de Aragón (siglos XII al XIV)', *VII C.H.A.*, vol. i (Barcelona, 1962) pp. 143–84; J. M. Lacarra, 'Los franceses en la reconquista y repoblación del valle del Ebro en tiempos de Alfonso el Batallador', *Cuadernos*, 2 (1968) 65–80; J. M. Font y Rius, 'El repartimiento de Orihuela', *Homenaje a Jaime Vicens Vives* (Barcelona, 1965) vol. i, pp. 417–30; J. González, *Repartimiento de Sevilla*, 2 vols (Madrid, 1951); J. Torres Fontes, *Repartimiento de la huerta y campo de Murcia en el siglo XIII* (Murcia, 1971); H. Sancho de Sopranis, 'La repoblación y el repartimiento de Cádiz por Alfonso X', *Hispania*, xv (1955) 483–539.

The indispensable work for institutions is García de Valdeavellano (B1) to which should be added the studies listed above (B3–*a*). See also: C. Sánchez-Albornoz, 'Imperantes y potestates en el reino astur-leonés (718–1037)', *C.H.E.*, xlv–vi (1967) 352–73; H. Grassotti, 'La ira regia en León y Castilla', *C.H.E.*, xli–ii (1965) 5–135; N. Guglielmi, 'La curia regia en León y Castilla', *C.H.E.*, xxiii–iv (1955) 116–267 and xxviii (1958) 43–101; A. Millares Carlo, 'La cancillería real en León y Castilla hasta fines del reinado de Fernando III', *A.H.D.E.*, iii (1926) 251–306; L. Sánchez Belda, 'La cancillería durante el reinado de Sancho IV (1284–1295)', *A.H.D.E.*, xxi (1951) 171–223; and W. Piskorski, *Las cortes de Castilla en el período de tránsito de la edad media a la moderna (1188–1520)* (Barcelona, 1930).

For the military orders there is the excellent study of D. Lomax, *La Orden de Santiago, 1170–1275* (Madrid, 1965) to which can be added Forey (A3–*b*), S. A. García Larragueta, *El gran priorato de Navarra de la Orden de San Juan de Jerusalen. Siglos XII–XIII*, 2 vols (Pamplona, 1957) and the survey by F. Gutton, *L'Ordre de Calatrava* (Paris, 1955).

For Muslim Spain the studies of the period up to the collapse of the caliphate provide an adequate picture but there is very little of use for the Taifas, Almoravids and Almohads. The fundamental work is Lévi-Provençal (B1). P. Guichard, 'Le peuplement de la région de Valence aux deux premiers siècles de la domination musulmane', *M.C.V.*, v (1969) 103–58 throws much new light on the Arab–Berber patterns of settlement. Ahmad Mujtār ʿAbd al-Fattāh al-ʿAbbādī, *Los eslavos en España* (Madrid, 1953) is a brief but useful study of the *saqāliba*. For the eleventh century there is H. Terrasse, 'La vie d'un royaume berbère au XIe siècle: l'émirat ziride de Grenade', *M.C.V.*, i (1965) 73–86, and – an article which I have not seen – idem, 'Caractères généraux des émirats espagnols au XIe siècle', *Revue de l'Occident musulman et de la Méditerranée*, no. 2 (1966) 189–98. See also: H. Monès, 'Consideraciònes sobre la época de los reyes de Taifas', *A.A.*, xxxi (1966) 305–28; R. H. Idris, 'Les zirides d'Espagne', *A.A.*, xxix (1964) 39–45; A. Huici Miranda, *Historia política del imperio almohade*, 2 vols (Tetuan, 1956–7); P. Guichard, 'Un seigneur musulman dans l'Espagne chrétienne: le "Raʾis" de Crevillente (1243–1318)', *M.C.V.*, ix (1973) 283–334.

(c) From c. 1300 to c. 1500

In addition to Suárez Fernández (B1) and the relevant volumes of Menéndez Pidal (B1), there is a brief and attractive analysis of later medieval Castilian politics in L. Suárez Fernández, *Nobleza y monarquía* (Valladolid, 1959). For the fourteenth-century Castilian crisis see: J. Gimeno Casalduero, *La imagen del monarca en la Castilla del siglo XIV* (Madrid, 1972); J. Valdeón Baruque, *Enrique II de Castilla. La guerra civil y la consolidación del régimen (1366–71)* (Valladolid, 1966); *idem, Los judíos de Castilla y la revolución Trastámara* (Valladolid, 1968); *idem,* 'Aspectos de la crisis castellana en la primera mitad del siglo XIV', *Hispania,* XXIX (1969) 5–24; L. Suárez Fernández, *Juan I, rey de Castilla (1379–1390)* (Madrid, 1955); S. Dias Arnaut, *A crise nacional do século XIV. A sucessão de D. Fernando* (Coimbra, 1960). For the fifteenth century see: E. Benito Ruano, *Los infantes de Aragón* (Madrid, 1952); C. Silió, *Don Alvaro de Luna y su tiempo* (Madrid, 1935) – useful in want of a modern study; L. Suárez Fernández, 'Un libro de asientos de Juan II', *Hispania,* XVII (1957) 323–68; *idem,* 'Las rentas castellanas del infante don Juan, rey de Navarra y de Aragón', *Hispania,* XIX (1959) 192–204. Tarsicio de Azcona, *Isabel la Católica* (Madrid, 1964) is the best work for the late fifteenth century, while Orestes Ferrara, *L'avènement d'Isabelle la Catholique* (Paris, 1958) is an immensely readable but highly biased study designed to debunk Isabella. J. Vicens Vives, *Juan II de Aragón (1398–1479)* (Barcelona, 1953) is a fine book which covers the whole field of Iberian politics. For the convulsions in Catalonia see the excellent studies of S. Sobrequés Vidal, 'Los orígenes de la revolución catalana del siglo XV. Las cortes de Barcelona de 1454–1458', *Estudios de Historia Moderna,* II (1952) 1–96; *idem, La alta nobleza del norte en la guerra civil catalana de 1462–1472* (Zaragoza, 1966).

Two fine studies of regional politics which have much wider implications are E. Benito Ruano, *Toledo en el siglo XV* (Madrid, 1961) and J. Torres Fontes, *Don Pedro Fajardo, adelantado mayor de Murcia* (Madrid, 1953).

C-E. Dufourcq (B4–a) is the outstanding work for Aragonese–Catalan policies towards North Africa. For Spain and the Hundred Years War there is, in addition to Russell's excellent book (A3–c), the brief and rather dated L. Suárez Fernández, *Intervención de Castilla en la guerra de los cien años* (Valladolid, 1950). The same author's *Navegación y comercio en el golfo de Vizcaya* (Madrid, 1959) is very useful for the politics of trade and shipping. F. Pérez-Embid, 'La marina real castellana en el siglo XIII', *A.E.M.,* VI (1969) 141–85, examines the origins of the Castilian royal navy and warns against exaggerating the debt to Genoese expertise. M. T. Ferrer I Mallol, 'Els corsaris castellans i la campanya de Pero Niño al Mediterrani. Documents sobre "El Victorial" ', *A.E.M.,* V (1968) 265–338, confirms that Díez de Games's account of Castilian naval exploits (A2) is remarkably accurate.

Homenaje al profesor Carriazo, vol. 1: *En la frontera de Granada* (Seville, 1971) is a collection of Carriazo's fascinating articles on the frontier. M. A. Ladero Quesada, *Castilla y la conquista del reino de Granada* (Valladolid, 1967) is a good analysis of the military organisation and course of the last campaigns of conquest. See also: J. Suárez Fernández, *Juan II y la frontera de Granada* (Valladolid, 1954); E. Mitre Fernández, 'La frontière de Grenade aux environs de 1400', *M.A.,* LXXVIII (1972) 489–522; *idem,* 'Enrique III, Granada y las cortes de Toledo de 1406', *Homenaje al Profesor Alarcos* (Valladolid, 1966) vol. II, pp. 733–9.

There are two good books on Nasrid Granada: Rachel Arié, *L'Espagne Musulmane au temps des Nasrides (1239–1492)* (Paris, 1973) and M. A. Ladero Quesada, *Granada. Historia de un país islámico (1232–1571)* (Madrid, 1969).

VIII C.H.A., vol. II, no. 2 (Valladolid, 1970) is devoted to studies on the institutions of the Crown of Aragon in the fourteenth century. A pioneering survey of Navarrese institutions is J. Zabalo Zabalegui, *La administración del reino de Navarra en el siglo XIV* (Pamplona, 1973).

M. A. Ladero Quesada, *La Hacienda Real de Castilla en el siglo XV* (La Laguna, 1973) is an excellent study based on the relevant fiscal documents. The important changes resulting from new methods of taxation emerge well from Salvador de Moxó, *La alcabala* (Madrid, 1963). For these and other aspects of late medieval institutions see also: Salvador de Moxó, 'Los cuadernos de alcabala. Orígenes de la legislación tributaria castellana', *A.H.D.E.*, xxxix (1969) 317–450; E. Mitre Fernández, *La extensión del régimen de corregidores en el reinado de Enrique III de Castilla* (Valladolid, 1969); J. Lalinde, *La gobernación general de la Corona de Aragón* (Zaragoza, 1963); idem, *La institución virreinal en Cataluña, 1471–1716* (Zaragoza, 1964); A. Masía de Ros, 'El maestre racional en la Corona de Aragón', *Hispania*, x (1950) 25–60. The late medieval *cortes* still await detailed study. In addition to Piskorski (B3–*b*) and the article by Sobrequés (cited above) see J. Valdeón, 'Las cortes de Castilla y las luchas del siglo XV (1419–1430)', *A.E.M.*, III (1966) 293–326.

4. SOCIAL AND ECONOMIC HISTORY

(a) General

The best surveys are the relevant volumes of Vicens Vives (B1) and the book by García de Cortazar (B1). An important work for many aspects of social and economic history is L. Vásquez de Parga, J. M. Lacarra and J. Uría Ríu, *Las peregrinaciones a Santiago de Compostela*, 3 vols (Madrid, 1948–9).

There is no general study for demography, but a useful bibliography is to be found in J. Carrasco Pérez, *La población de Navarra en el siglo XIV* (Pamplona, 1973) pp. 58–9. R. Pastor de Togneri, 'Historia de las familias en Castilla y León y su relación con la formación de los grandes dominios eclesiásticos', *C.H.E.*, XLIII–IV (1967) 88–118 covers the period from the tenth to the fourteenth centuries. N. Cabrillana, 'Los despoblados en Castilla la Vieja', *Hispania*, xxxi (1971) 485–550 and 5–60 ranges widely in time and tries to deal with problems which have attracted hardly any attention. See also the studies listed below (B4–*b*, *c*).

For feudalism, vassalage and immunities in general see García de Valdeavellano (B3–*a*) and idem, 'Les liens de vassalité et les immunités en Espagne', *Recueils de la Société Jean Bodin: Les liens de vassalité et les immunités* (Brussels, 1958) vol. I, pp. 223–55.

Although there is no good general book on agrarian history, three fine studies, which range far more widely than their titles suggest, are: Salustiano Moreta, *El monasterio de San Pedro de Cardeña. Historia de un dominio monástico castellano (902–1338)* (Salamanca, 1971); idem, *Rentas monásticas en Castilla: Problemas de método* (Salamanca, 1974); J. A. García de Cortazar, *El dominio del monasterio de San Millán de la Cogolla (siglos X a XIII). Introducción a la historia rural de Castilla alto medieval* (Salamanca, 1969). See also J. Gautier-Dalché, 'Le Domaine du monastère de Santo Toribio de Liébana: formation, structures et modes d'exploitation', *A.E.M.*, II (1965) 63–117.

On the nobility there is a good study by Salvador de Moxó, 'De la nobleza vieja a la nobleza nueva. La transformación nobiliaria castellana en la baja edad media', *Cuadernos*, 3 (1969) 1–210, which ranges back as far as the twelfth century. See also idem, 'La nobleza castellano–leonesa en la edad media', *Hispania*, xxx (1970) 5–68; idem, 'En torno a una problemática para el estudio del régimen señorial', *Hispania*, xxiv (1964) 138–236 and 399–430; María del Carmen Carlé, 'Infanzones e hidalgos', *C.H.E.*, xxxiii–iv (1961) 56–100; Carmela Pescador, 'La caballería popular en León y Castilla', *C.H.E.*, xxxiii–iv (1961) 101–238, xxxv–vi (1962) 56–201, xxxvii–viii (1963) 88–198 and xxxix–xl (1964) 169–260.

L. Torres Balbás, L. Cervera, F. Chueca, P. Bidagor, *Resumen histórico del urbanismo en España* (Madrid, 1954) is invaluable because it contains the conclusions of Torres Balbás on urban development in medieval Iberia. For urban institutions and *fueros* see: María del Carmen Carlé, *Del concejo medieval castellano–leonés* (Buenos Aires, 1968); and A. García Gallo, 'Aportación al estudio de los fueros', *A.H.D.E.*, xxvi (1956) 387–446. Good studies on specific towns are: H. Sancho de Sopranis, *Historia social de Jerez de la Frontera al fin de la edad media*,

3 vols (Jerez, 1959); M. A. Irurita Lusarreta, *El municipio de Pamplona en la edad media* (Pamplona, 1959).

C-E. Dufourcq, *L'Espagne catalane et le Maghrib au XIIIe et au XIVe siècles* (Paris, 1966) is a brilliant work which covers everything from Christian mercenaries in the service of Muslim rulers to the important gold routes from the Sudan and the activities of Christian merchants in North Africa. See also María del Carmen Carlé, 'Mercaderes en Castilla (1252–1512)', *C.H.E.*, XXI–II (1954) 146–328.

For Mozarabs and Mudejars in general see: I. de la Cagigas, *Los mozárabes*, 2 vols (Madrid, 1947–8); and *idem*, *Minorías étnico-religiosas de la edad media española*. *Los mudéjares*, 2 vols (Madrid, 1948–9). The best general work on the Jews is Baer (A4–*a*) but, while in Germany, the same author – using the Christian name Fritz instead of Yitzhak – produced *Die Juden im Christlichen Spanien: Urkunden und Regesten*, 2 vols (Berlin, 1922–36; reprinted Farnborough: Gregg International, 1971) which contains a mass of documentary material of great value. José Amador de los Ríos, *Historia social, política y religiosa de los judíos de España y Portugal*, 3 vols (Madrid, 1875) remains useful.

For slavery see C. Verlinden, *L'Esclavage dans l'Europe médiévale*, vol. 1: *Péninsule Ibérique-France* (Bruges, 1955).

(b) Down to c. 1300

For demographic history see the studies already cited (B4–*a*) and those dealing with repopulation and *repartimientos* (B3–*b*). See also L. C. Kofman and M. I. Carzolío, 'Acerca de la demografía astur-leonesa y castellana en la alta edad media', *C.H.E.*, XLVII–VIII (1968) 136–70; S. M. Belmartino, 'Estructura de la familia y "edades sociales" en la aristocracia de León y Castilla según las fuentes literarias e historiográficas (siglos X–XIII)', *C.H.E.*, XLVII VIII (1968) 256–328; Pastor de Togneri (B3–*b*).

For agrarian society and economy see the works by Salustiano Moreta and García de Cortazar (B4–*a*); E. Pontieri, 'Una familia de propietarios rurales en la Liébana del siglo X', *C.H.E.*, XLIII–IV (1967) 119–32; and N. Guglielmi, 'La dependencia del campesino no-proprietario (León y Castilla–Francia, siglos XI–XIII)', *Anales de historia antigua y medieval*, XIII (1967) 95–187.

N. Guglielmi, 'Cambio y movilidad social en el Cantar del mio Cid', *Anales de historia antigua y medieval*, XII (1963–5) 43–65, uses the literary text to illustrate some of the more interesting features of noble groupings in relation to war and social mobility.

On monetary problems see: J. Gautier-Dalché, 'L'Histoire monétaire de l'Espagne septentrionale et centrale du IXe au XIIe siècles: quelques réflexions sur diverses problèmes', *A.E.M.*, VI (1969) 43–95; C. Sánchez-Albornoz, '¿Devaluación monetaria en León y Castilla al filo del 1200?', *Homenaje a Jaime Vicens Vives* (Barcelona, 1965) vol. 1, pp. 607–17; and María del Carmen Carlé, 'El precio de la vida en Castilla del Rey Sabio al Emplazado', *C.H.E.*, XV (1951) 132–56.

For some of the basic commodities of the economy see: R. Pastor de Togneri, 'Ganadería y precios: consideraciones sobre la economía de León y Castilla (siglos XI–XIII)', *C.H.E.*, XXXV–VI (1962) 37–55; *idem*, 'La lana en Castilla y León antes de la organización de la Mesta', *Moneda y Crédito*, 112 (1970) 47–69; M. Gual Camarena, 'Para un mapa de la industria textil hispana en la edad media', *A.E.M.*, IV (1967) 109–68; *idem*, 'El comercio de las telas en el siglo XIII hispano', *Anuario de historia económica y social*, I (1968) 85–106; R. Pastor de Togneri, 'La sal en Castilla y León. Un problema de la alimentación y del trabajo y una política fiscal (siglos X–XIII)', *C.H.E.*, XXXVII–VIII (1963) 42–87; M. Gual Camerena, 'Para un mapa de la sal hispana en la edad media', *Homenaje a Jaime Vicens Vives* (Barcelona, 1965) vol. 1, pp. 483–97.

There is very little on commercial practices and techniques. E. Benito Ruano, *La banca toscana y la Orden de Santiago en el siglo XIII* (Valladolid, 1961) is a brief but valuable study of loans given by Italian financiers to the master of Santiago; this helps to complement the interesting information of a similar nature in Linehan (A5–*b*).

The best survey of the early growth of towns and urban society is L. García de Valdeavellano, *Orígenes de la burguesía en la España medieval* (Madrid, 1969). On communal movements and urban unrest see: J. Gautier-Dalché, 'Les Mouvements urbains dans le nord-ouest de l'Espagne au XIIe siècle. Influences étrangères ou phénomènes originaux?', *Cuadernos*, 2 (1968) 51–64; R. Pastor de Togneri, 'Las primeras rebeliones burguesas en Castilla y León (siglo XII)', *Estudios de historia social*, 1 (1965) 29–106; and P. Wolff, 'L'Épisode de Berenguer Oller à Barcelone en 1285. Essai d'interprétation sociale', *A.E.M.*, v (1968) 207–22. See also J. M. Font y Rius, 'Orígenes del municipio medieval en Cataluña', *A.H.D.E.*, xvi (1945) 389–529 and xvii (1946) 229–585.

In addition to the studies already cited on ethnic and religious minorities (B4–*a*) see A. González Palencia, *Los mozárabes de Toledo en los siglos XII y XIII*, 4 vols (Madrid, 1926–30); R. Pastor de Togneri, 'Problèmes d'assimilation d'une minorité. Les mozarabes de Tolède de 1085 à la fin du XIIIe siècle', *A.E.S.C.*, xxv (1970) 351–90; and M. Defourneaux, *Les Français en Espagne aux XIe et XII siècles* (Paris, 1949).

An absorbing book on early Islamic social and economic history, which contains sections on Spain as well as excellent maps and diagrams, is M. Lombard, *L'Islam dans sa première grandeur (VIIIe–XIe siècles)* (Paris, 1971). A. Ashtor, 'Prix et salaires dans l'Espagne musulmane aux Xe et XIe siècles', *A.E.S.C.*, xx (1965) 664–79, uses fragmentary evidence to build up a convincing argument. E. Lévi-Provençal (B1) remains fundamental and the articles by Guichard (B3–*b*) contain much on such varied problems as patterns of settlement and family structures.

(c) From c. 1300 to c. 1500
The theme of *Cuadernos*, 1 (1967) is the transition from the late medieval to the early modern period and the volume contains useful studies on crusading ideals, relationships between Christians, Jews and Moors, and continuity in the structure of lordships. *Cuadernos*, 3 (1969) is devoted to later medieval society and includes good studies on the Castilian nobility, the towns of Murcia and Salamanca, Nasrid Granada, and the Castilian Jews. C. Verlinden, *Précédents médiévaux de la colonie en Amérique* (Mexico, 1954) is brief but stimulating. Also stimulating but rather dated is C. Viñas Mey, 'De la edad media a la moderna: el Cantábrico y el estrecho de Gibraltar en la historia política española', *Hispania*, 1 (1940) no. 1, 52–70; no. 2, 64–101; no. 3, 41–105. *VIII C.H.A.*, vol. 11, no. 1 (Valencia, 1969) pp. 9–220, contains studies on the Black Death and on urban developments in the fourteenth century. Two excellent surveys of the economy of the Crown of Aragon are: P. Vilar, 'Le Déclin catalan du bas moyen âge', *Estudios de Historia Moderna*, vi (1956–9) 1–62; J. Vicens Vives, L. Suárez, C. Carrère, 'La economía de los países de la Corona de Aragón en la baja edad media', *VI C.H.A.* (Madrid, 1957) pp. 103–35. For Valencia see L. Piles Ros, *Apuntes para la historia económico-social de Valencia durante el siglo XV* (Valencia, 1969). For the Basque area there is J. A. García de Cortazar, *Vizcaya en el siglo XV. Aspectos económicos y sociales* (Bilbao, 1966).

C. Verlinden, 'La grande peste de 1348 en Espagne. Contribution à l'étude de ses conséquences économiques et sociales', *Revue belge de philologie et d'histoire*, xvii (1938) 103–46 remains useful but needs to be supplemented by more recent studies on demography. N. Cabrillana, 'La crisis del siglo XIV en Castilla: La Peste Negra en el obispado de Palencia', *Hispania*, xxviii (1968) 245–58 discusses the considerable depopulation in the bishopric and contains a map of *lugares despoblados*. J. P. Cuvillier, 'La Population catalane du XIVe siècle', *M.C.V.*, v (1969) 159–85 is an important article which covers many aspects of Catalan economy and society. J. Carrasco Pérez, *La población de Navarra en el siglo XV* (Pamplona, 1973) is a massive study, but the population movement for the crucial period 1330–50 can only be determined for the area of the *merindad* of Estella. See also: A. López de Meneses, 'Documentos acerca de la Peste Negra en los dominios de la Corona de Aragón', *Estudios de Edad Media de la Corona de Aragón*, VI (1956), 291–447; A. Santamaría, 'La peste negra en Mallorca', *VIII C.H.A.*, vol. II, no. 1 (Valencia, 1969) pp. 103–30. For related monetary and price problems see the studies by Hamilton (A4–*c*); MacKay (A4–*c*); J. Valdeón Baruque, 'Las reformas monetarias de Enrique II de Castilla', *Homenaje al profesor Alarcos* (Valladolid, 1967) vol. II, pp. 829–945; and J. Torres Fontes, 'La vida en la ciudad de Murcia en 1422–1444. Precios y salarios', *Anuario de historia económica y social*, 1 (1968) 691–714.

E. Mitre Fernández, *Evolución de la nobleza en Castilla bajo Enrique III (1396–1406)* (Valladolid, 1968) deals with problems which have been only partially examined by other historians. M. C. Gerbet, 'Les Guerres et l'accès à la noblesse en Espagne de 1465 à 1592', *M.C.V.*, VIII (1972) is a remarkable study of social mobility within the context of the geographical and chronological rhythms created by war. J. P. Cuvillier, 'La Noblesse catalane et le commerce des blés aragonais, 1316–1318', *M.C.V.*, VI (1970) 113–30, deals with trade-orientated nobility and is useful for contrasting with Castilian patterns. Two articles which throw light on the military orders and the structure of agrarian exploitation are: M. A. Ladero Quesada, 'Algunos datos para la historia económica de las órdenes militares de Santiago y Calatrava en el siglo XV', *Hispania*, XXX (1970) 639–62; M. Góngora, 'Régimen señorial y rural en la Extremadura de la orden de Santiago en el momento de la emigración a Indias', *Jahrbuch für Geschichte von Staat, Wirtschaft und Gesellschaft Lateinamerikas*, II (1965) 1–29. J. P. Cuvillier, 'Les Communautés rurales de la plaine de Vich', *M.C.V.*, IV (1968) 73–105, is an excellent study of the background of the *remensa* troubles for which the indispensable work is J. Vicens Vives, *Historia de los remensas en el siglo XV* (Barcelona, 1945).

An outstanding work which throws a flood of light on a hitherto neglected aspect of the Castilian economy is P. Iradiel Murugarren, *Evolución de la industria textil castellana en los siglos XIII–XVI* (Salamanca, 1974). J. Heers, *Gênes au XVe siècle* (Paris, 1961) has much of value for Spanish trade and Genoese activities in Iberia. See also: Suárez Fernández (*Navegación*, B3–*c*); Carmen Carlé ('Mercaderes', B4–*a*); J. Heers, 'Le Commerce des Basques en Méditerranée au XVe siècle', *Bulletin Hispanique*, LVII (1955) 292–324; *idem*, 'Le Royaume de Grenade et la politique marchande de Gênes en Occident au XVe siècle', *M.A.*, LXIII (1957) 87–121; and F. Melis, 'Málaga sul sentiero economico del XIV e XV secolo', *Economia e Storia*, II (1956) 19–59.

An indispensable work for Barcelona, the Catalan economy and the origins of the civil war is C. Carrère, *Barcelone, centre économique à l'époque des difficultés, 1380–1462*, 2 vols (Paris, 1967). Good studies of the *Busca* are C. Battle, 'La ideología de la Busca. La crisis municipal de Barcelona en el siglo XV', *Estudios de Historia Moderna*, v (1955) 165–96; *idem*, 'La Busca. Aspectos de la reforma municipal de Barcelona', *Homenaje a Jaime Vicens Vives* (Barcelona, 1965) vol. I, pp. 337–50. For the urban history of Castile see: R. Carande, 'Sevilla, fortaleza y mercado', and 'El obispo, el concejo y los regidores de Palencia (1352–1422)' in R. Carande, *Siete estudios de historia de España* (Barcelona, 1969); J. Torres Fontes, 'El concejo murciano en el reinado de Alfonso XI', *A.H.D.E.*, XXIII (1953) 139–59; *idem*, 'El concejo murciano en el reinado de Pedro I', *C.H.E.*, XXV–VI (1957) 251–78.

Valdeón (*Los judíos*, B3–*c*) and Benito Ruano (*Toledo*, B3–*c*) both throw valuable ight on the Jews and *conversos*. In addition see the studies by F. Cantera Burgos, *Alvar García de Santa María y su familia de conversos* (Madrid, 1952); E. Benito Ruano, 'La "Sentencia–Estatuto" de Pero Sarmiento contra los conversos toledanos', *Revista de la Universidad de Madrid*, vi (1957) 277–306; and R. Márquez Villanueva, 'Conversos y cargos concejiles en el siglo XV', *R.A.B.M.*, lxiii (1957) 503–40.

5.　RELIGION, THE CHURCH AND CIVILISATION

(a) General

The contrasting views of Castro (A1) and Sánchez-Albornoz (B1) are central to any discussion of these topics and much relevant material is also to be found in the works of Maravall (B1).

There is no good general survey for religion or the Church. The *Diccionario de historia eclesiástica* (B1) is indispensable and the studies by García de Cortazar and Gautier-Dalché (B4–*a*) are useful for the social and economic aspects relating to monastic life. See also M. Cocheril, *Etudes sur le monachisme en Espagne et au Portugal* (Paris, 1966); E. Duro Peña, 'Las antiguas dignidades de la Catedral de Orense', *A.E.M.*, 1 (1964) 289–332, which covers from the twelfth to the fifteenth centuries and is, as far as I know, the only good study of its kind; D. Mansilla, 'Disputas diocesanas entre Toledo, Braga, y Compostela en los siglos XII al XIV', *Anthológica Annua*, iii (1955) 89–143; and *idem*, 'La reacción del cabildo de Burgos ante las visitas y otros actos de jurisdicción intentados por sus obispos', *Hispania Sacra*, x (1957) 135–59.

For the general relationship between history, literature and the arts see: J. L. Alborg, *Historia de la literatura española*, vol. i, 2nd ed. (Madrid, 1970); M. R. Lida de Malkiel, *La idea de la fama en la edad media castellana* (Mexico and Buenos Aires, 1952); J. M. Garate Córdoba, *Espíritu y milicia en la España medieval* (Madrid, 1967); and H. Terrasse, *L'Espagne du Moyen Age* (Paris, 1966).

For Muslim Spain and its impact there is, in addition to the brief study by Vernet (B1), the excellent work by H. Terrasse, *Islam d'Espagne. Une rencontre de l'Orient et de l'Occident* (Paris, 1958). A. González Palencia, *Historia de la literatura arábigo-española*, 2nd ed. (Barcelona, 1945) is comprehensive but dated. Although E. García Gómez, *Poemas arábigoandaluces*, 4th ed. (Madrid, 1959) only goes down to the thirteenth century, this deficiency is in part made up by *idem*, *Cinco poetas musulmanes* (Madrid, 1944). E. Lévi-Provençal, *La civilisation arabe en Espagne* (Cairo, 1938; new ed. Paris, 1948) gives a general survey in three essays. The article by J. M. Millás Vallicrosa (A5–*b*) usefully summarises some of the material in the same author's *Estudios de historia de la ciencia española* (Barcelona, 1949) and *Nuevos estudios sobre la historia de la ciencia española* (Barcelona, 1960).

(b) Down to c. 1300

C. J. Bishko, 'Fernando I y los orígenes de la alianza castellano-leonesa con Cluny', *C.H.E.*, xlvii–viii (1968) 31–135, begins a highly interesting and meticulous analysis of the role of the Cluniacs in Castile–León. A good survey of some aspects of the conflicts over rites is given in R. Hitchcock, 'El rito hispánico, las ordalías y los mozárabes en el reinado de Alfonso VI', *Estudios Orientales*, viii (1973) 19–41. A good study on the Cistercians is M. Cocheril, 'L'implantation des abbayes cisterciennes dans la péninsule ibérique', *A.E.M.*, 1 (1964) 217–87. On other aspects of religious history see, in addition to Burns (A4–*b*) and Linehan (A5–*b*), J. Orlandis, 'Los monasterios familiares en España durante la edad media', *A.H.D.E.*, xxvi (1956) 1–46; J. F. Rivera, *La iglesia de Toledo en el siglo XII (1086–1208)* (Rome, 1966); J. Torres Fontes, 'El obispado de Cartagena en el siglo XIII', *Hispania*, xiii (1953) 339–401, 515–80.

In addition to the studies on cultural developments already cited (A5–*a*, *b*;

B5–*a*) see H. Davenson, *Les Troubadours* (Paris, 1961); R. Lemay, 'A propos de l'origine arabe de l'art des troubadours', *A.E.S.C.*, xxi (1966) 990–1011; *idem*, 'Dans l'Espagne du XIIe siècle. Les traductions de l'arabe au latin', *A.E.S.C.*, xviii (1963) 639–65.

(*c*) *From* c. *1300 to* c. *1500*

L. Suárez Fernández, *Castilla, el cisma y la crisis conciliar* (*1378–1440*) (Madrid, 1960) relates Castilian reactions to the Great Schism within a political context. For changes in the nature of the late medieval hierarchy there is much of value in Tarsicio de Azcona, *La elección y reforma del episcopado español en tiempo de los Reyes Católicos* (Madrid, 1960). On reform there is *Introducción a los orígenes de la Observancia en España. Las reformas en los siglos XIV y XV* which takes up one volume of a periodical – *Archivo Ibero-Americano*, xvii (1970). J. L. Santos Díez, *La encomienda de monasterios en la corona de Castilla* (Rome and Madrid, 1961) is useful for the 'protection' system exercised over monastic property. See also: J. Goñi Gaztambide, 'Recompensas de Martín V a sus electores españoles', *Hispania Sacra*, xi (1958) 259–97; J. Fernández Alonso, 'Los enviados pontificios y la colectoría en España de 1466 a 1475', *Anthológica Annua*, ii (1954) 55–122; *idem*, 'Nuncios, colectores y legados pontificios en España de 1474 a 1492', *Hispania Sacra*, x (1957) 33–90.

Three articles are of great interest for the quality of religious life and sentiment outside the structures of the official Church: M-C. Gerbet, 'Les confréries religieuses à Cáceres de 1467 à 1523', *M.C.V.*, vii (1971) 75–113; J. B. Avalle-Arce, 'Los herejes de Durango', *Homenaje a Rodríguez-Moñino* (Madrid, 1966) vol. i, pp. 39–55; and N. G. Round, 'La rebelión toledana de 1449', *Archivum*, xvi (1966) 385–446.

For a general view of cultural developments see M. de Riquer, 'La culture au bas moyen âge', *J.W.H.*, vi (1961) 771–86. J. Rubió y Balaguer, *Vida española en la época gótica* (Barcelona, 1943) has an unusual and useful focus. In R. B. Tate, *Ensayos sobre la historiografía peninsular del siglo XV* (Madrid, 1970) the author's articles are collected into one handy volume. M. de Riquer, *Caballeros andantes españoles* (Madrid, 1967) is an interesting introduction to the world of chivalry. Chivalric ideals can be usefully contrasted with the frontier practices described by Carriazo (B3–*c*). The cultural world of the merchant emerges well in C. Carrère, 'La Vie privée du marchand barcelonais dans la première moitié du xve siècle', *A.E.M.*, iii (1966) 263–91. Although somewhat cumbersome, the work by Cantera Burgos (B4–*c*) is a mine of information on all aspects of the religious and cultural life of *conversos*.

Addenda

Three recent and encyclopaedic works are extremely useful in providing that detailed coverage of various aspects of medieval Spanish history which has hitherto not been available in English. Anwar Chejne, *Muslim Spain. Its History and Culture* (Minneapolis, 1974) contains a magnificent accumulation of facts but suffers from a minimum of analysis and structural order. J. F. O'Callaghan, *A History of Medieval Spain* (London, 1975) starts in the fifth century and is particularly valuable for the detailed treatment which it devotes to political history and the development of institutions. For the later medieval period an even more detailed survey is to be expected from the two-volume work of J. N. Hillgarth, *The Spanish Kingdoms, 1250–1516* of which only the first volume (Oxford, 1976) has so far been published.

References to Quotations

1   E. Lévi-Provençal, 'Les "Mémoires" de ʿAbd Allāh, dernier roi zīride de Grenade', *Al-Andalus,* IV (1936–9) 35–6.
2   *Ibid.,* 35.
3   *Ibid.,* 39–40.
4   *Poema de mio Cid,* ed. Colin Smith (Oxford, 1972) lines 1613–17.
5   Cited in R. Menéndez Pidal and E. García Gomez, 'El conde mozárabe Sisnando Davídiz y la política de Alfonso VI con los Taifas', *Al-Andalus,* XII (1947) 29.
6   *Ibid.,* 31–2.
7   *Ibid.,* 38.
8   *La Péninsule Ibérique au moyen-âge d'après le Kitab ar-Rawd al-mi ʿtār,* trans. and ed. E. Lévi-Provençal (Leiden, 1938) p. 193.
9   Cited in M. Asín Palacios, 'Un códice inexplorado del cordobés Ibn Hazm', *Al-Andalus,* II (1934) 42.
10   Cited in J. M. Lacarra, 'La conquista de Zaragoza por Alfonso I', *Al-Andalus,* XII (1947) 79.
11   *Primera Crónica General de España que mandó componer Alfonso el Sabio,* ed. R. Menéndez Pidal (Madrid, 1955) vol. II, p. 696.
12   C. Gutiérrez del Arroyo, 'Fueros de Oreja y Ocaña', *Anuario de Historia de Derecho Español,* XVII (1946) 651–62.
13   *Poema de mio Cid,* ed. cit., lines 946–7.
14   *Primera Crónica General,* ed. cit., vol. II, p. 375.
15   *Poema de mio Cid,* ed. cit., lines 1187–99.
16   *Ibid.,* lines 1211–14.
17   *Ibid.,* lines 1861–5.
18   *Ibid.,* lines 3296–300.
19   Cited in R. Pastor de Togneri, 'Las primeras rebeliones burguesas en Castilla y León (siglo XII)', *Estudios de historia social,* I (1965) 63–4.
20   *Ibid.,* 95.
21   *Crónica de la población de Avila,* ed. A. Hernández Segura (Valencia, 1966) pp. 25–6.
22   *Ibid.,* p. 23.
23   *Primera Crónica General,* ed. cit., vol. II, p. 747.
24   *Ibid.,* pp. 772–3.
25   *Ibid.,* pp. 733–4.
26   R. I. Burns, *Islam under the Crusaders. Colonial Survival in the Thirteenth-century Kingdom of Valencia* (Princeton, 1973) p. 9.
27   *The Chronicle of James I of Aragon,* trans. J. Forster, 2 vols (London, 1888) vol. II, p. 560.
28   *Ibid.,* pp. 567–8.
29   *Primera Crónica General,* ed. cit., vol. II, p. 748.
30   Burns, *op. cit.,* p. 304.
31   *Crónica de don Alfonso el Onceno* (B.A.E., vol. LXVI; Madrid, 1877) p. 347.
32   *Primera Crónica General,* ed. cit., vol. II, pp. 746–7.
33   *The Chronicle of James I of Aragon,* ed. cit., vol. II, pp. 434 and 437.
34   *Primera Crónica General,* ed. cit., vol. II, p. 769.

35 Cited in *A Source Book in Medieval Science*, ed. E. Grant (Cambridge, Mass., 1974) p. 35.

36 Averroes, *On the Harmony of Religion and Philosophy*, trans. and ed. G. F. Hourani (London, 1961) pp. 12–13.

37 *Séville musulmane au début du XIIe siècle. Le traité d'Ibn 'Abdun*, trans. and ed. E. Lévi-Provençal (Paris, 1947) p. 128.

38 Ramón d'Abadal, 'Pedro el Ceremonioso y los comienzos de la decadencia política de Cataluña' in *Historia de España*, ed. R. Menéndez Pidal, vol. XIV, p. cxxiv.

39 *Las Siete Partidas del rey don Alfonso el Sabio*, published by the Real Academia de la Historia (Madrid, 1807; reprinted 1972), Part I, Tit. I, Ley xii.

40 *Crónica de don Alfonso el Onceno*, ed. cit., pp. 180–1.

41 *The Chronicle of James I of Aragon*, ed. cit., vol. II, p. 617.

42 Cited in J. Rodríguez-Puértolas, *De la edad media a la edad conflictiva* (Madrid, 1972) p. 43.

43 For this and the following quotations from Eiximenis see Ramón d'Abadal, *op. cit.*, pp. cxviii and cxxi.

44 *Ibid.*, p. cxxii.

45 *The Chronicle of James I of Aragon*, ed. cit., vol. II, p. 519.

46 J. Rodríguez-Puértolas, *op. cit.*, p. 41.

47 *Las Siete Partidas*, ed. cit., Part. II, Tit. I, Leyes v and viii.

48 *Crónica de don Pedro Primero* (B.A.E., vol. LXVI; Madrid, 1877) p. 556.

49 Pedro Carrillo de Huete, *Crónica del Halconero de Juan II*, ed. J. de Mata Carriazo (Madrid, 1946) p. 267.

50 *Cortes de los antiguos reinos de León y Castilla*, published by the Real Academia de la Historia (Madrid, 1861–1903) vol. III, p. 458.

51 *Ibid.*, pp. 483–4.

52 *Ibid.*, pp. 491–2.

53 *Crónica de don Juan Segundo* (B.A.E., vol. LXVIII; Madrid, 1877) p. 560.

54 *Crónica del Halconero de Juan II*, ed. cit., p. 521.

55 *Crónica de don Juan Primero* (B.A.E., vol. LXVIII; Madrid, 1877) pp. 147–8.

56 Pero López de Ayala, *Rimado de Palacio* (B.A.E., vol. LVII; reprinted Madrid, 1952) p. 434.

57 See J. Hernández Díaz, A. Sancho Corbacho and F. Collantes de Teran, *Colección diplomática de Carmona* (Seville, 1941) pp. 62–3.

58 *The Travels of Leo of Rozmital*, trans. and ed. M. Letts (Cambridge: Hakluyt Society, 1957) p. 85.

59 C. J. Bishko, 'The Peninsular Background of Latin American Cattle Ranching', *Hispanic American Historical Review*, XXXII (1952) p. 494.

60 *The Travels of Leo of Rozmital*, ed. cit., p. 94.

61 Fernán Pérez de Guzmán, *Generaciones y Semblanzas*, ed. R. B. Tate (London, 1965) p. 47.

62 *Ibid.*, p. 28.

63 See J. Vicens Vives, *Historia de los remensas en el siglo XV* (Barcelona, 1945) pp. 52–3.

64 Claude de Seyssel, *La monarchie de France*, ed. J. Poujol (Paris, 1961) p. 123.

65 This famous poem is included in many anthologies; see, for example, *Antología de la poesía lírica española*, ed. E. Moreno Baez (Madrid, 1952) pp. 68–9, 73.

66 *Ibid.*, p. 71.

67 H. Sancho de Sopranis, *Historia social de Jerez de la Frontera al fin de la edad media* (Jerez, 1959) vol. II, p. 29.

68 *Los Anales de Garci Sánchez, jurado de Sevilla*, ed. J. de Mata Carriazo (Seville, 1953) p. 50.

[69] J. de Mata Carriazo, 'Relaciones fronterizas entre Jaén y Granada en el año 1479', in *Homenaje al profesor Carriazo* (Seville, 1971) vol. I, p. 274.
[70] *Ibid.*, p. 280.
[71] *Ibid.*, p. 289.
[72] Diego de Valera, *Memorial de diversas hazañas*, ed. J. de Mata Carriazo (Madrid, 1941) p. 45.
[73] *Memorias de don Enrique IV de Castilla*, vol. II. *Colección diplomática,* published by the Real Academia de la Historia (Madrid, 1835–1913) pp. 364–5.
[74] *Poema de mio Cid*, ed. *cit.*, lines 1211–14.

Rulers of the Period

Rulers of Castile and León

Ferdinand I of Castile (1035–65) and León (1037–65)
Sancho II of Castile (1065–72)
Alfonso VI of León (1065–1109) and Castile (1072–1109)
Urraca (1109–26)
Alfonso VII (1126–57)
Sancho III of Castile (1157–8)
Alfonso VIII of Castile (1158–1214)
Ferdinand II of León (1157–88)
Alfonso IX of León (1188–1230)
Henry I of Castile (1214–17)
Ferdinand III of Castile (1217–52) and León (1230–52)
Alfonso X (1252–84)
Sancho IV (1284–95)
Ferdinand IV (1295–1312)
Alfonso XI (1312–50)
Peter I (1350–69)
Henry II (1369–79)
John I (1379–90)
Henry III (1390–1406)
John II (1406–54)
Henry IV (1454–74)
Isabella (1474–1504)

Rulers of Aragon

Ramiro I (1035–63)
Sancho I (1063–94)
Peter I (1094–1104)
Alfonso I (1104–34)
Ramiro II (1134–7)
Petronila (1137–62)

Rulers of Aragon and Counts of Barcelona

Petronila of Aragon
Ramón Berenguer IV of Barcelona } (1137–62)
Alfonso II (1162–96)
Peter II (1196–1213)
James I (1213–76)
Peter III (1276–85)
Alfonso III (1285–91)
James II (1291–1327)

Alfonso IV (1327–36)
Peter IV (1336–87)
John I (1387–95)
Martin I (1395–1410)
Interregnum (1410–12)
Ferdinand I (1412–16)
Alfonso V (1416–58)
John II (1458–79)
Ferdinand (1479–1516)

Glossary

Adelantado (*mayor*) Regional governor with military powers as well as some administrative functions.

Alcabala Royal tax on commercial transactions.

Alcaide Commander of a fortress; castellan.

Alcaldes Judges; especially municipal judges with administrative as well as judicial functions.

Aldea Village.

Alfaqueques Christian and Muslim officials encharged with the task of arranging for the exchange or ransom of captives.

Alfaquíes Jurists and spiritual leaders; upholders of religious orthodoxy in al-Andalus.

Aljama Settlement or district of Jews or Moors.

Arrendador Tax-farmer.

'Asabiya Spirit of group unity based on religious conviction and tribal loyalty.

Audiencia Supreme royal court with jurisdiction over a kingdom or a province.

Ayuntamiento The governing body of a town.

Barrio District or quarter of a town.

Battle Local administrative official.

Behetría Seigneurial area in which the inhabitants had some say in choosing or changing their lord.

Biga Name given to the oligarchical party in Barcelona during the fifteenth century.

Brazo An estate of the *cortes*.

Busca Name given to the 'popular' and 'reforming' party in Barcelona during the fifteenth century.

Caballero Knight.

Caballeros villanos 'Commoner knights'; men enjoying privileges akin to those of the nobility by virtue of maintaining the appropriate horse and armour and performing mounted military service.

Camino francés The pilgrim route to Santiago de Compostela.

Cartas de población Settlement charters.

Chancillería See *Audiencia*.

Ciutadans honrats Privileged group of townsmen whose members were 'apt' for office.

Consell de cent 'The council of one hundred' in Barcelona.

Consellers Municipal magistrates; urban office-holding oligarchs.

Contadores mayores (*de hacienda* or *de cuentas*) Chief officials of the central (financial or accounting) administration of the Crown.

Contaduría de cuentas The accounting section of the central financial administration.

Contrafuero Illegal action violating the laws and customs of a *fuero*.

Conversos Converted Jews or their descendants.

Corregidor Royal official appointed to preside over urban affairs and having extensive powers to intervene in town government.

Cortes Representative assembly of the estates of society; 'parliament'.

Diputació See *Generalitat*.

Fonsadera Tax levied in lieu of military service.

Fueros Laws, customs and privileges applying to a particular region or to a social grouping; the charter containing the privileges and customs of a town.

Generalitat A powerful 'watchdog' institution which, emerging as a temporary committee to deal with outstanding problems between *cortes* meetings, eventually acquired a share in sovereign power (especially in Catalonia).

Gerenti vices Officials exercising delegated royal powers in the various states of the Aragonese federation.

Hermandad Brotherhood, confederation or association.

Hidalgo A noble; member of the lesser nobility.

Hidalguía Nobility.

Huertas Irrigated lands or regions.

Infante Prince.

Infanzón A member of the lesser nobility by birth.

Juros Sums of money assigned on royal revenues and alienated by the Crown in *mercedes*.

Justicia (of Aragon) Powerful official who in theory protected traditional liberties and privileges from the illegal acts of the king and his officials.

Kharja Fragment of lyrical poetry, composed in either colloquial Arabic or the Romance language of al-Andalus, and forming the concluding lines of a *muwashshaha*.

Letrados Legists; learned men.

Malikite rite One of the main four Muslim rites or schools; rite named after Mālik (d. 795) and becoming the official rite in al-Andalus from the reign of al-Hakam I (796–822).

Maravedí Coin adapted from the Almoravid gold *morabitín* and which, once it ceased to be minted, became the Castilian money of account.

Martiniega Seigneurial tax payable on St Martin's day.

Mayorazgo Entailed estate.

Mercedes Royal privileges, usually of a financial nature.

Moneda forera In theory, a tax voted every seven years by the Castilian *cortes* in order to avoid excessive royal manipulation of the coinage.

Mozarab Term used to denote Christians living in al-Andalus or, in a more general sense, a person or pattern of life which, while being Christian, is characterised by the assimilation of Muslim habits and customs.

Mrs Abbreviation for *maravedís*.

Mudejars Muslims living under Christian rule.

Muwallads Spanish converts to Islam.

Muwashshaha Hispano-Arabic verse-form composed in classical Arabic or Hebrew apart from the Vulgar Arabic or Spanish of the final stanza (*kharja*).

Oidor A judge of the *audiencia*.

Parias Tribute money paid by Muslim rulers to Christian princes.

Payés de Remensa Serf-like Catalan peasant unable to leave his land without first buying personal redemption from his lord.

Pedido Subsidy voted by the Castilian *cortes*.

Poble menut or *pueblo menudo* Unprivileged and inferior sections of urban society.

Poder real absoluto Absolute royal power.

Portazgo Tax levied on the circulation of goods.

Procuradores Town representatives attending the *cortes*.

Qasīda The standard or 'classical' form of Arabic poetry.

Rastreros Scouts.

Regidor Alderman.

Remensa See *payés de remensa*.

Repartimiento Distribution of land among Christians after its reconquest.

Ricos hombres Great nobles or magnates.

Romances fronterizos Frontier ballads.

Routiers French term denoting professional soldiers whose abiding interest was in the profits of war (booty, ransoms, etc.) and whose loyalties lay primarily to the captains and others who recruited and paid them.

Saqāliba 'Slaves', imported into al-Andalus from eastern and western Europe, many of whom played an important role in the army and civil service of the caliphate of Córdoba.

Servicio Subsidy voted by the *cortes*.

Taifa rulers/states The rulers of small 'party' states which emerged in al-Andalus after the breakdown of caliphal authority in the early eleventh century.

Taula de Canvi Deposit bank established in Barcelona in 1401.

Tercias The royal share of ecclesiastical tithes.

Tierras Money benefices granted by the Crown in return for the promise to fulfil military service.

Usatges Law code, compiled in Barcelona, which became one of the fundamental texts of Catalan law.

Villani Non-noble freemen.

Yantar Tax: originally the obligation to give hospitality (food and lodging) to a superior.

Zajal Verse-form, similar to the *muwashshaha*, but composed in Vulgar Arabic and lacking a *kharja*.

Index